Compelling Counseling Interventions: VISTAS 2009

Edited by

Garry R. Walz
Jeanne C. Bleuer
Richard K. Yep

Counseling Outfitters, LLC

AMERICAN COUNSELING
ASSOCIATION

Compelling Counseling Interventions: VISTAS 2009
Edited by Garry R. Walz, Jeanne C. Bleuer, and Richard K. Yep

10   9   8   7   6   5   4   3   2   1

American Counseling Association
5999 Stevenson Avenue
Alexandria, VA 22304

Cover Photo by Garry R. Walz

Cover design by Martha Woolsey

Library of Congress Cataloging-in-Publication Data
Compelling counseling interventions : VISTAS 2009 / edited by Garry R. Walz, Jeanne C. Bleuer, and Richard K. Yep.
    p. cm.
Includes bibliographical references.
ISBN 978-1-55620-302-2 (alk. paper)
1. Counseling psychology. 2. Counseling psychologist. I. Walz, Garry Richard.
II. Bleuer, Jeanne. III. Yep, Richard, 1956-
    BF636.6.C64 2009
    158'.3—dc22
                        2009000640

Compelling Counseling Interventions:
VISTAS 2009

Table of Contents

Section I. Career Counseling and Development

Section II. Client Characteristics and Needs

Section III. Counselor Education and Supervision

Section IV. Effective Counseling Interventions

Section V. Research and Evaluation

Section VI. Technology and Counseling

Greetings from the Presidents

Greetings from Dr. Colleen Logan, President
American Counseling Association

For the past five years the *VISTAS* program has been an invaluable resource to the counseling profession. I am proud to say that this year is no different! I am excited to report that with this year's publication, the American Counseling Association presents a rigorous compilation of the current challenges we, as professional counselors, face today such as working with military families, counseling across the multi-generational divides, and the emerging role of the counseling professional as a member of disaster response teams. In these changing and often turbulent times, counselors are called upon to serve on the front line and many of these articles provide practical and innovative ways to help everyday people who are experiencing extraordinary problems in today's world.

These 86 articles come from experienced authors and leaders of ACA as well as emerging new professionals—the proverbial future of our great profession. All articles will be added to the online database, available to our members with a click of a mouse or tap of a button on a hand-held device. These are indeed changing and hopeful times and I am thrilled to say that the *VISTAS* program is staying in touch and meeting the needs of the counseling profession. It is my belief that this most recent edition of *VISTAS* truly reflects the theme of this year's convention, *One Counselor, One World.* My heartfelt thanks to you from the American Counseling Association for making this dream a reality.

Greetings from Dr. Judith Hoppin, President
National Career Development Association

It is my pleasure to join in the celebration of *VISTAS'* sixth anniversary and the publishing of *Compelling Counseling Interventions: VISTAS 2009.* It is also my privilege to write about the value of the *VISTAS* publications produced for the American Counseling Association by Counseling Outfitters (Garry Walz and Jeanne Bleuer). To date, *VISTAS* provides 309 exceptional and reviewed articles of importance to the counseling profession.

Recent years have provided many challenges for counselors and counselor educators. Those challenges have included helping clients and students cope with natural, economic, employment, and personal disasters. To make a difference in the lives of those we serve, we need up to date knowledge and tools to assist all of us in the work we do.

Personally, the resources provided through *VISTAS* give me an opportunity to seek out selected articles relevant to my practice as a counselor and instructor. Having them online from years 2004 to the present provides instant accessibility for in-service and pre-service counselor training. Practitioners can sort articles by title, author, or subject and find an article relevant to many settings and client issues.

It is essential that we continually add to this counseling knowledge base, and it is most important for those who are new to ACA and to the profession (as well as veteran members) to contribute by authoring an article for *VISTAS*.

Congratulations, *VISTAS*, on your sixth anniversary and the important contribution you make through ACA to the counseling profession.

Greetings from Dr. David Kleist, President and Dr. Thomas Scofield, President-Elect Association for Counselor Education and Supervision

The ACA *VISTAS* project represents ACA's continued focus on the production and delivery of quality scholarship. *VISTAS* provides ACA members, from counselors in training, to site supervisors, to seasoned counselors, an accessible avenue for contributing to the knowledge base of the counseling profession. ACES strongly supports ACA's attention to scholarship, and we are particularly excited about the *VISTAS Online* database. The future of knowledge dissemination and access lies in such internet-based venues.

It is a pleasure to acknowledge the ongoing and evolving relationship between ACES and the ACA *VISTAS* project. The usefulness of this system is evident as it captures the innovative ideas, developing information, and diverse experiences that are generated by the annual ACA conference and exposition.

Preface

The *VISTAS* program was inaugurated six years ago because a great deal of valuable information presented in the 500+ convention programs each year – much of it cutting edge and previously unreported – was available to only a select few people who were able to attend the sessions. *VISTAS* was created to provide a means for ACA program presenters to share their ideas, experiences, and research outcomes with a much larger audience, people who can put the information to immediate use to improve counselor preparation and counseling practice. Full details of the *VISTAS* information system, including how to access it and how to contribute to it, are presented in Appendix II.

This publication celebrates the sixth year that Counseling Outfitters, working in close partnership with ACA, has collected articles for inclusion in the ongoing development of the *VISTAS* database. All of the articles that are selected for *VISTAS* are entered into the online ACA library; and, for five of the past six years, a print publication has been produced to highlight articles that are especially well written and contain particularly valuable information. By the *time this book is published, the VISTAS* database will contain the full text of nearly 400 articles that ACA members can access through the ACA web site.

ACA is unique among professional organizations in offering its members a quick and easy way to share information with one another – information that is frequently breaking new ground and previously unpublished. It also provides graduate students, counselor educators, and practicing counselors a valuable source for searching and acquiring highly useful and unique resources on current and emerging issues in the field.

This year's edition of *VISTAS* contains 30 articles organized under six major sections and is noteworthy for its attention to major challenges currently facing counselors. There are three important characteristics that make this selection of articles notable. First, having survived both the rigorous reviews of the convention program reviewers and also the *VISTAS* peer review panel, *they are strong in substance*. Second, they focus on topics that are the bread and butter of today's counselors; but often *they call for counselors to change how they view counseling and how services should be delivered*. Third, *they are succinct and pithy*. They offer a quick read and a concentrated load of useful information.

The group of authors contains both experienced ACA authors and leaders as well as young professionals new to ACA. If you don't recognize some of the names, take note because they will clearly become the idea-generators and leaders of tomorrow.

In 2009, we will add 86 new full-text articles to the database. The first group of 30 articles is contained in this publication and will also be entered into the online database. The authors and titles of the second group of 56 articles are presented in Appendix I. These articles are equally important, substantive, and well written; but for a variety of reasons, not the least of which was limited space, they were selected for "*VISTAS Online* only" inclusion. Together, the two groups of articles constitute a valuable set of resources and do an excellent job of describing where counseling is today and what can be done to improve our programs and practices.

If I have had even a modicum of success in writing this preface, two things will have occurred. First, you will want to explore and experiment with the ideas and interventions available to you in the *VISTAS* database, particularly those that are relevant to your own counseling and/or teaching in this year's publication. Secondly, you will be turned on by what you find and will tell yourself "I, myself, have important ideas and resources that I can share with others." Then, when the next "Call for *VISTAS*" is issued, you will use it as a means to reach a far broader audience of "idea hungry counselors" than you can through your presentation alone.

Thanks for reading this. We hope to see you – both in person and in print!

Garry R. Walz, Ph.D.
Senior Editor

About the Editors

Garry R. Walz, PhD, NCC, is past director of the ERIC Counseling and Student Services Clearinghouse and a professor emeritus of the University of Michigan. He established the clearinghouse at the University of Michigan in 1966 and moved it to the University of North Carolina at Greensboro in 1993, where it continued until 2004 when the U.S. Department of Education discontinued funding for all ERIC clearinghouses. He is currently CEO of Counseling Outfitters, LLC, and CAPS Press, LLC.

Walz has authored and coauthored numerous books and articles including *Promoting Student Resiliency* (with Kris Bosworth, published by the ACA Foundation); *Cybercounseling and Cyberlearning: Strategies for the Millennium* and *Cybercounseling and Cyberlearning: An Encore* (both with John Bloom and published by ACA); and *Measuring Up: Assessment Issues for Teachers, Counselors, and Administrators* (with Janet Wall). He also initiated and directed the ERIC/CASS Virtual Libraries, including the International Career Development Library (ICDL) and the Cybercounseling Web site (jointly hosted with ACA).

He is a past president of the American Counseling Association and the Association for Counselor Education and Supervision, as well as a past chair of the Counseling and Human Development Foundation. He has been recognized through numerous awards including ACA's Gilbert and Kathleen Wrenn Humanitarian Award, the National Career Development Association's Eminent Professional Career Award, and ACA's Distinguished Professional Service Award and Fellow Award.

Jeanne C. Bleuer, PhD, NCC, is past co-director of the ERIC Counseling and Student Services Clearinghouse at the University of North Carolina at Greensboro and past associate director of the ERIC Counseling and Personnel Services Clearinghouse at the University of Michigan. She is currently CFO of Counseling Outfitters, LLC, and CAPS Press, LLC.

Bleuer has worked as a school counselor, vocational rehabilitation counselor, and social worker in a variety of settings including elementary and secondary schools, residential treatment facilities, and community counseling agencies.

She is the author of *Counseling Underachievers* and the coauthor of numerous publications including *Activities for Counseling Underachievers*, *Counseling Young Students at Risk*, and *Assessment: Issues and Challenges for the Millennium*. She and Walz have designed and conducted numerous national conferences and training workshops on assessment, comprehensive guidance programs, and the use of computers in counseling.

She has received the ACA Distinguished Professional Service Award and Fellow Award, the IAMFC Professional Development Award, the RACC Exemplary Contribution to Research in Counseling Award, the AAC Exemplary Practices Award, and the ACES Publication in Counselor Education and Supervision Award.

Richard K. Yep, MPA, is the executive director of the American Counseling Association in Alexandria, Virginia, the largest membership organization of professional counselors in the world. He currently oversees a 53-member staff and an $8 million budget. In addition to management of all staff functions, Yep works closely with ACA governance in implementing the policies that they adopt.

Yep is also the chief staff officer for the ACA Foundation. He served as ACA interim executive director for 18 months before his appointment as executive director in 1999. Prior to his most recent appointment, Yep served ACA in a variety of positions including director of government relations, assistant executive director, and senior associate executive director for corporate planning.

For more than 20 years, Yep has been involved in not-for-profit organizations. He began his career in a human service agency working with the Native American population in northern Arizona as a Volunteer in Service to America (VISTA). He then went on to do direct service work in summer youth employment programs and the TRIO programs that focused on youth from underrepresented populations as they transitioned from high school to postsecondary education. He also served as project director for an Asian American AIDS education program.

Yep worked in the California State Legislature and in the U.S. Congress as a legislative assistant, where he focused on education, human service, and civil rights issues.

Yep received his bachelor's degree from the University of California, Santa Barbara, and a master's degree in public administration from the University of Southern California.

About the Authors

Albrecht, Annette C., is a Professor in the Department of Psychology and Counseling at Tarleton State University. As a faculty member in the institution's professional counselor program, she has conducted research for over 15 years using a variety of research methodologies and data collection tools. Recently, she served on a research team that collected data using a web-based tool from school district personnel from across the state of Texas. (Article 30)

Alexander-Albritton, Carrie, is an Assistant Professor at Western Illinois University. She specializes in mental health counseling and is a nationally Certified Counselor, a Licensed Professional Counselor, and a Certified Alcohol and Other Drug Abuse Counselor. (Article 16)

Astramovich, Randall L., is an Associate Professor of Counselor Education at the University of Nevada, Las Vegas. He has published numerous articles and a book on the topic of counseling program evaluation. His current research interests focus on self-advocacy and advocacy evaluation methods in counseling. (Article 23)

Audet, Cristelle T., is an Assistant Professor in Educational Counselling at the University of Ottawa. She is interested in pedagogical processes that facilitate and enhance counselor education. She is also interested in applying her informal background in web-based technologies and design to create collaborative learning environments. (Article 27)

Bastian Hanks, Brooks, is an Assistant Professor at West Texas A&M University. She is a Licensed Clinical Professional Counselor and holds national certification as a Sign Language Transliterater. Her scholarly interests include training students in marriage and family counseling, sexual abuse, and counseling adolescents. (Article 16)

Bishop, Michael A., is a first year doctoral student at the University of Wyoming. His interest and counseling experience is in working with adolescents in residential settings with a research focus in the area of adolescent resiliency. (Articles 11 & 21)

Brennan, Cecile, is an Assistant Professor of Art Therapy & Counseling at Ursuline College. Her areas of scholarly interest are ethics education, counselor education, and the psychological disorders which have emerged as a result of the complexity of our postmodern culture. She has a highly diversified clinical practice that reflects her longstanding interest in depth psychology. (Article 13)

Brown, Jessica A., is a second year master's student in Community Counseling at North Dakota State University. She has personal and professional experience with military couple communication. Her past research experience explored women's experiences with their partner's deployment. (Article 6)

Brumfield, Kristy A., is an Assistant Professor at Xavier University of Louisiana in New Orleans. Her professional interests include play therapy, multicultural counseling, work with preschool age children, filial therapy, and group therapy with adolescents. (Article 17)

Choudhuri, Devika Dibya, is an Associate Professor at Eastern Michigan University. She received her Ph.D. in Counselor Education from Syracuse University in 2001. Her focus on multicultural counseling includes researching effective counselor pedagogy, counseling issues, and clinical supervision. (Article 15)

Clark, Jean N., is an Associate Professor in the Department of Professional Studies at the University of South Alabama. She continues to conduct research in disaster and crisis intervention. (Article 5)

Cohen-Posey, Kate, is a Licensed Mental Health Counselor and Marriage and Family Therapist who has been practicing in Central Florida since 1973. Her most recent books, *Making Hostile Words Harmless* and *Empowering Dialogues Within*, support and extend the material presented in this paper. (Article 22)

Devlin, James M., is an Assistant Professor in the Department of Counselor Education at Seattle Pacific University. Dr. Devlin serves on the Executive Board of the IAMFC and is the Chair of the ACA Standing Committee. He is the founder and lead consultant for the Counselor Education Research Consortium. (Article 25)

Dinsmore, Julie A., is a Professor and the Counselor Education Program Director in the Department of Counseling & School Psychology at the University of Nebraska-Kearney. Her instructional and research interests include multicultural counseling, social justice and advocacy issues in counseling, and school counseling. She has practiced for over 16 years as a therapist to include clinically supervising and directing an adolescent sex offender program in Minnesota. (Articles 11 & 21)

Douglas, Kristin I., is a Licensed Professional Counselor at Laramie County Community College in Cheyenne, Wyoming and a doctoral student at the University of Wyoming. (Article 9)

Dufrene, Roxane L., is an Assistant Professor at the University of New Orleans. Dr. Dufrene is a Licensed Professional Counselor, a National Certified Counselor, and has supervised master's, doctoral, and post-master's counselor interns in various counseling settings in Louisiana and West Virginia. (Article 14)

Fox, Joy R., is a doctoral candidate at the University of Wyoming. Her research focuses on creativity, diversity, and culture. (Article 9)

Froeschle, Janet G., joins the faculty at Texas Tech University as an Assistant Professor in 2009. She previously worked as a school counselor and educator in the public schools for over 14 years. She received her Ph.D. in counselor education from Texas A&M University-Corpus Christi in 2005. (Article 2)

Hall, Brenda S., is an Associate Professor of Counseling in the School of Education at North Dakota State University and a Nationally Certified Counselor. Brenda has served as a counselor and educator in a variety of community and educational settings. Other areas of scholarship and consultation include: intimate partner violence, community/school partnerships, and collaborative group processes. (Article 6)

Henderson, Kathryn L., is a doctoral student at the University of New Orleans. Ms. Henderson is a National Certified Counselor and a

Counselor Intern with the Louisiana LPC Board and has supervised master's trainees in practicum and internship. (Article 14)

Hill, Nicole R., is an Associate Professor at Idaho State University. Her scholarly and research interests include multicultural counseling competencies, play therapy, mental health counseling, working with children and adolescents, and professional development of faculty and graduate students. (Article 16)

Hock, Catherine M., is a graduate student in the Counseling and School Psychology Department at the University of Nebraska at Kearney. Catherine is the 2008 winner of the Graduate Student Essay Contest sponsored by ACA and has research interests in the areas of children and adolescent treatment. (Articles 11 & 21)

Hof, David D., is an Associate Professor at the University of Nebraska at Kearney and the current president-elect of the Midwest Region of the American Counseling Association. He has practiced for over 16 years as a therapist to include clinically supervising and directing an adolescent sex offender program in Minnesota. (Articles 11 & 21)

Hoskins, Wendy J., is an Assistant Professor of Counselor Education at the University of Nevada, Las Vegas. She has contributed to the counseling program evaluation literature through collaborative research. In addition, she has disseminated information through national and international presentations on counseling program evaluation and advocacy. (Article 23)

Husson, Marlene A., is an administrator at a community mental health center in the Denver metropolitan area. She is the local mental health coordinator for disaster response for Colorado Division of Mental Health and lead for mental health for the Mile High Chapter of the American Red Cross. Additionally she is an instructor for Psychological First Aid and TF/CBT. (Article 24)

Ishii, Harue, is an Assistant Professor at the University of New Mexico. She has extensive working experience with international students at a university career counseling center. Her expertise includes multicultural training research and cultural immersion studies. (Article 1)

Jones, Dennis G., is a Professor in the Department of Computer Information Systems at Tarleton State University. Through a series of research grants, he received funding to purchase a web-based survey tool that is now used by all researchers at his institution. Additionally, he serves on a University committee that reviews web-based surveys prior to their publication. (Article 30)

Kegel, Karen A., is a graduate student in Community Counseling at Wake Forest University. (Article 7)

Keim, Jeanmarie, is an Assistant Professor at the University of New Mexico. She has 20 years experience with the application of career models to counseling in university, rehabilitation, and community settings. (Article 1)

LeBeauf, Ireon, is an Assistant Professor of Counseling and Educational Psychology at the University of Nevada, Reno. Her expertise is multicultural counseling. (Article 4)

Maddux, Cleborne D., is a Foundation Professor of Counseling and Educational Psychology at the University of Nevada, Reno. He teaches a variety of statistics courses and his research interests are on moral development and the use of technology in education. (Article 4)

Mascari, J. Barry, is an Assistant Professor and Acting Chair of the Counselor Education Department at Kean University in Union, New Jersey. He is a former President of the American Association of State Counseling Boards, current Chair of the New Jersey Professional Counselor Examiners Committee, a certified NJ Disaster Response Crisis Counselor, and American Red Cross Disaster Mental Health Specialist. (Article 12)

Miller, Kenneth L., is an Associate Professor in the Department of Counseling and Special Education at Youngstown State University. He is a Supervising Professional Clinical Counselor, National

Certified Counselor, and an Approved Clinical Supervisor. His research interests include technology use in counselor supervision, measurement of cultural bias and discrimination, and child abuse prevention. (Article 28)

Miller, Susan M., is an Assistant Professor in the Department of Educational Foundations and Special Services at Kent State University. She teaches graduate education and counseling courses in human development, cognition, and research methods. Her research interests are assessment of intentionality to report child abuse, measurement of cultural bias and discrimination, and technology-based approaches to promote scientific reasoning. (Article 28)

Millner, Vaughn S., is Chair and Associate Professor in the Department of Interdisciplinary Studies with a joint appointment in the College of Education at the University of South Alabama. (Article 5)

Olguin, David L., is an Assistant Professor at the University of New Mexico. He has extensive experience as a university career counselor where he worked with international students. He also teaches graduate-level courses in career counseling and multicultural counseling. (Article 1)

Osborn, Debra, S., is a tenured Associate Professor in the Counselor Education program at the University of South Florida. She has been teaching online courses for more than 10 years, and has designed and provided the e-training curriculum for NCDA's Career Development Facilitator's instruction for those wishing to provide the CDF training in a hybrid format. (Article 29)

Paré, David A., is an Associate Professor and Coordinator of Educational Counselling at the University of Ottawa. He has a longstanding interest in collaborative approaches to counseling and therapy. His current research centers on the creation of counselor collaborative practice groups and other processes for creating communities among working counselors. (Article 27)

Perera-Diltz, Dilani M., is an Assistant Professor of Counselor Education at Cleveland State University. She is licensed as a Professional Clinical Counselor, Licensed Independent Chemical Dependency Counselor, and Professional School Counselor. Her current research interests include assessment, substance abuse, trauma, and school counselor role. (Article 10)

Perkins, Gerra, is an Assistant Professor at Northwestern State University in Natchitoches, Louisiana. Her research interests include service learning integration into counselor education curriculum, working with children and adolescents, and school counseling. (Article 17)

Ponton, Richard F., is the Director of Human Services for the Township of Ocean, New Jersey. Dr. Ponton has been a counselor for over 30 years, and for over 25 years has been a counselor-manager. Having served as a supervisor, counselor-educator, and program director, his professional interests include counselor development, professional identity, and ethics. (Article 19)

Ricard, Richard, is a Professor in the Department of Counseling and Educational Psychology at Texas A&M University-Corpus Christi. (Article 25)

Sanders, Salvatore A., is an Assistant Professor in the Department of Health Professions and the director of distance learning for the Bitonte College of Health & Human Services at Youngstown State University. He often teaches in online learning environments. His current research interests include ways to utilize technology to better serve students, faculty members, and learning communities. (Article 28)

Scofield, Thomas R., is an Associate Professor/Clinical Instructor and program coordinator of the Community Counseling emphasis in the Department of Professional Counseling at the University of Wisconsin, Oshkosh. Areas of interest include counselor training and outcome research, social and professional advocacy, instructional/transformational training strategies for predominantly white counselor education programs. (Articles 11 & 21)

Scott, David A., is currently the Community Counseling Program Coordinator and an Assistant Professor at Clemson University. His areas of interest include career and community counseling, identity development, and at-risk youth. (Article 3)

Smaby, Marlowe H., is a Professor of Counseling and Educational Psychology at the University of Nevada, Reno. His expertise is counseling skills. (Article 4)

Smith, Robert L., is the Chair of the Counseling and Educational Psychology Program as well as Director of the Counselor Education Program at Texas A&M University-Corpus Christi. (Article 25)

Southern, Stephen, is the Chair of the Masters and Undergraduate Psychology Program at Mississippi College in Jackson, Mississippi. (Article 25)

Taylor, Adetura, is a counselor in the mental illness management services program at the Weems Community Mental Health Center in Meridian, Mississippi. Ms. Taylor has been in her current position in the mental illness management services program for two years and has ten years of work experience with the Weems Community Mental Health Center. Ms. Taylor is a recent graduate of the Counselor Education Program (Ed.S., Community) at Mississippi State University-Meridian Campus. (Article 20)

Thompson, Mary J., is a licensed counselor and registered play therapist supervisor at a full-time private practice in Statesboro, Georgia, that specializes in providing counseling services to children, adolescents, and their families. She has 10 years of clinical experience, is the Vice President of the South Georgia Association for Play Therapy, and is a founding member of a local volunteer therapy dog program. She established the Paws for Healing program, provides training for therapist-canine teams, and conducts research in the field of canine-assisted play therapy. (Article 18)

Trotman, Frances K., is a Professor and Chair of the Psychological Counseling Department of Monmouth University, West Long Branch, New Jersey. (Article 8)

Uhernik, Julie A., is a Disaster Behavioral Health Responder for the American Red Cross and has been active in public health emergency response and planning in the greater Denver metropolitan area. Additionally, she is a Licensed Professional Counselor and Registered Nurse in private practice in Parker, Colorado. (Article 24)

Warchal, Judith, is a Professor in the Psychology and Counseling Department at Alvernia University in Reading, Pennsylvania. Dr. Warchal is a Licensed Psychologist and Coordinator of the Master of Arts in Community Counseling Program. (Article 26)

Webber, Jane M., is an Associate Professor of Counseling at the New Jersey City University in Jersey City, New Jersey. She was Chair of the American Counseling Association Foundation on 9/11/01, and is a certified NJ Disaster Response Crisis Counselor and American Red Cross Disaster Mental Health Specialist. (Article 12)

West, Paul L., is an Assistant Professor in the Psychology and Counseling Department at Alvernia University in Reading, Pennsylvania. Dr. West is a Licensed Professional Counselor and a National Certified Counselor. (Article 26)

Wozny, Darren A., is an Assistant Professor of counselor education at Mississippi State University-Meridian Campus. Dr. Wozny is the principal investigator and project director of the Mississippi State University-Meridian Campus Suicide Prevention Program (three year SAMHSA grant). His areas of specialty include ethics, marriage and family therapy, multicultural issues in counseling, and suicide prevention/intervention. (Article 20)

Yeager, Clancy J., is the Forensic Program Manager at Behavioral Connections in Wood County, Ohio. He is licensed as a Professional Clinical Counselor and an Independent Chemical Dependency Counselor. His current areas of clinical interest are the assessment and treatment of adults who have committed sex offenses. (Article 10)

About the Reviewers

We wish to thank the following ACA professional leaders for their excellent assistance in reviewing and evaluating the articles that were submitted for VISTAS 2009. They undertook this daunting task (so many good articles to choose from!) under a great time press. They deserve great credit for contributing their professional expertise to insure the outstanding quality of the ACA professional counseling database. We owe all of them a great debt of gratitude for their selfless work.

Garry R. Walz, Jeanne C. Bleuer, and Richard K. Yep, Editors

Dr. Doris Coy, Ph.D., School Counseling Coordinator, Northern Kentucky University, Past President, ACA; Past President, American School Counselor Association.

Dr. Carol Dahir, Ed.D., Associate Professor, New York Institute of Technology, National Career Development Association, Regional Trustee.

Dr. Bradley T. Erford, Ph.D., NCC, LCPC, Professor, Loyola University, ACA Governing Council Representative; Past President and Past Treasurer, Association for Assessment in Counseling and Education; Past Chair, ACA-Southern Region.

Ms. Donna Ford, Retired Community College Counselor, Past President ACA; Past President, American College Counseling Association; Past President, Association for Adult Development and Aging; Past Chair, ACA-Western Region; ACA Governing Council.

Dr. Sally Gelardin, Ed.D., Career Educator, Chair, ACA Cybertechnology Task Force.

Dr. Samuel T. Gladding, Ph.D., Professor of Counseling, Wake Forest University, Past President, ACA.

Dr. Norman C. Gysbers, Ph.D, Curators' Professor, Department of Educational, School, & Counseling Psychology, University of Missouri, Columbia; Former Editor, *Career Development Quarterly*; Past President, National Career Development Association; Past President, ACA.

Dr. Cheryl Holcomb-McCoy, Ph.D., Professor, Department of Counseling and Human Services, Johns Hopkins University, Chairperson, American School Counselor Association Diversity Professional Interest Network.

Dr. Gerald Juhnke, Ed.D., Professor and Doctoral Program Director, Department of Counseling, The University of Texas at San Antonio. Past President, International Association of Addictions and Offender Counselors; Past President, Association for Assessment in Counseling and Education.

Dr. Courtland C. Lee, Ph.D., Professor, Counselor Education Program, University of Maryland at College Park, Past President-Elect, International Association for Counseling; Past President, ACA.

Dr. David Lundberg, Ph.D., Associate Professor of Counseling, North Carolina A&T State University, Past President and Executive Board member, Association for Assessment in Counseling and Education.

Dr. Martin Ritchie, Ed.D., Professor and Chairperson, Department of Counselor Education and School Psychology, The University of Toledo.

Ms. Martha Russell, M.S., Career Counselor, Russell Career Services, Past President, National Career Development Association.

Dr. Thomas R. Scofield, Ph.D., LPC, NCC, Associate Professor/Clinical Supervisor, Department of Professional Counseling, University of Wisconsin Oshkosh, President Elect, Association for Counselor Education and Supervision.

Dr. Janet Wall, Ed.D., CDFI, President and Founder, Sage Solutions; Past President, Association for Assessment in Counseling and Education; President-Elect, Association for Counselors and Educators in Government.

Section I

Career Counseling and Development

Article 1

Career Assessment With International Students: International Student Card Sort (ISCS)

Paper based on a program presented at the 2009 American Counseling Association Annual Conference and Exposition, March 19-23, Charlotte, North Carolina.

Harue Ishii, David L. Olguin, and Jeanmarie Keim

Since the 1950s, the number of international students attending U.S. universities has consistently increased (Bhandari & Chow, 2007). During the 2006-2007 academic year, 582,984 international students studied in the United States (Bhandari & Chow, 2007). As globalization increases, the increasing trend of students pursuing cross-national higher education is likely to continue. In recent years, English speaking nations such as Australia, Canada, and the United Kingdom launched vigorous recruitment strategies to attract talented, mobile students from abroad. Although the United States historically has been a leading host country for students seeking international education, recent declines in the enrollment of international students have led governmental and academic institutions to implement proactive recruitment strategies to ensure that the U.S. remains competitive in the global market of higher education (Obst & Forster, 2005).

International students increasingly play an important role in the U.S. higher education and economy. As a group, they comprise more than 16% of all graduate enrollment (Bhandari & Chow, 2007). Many of them are involved in teaching and conducting research as

1

teaching and research assistants. This trend is particularly evident in science and technological fields (Obst & Forster, 2005). They bring different perspectives and enhance the internationalization and diversification of universities (Obst & Forster, 2005). Those who return to their home country facilitate globalization of their field by serving as a cultural broker between their country and the U.S. International students also make contributions to the U.S. economy, with more than $13 billion expenditures annually (Bhandari & Chow, 2007). Despite these positive contributions and recent efforts to recruit international students, their contributions and lived experiences are not widely recognized. Research on international students generally focuses on acculturation and adjustment issues, and information on their career development is scant in the counseling literature (Reynolds & Constantine, 2007; Singaravelu, White, & Bringaze, 2005).

The prospect to expand their career opportunities at home or internationally is one of the major reasons for international students to decide to study abroad (Obst & Forster, 2005). However, although many international students express the need for assistance in their career decision-making, they seldom seek it through their university (Mori, 2000; Singaravelu et al., 2005; Spencer-Rodgers, 2000). Thus, in order to better serve this population it is critical counselors gain an understanding of factors that influence international student career development. Given that research is limited, we believe it is essential to first grasp common career concerns and factors that may influence the career development of international students. To meet this goal, we used Super's Archway of career determinants (1990) to conceptualize different aspects of career development and present a comprehensive picture of the relevant factors. Next, we developed a list of traits for a card sort that encompasses these factors. The card sort can be used as an assessment tool, with the emphasis on the whole personhood of international students.

Common Factors Associated With International Students' Career Development

Super (1990) developed the Archway of career determinants model to portray the biographical, psychological and socioeconomic factors in career choice and development. The archway consists of two columns, their capitals, and an arch that connects the two columns. The model conceptualizes that each component interacts with each other to influence the person's career decision. The biographical column includes personal needs, values, interests, intelligence, and aptitudes, with achievement and personality serving as the capital. The socioeconomic or geographical pillar represents the economy, society, labor market, community, school, family, and peer group, which influence current employment practices and social policy. The arch of the model symbolizes one's career including developmental stages, role self-concepts, and the self. The two columns and capitals illustrate that career decisions are influenced by both individual and environmental factors. Successful career transition and decision-making are facilitated by helping the person to gain a better understanding of the effects of all the determinants of her or his career (Super, 1990).

In addition to common career transition challenges experienced by domestic students, international students encounter unique challenges such as communication and acculturation issues (Reynolds & Constantine, 2007; Spencer-Rodgers, 2000). These issues affect international students making successful career transitions, and thus, it is vital that counselors understand these factors. In the following sections, factors impacting international students' career development are classified into the three domains of Super's (1990) model.

Geographical Factors

The career development of international students is affected by the geographical and socioeconomic factors of their home and host countries. Economic gaps between the two countries can affect choice of university and career decisions. For example, students from less affluent nations are likely to select universities with more affordable tuition and financial support. Governmental support from home countries may also determine field of study and future career options. Their home society, community, and family may perceive certain occupations as more prestigious. This can have a significant impact on the student especially if he or she comes from a collectivistic culture (Singaravelu et al., 2005; Yoon & Portman, 2004). Further, some cultures value parental or familial involvement in individuals' career choices, and thus, international students may experience family pressure (Singaravelu et al., 2005). Others come from countries where formal career guidance systems do not exist and career exploration opportunities are limited. International students may need to reassess career choices if they experience any career incongruence as a result of cultural adjustment (Singaravelu et al., 2005).

Perceived discrimination at both societal and university levels can negatively impact international students' well-being (Mori, 2000; Yoon & Portman, 2004), educational experience (Wadsworth, Hecht, & Jung, 2008), and career development (Reynolds & Constantine, 2007). Given that some international students were the majority group in their country, they might lack coping skills to deal with discrimination and stereotypes (Yoon & Portman, 2004), which can adversely affect optimal career development. Further, their immigration may result in a loss of their primary support systems (e.g., family, friends, and community), which can lead to difficulty focusing on career-related planning (Reynolds & Constantine, 2007).

Because immigration law tends to be complex, international students who plan to reside in the U.S. have great needs to learn about current regulations (Spencer-Rodgers, 2000). Further, social policy impacts these regulations and may limit career options for those who wish to work in the U.S. Students who plan to stay in the U.S. often desire to learn about the American job market and American-style interviewing techniques, whereas students planning to return to their home country are likely to need information about country-specific resumes and foreign job markets (Spencer-Rodgers, 2000). Unfamiliarity with the employment practices of the country in which students plan to seek employment can also pose challenges.

Biographical Factors

The most salient biographical factors for international students are language skills and intercultural competence, which can be conceptualized as special aptitudes. English proficiency was found to serve as a significant source of distress for many international students (Lin & Yi, 1997) and can be perceived as a potential career barrier for some international students (Reynolds & Constantine, 2007). Greater concerns about intercultural competence were associated with lower career aspirations and lower career outcome expectations (Reynolds & Constantine, 2007). Thus, issues related to language and intercultural competence can be significant career determinants.

Two other areas, personality and spirituality, may have indirect effects on international students' career development. For example, personality has been related to intercultural adjustment (Ward, Leong, & Low, 2004), which can impact the person's career-related behavior. Spiritual or religious orientation may also serve as a buffer against negative consequences of acculturation stress or add to it depending on the 'acceptability' of the religion by the mainstream. In addition, assuming that the geographical factors influence students' personal needs, values, and interests, it is possible that the process of adjusting to a new geographical context changes biographical factors such as values.

Psychological Factors

Various developmental aspects in Super's (1990) arch model are relevant for the career development of international students, including the stage of career development, racial/cultural identity development, personal identity development, cognitive development, and psychosocial development. Cultural adjustment and stress also have significant impact on international students (Reynolds & Constantine, 2007; Yoon & Portman, 2004). The challenges associated with adapting to a foreign country include culture shock, confusion about new role expectations, homesickness, loss of social support, discrimination, and language barriers leading to acculturative stress (Reynolds & Constantine, 2007). Acculturative stress has been associated with psychological distress, somatoform complaints, depression, anxiety (Mori, 2000; Wei et al., 2007; Yi, Giseala, & Kishimoto, 2003), poor work-related and socio-cultural adaptation (Shupe, 2007), and lower levels of career outcome expectations (Reynolds & Constantine, 2007). In addition, international students often experience the challenges of balancing the need to acculturate to become competitive in the U.S. job market with the need to maintain cultural identity. As they acculturate and modify career interests, they may also have to negotiate the gap between personal interests, family, and cultural values. Thus, acculturation issues have far-reaching impact on the whole personhood. Given that some studies found a positive relationship between cultural identity and vocational identity (Shih & Brown, 2000), connectedness to their cultural identity may serve as a protective factor. Because the process of acculturation can result in considerable changes in the various aspects of the person, it may impact students' racial/cultural identity, personal identity, cognitive, and psychosocial development that influence their career decisions.

International Student Card Sort

Card Sort Approach

Card sorts can be used to clarify students' values, interests, personal traits and perceived abilities. Unlike standardized career instruments or preset survey items, this approach allows students to interpret and give their stories on certain aspects of themselves. Thus, card sorts tend to enhance students' level of engagement and enrich the counseling process. This activity allows counselors to verify student-constructed meanings, providing the opportunities to develop a collaborative counseling relationship. It also helps both counselors and students gain a holistic understanding of the students through personal narratives (Brott, 2004).

The International Student Card Sort

Because we attempted to develop a card sort as a comprehensive assessment tool, counselors can use this card sort to assess various aspects of the international student beyond occupational information. The author-developed International Student Card Sort (ISCS) can be used to identify potential career development barriers. It can also be used to identify strengths of the international student. The instructions and 69 terms of the ISCS are described below.

First, students are asked to lay the four category title cards across the table, ranging from very important, reasonably important, not very important, and not important at all. Second, students go through each card while simultaneously thinking about the definition of the term, decide whether the particular concept is something they value, and then places the particular card under the respective category (e.g., very important). The students continue the sorting process until all cards are used. Third, once the students sort the entire deck of cards, the counselor helps them explore their values and traits to determine their strengths and challenges. The counselor helps them become aware of their values, strengths, and challenges, and how these factors may relate to their career development and educational opportunities. Fourth, the counselor develops a list of process questions to help students become clear as to how their values, traits, and challenges influence their decisions and life-as-a-whole (past, present and future-oriented).

The following is the list of terms developed for the ISCS. They represent various values, traits, and challenges salient to the career development of international students.

1. Worldview
2. Collectivist Environment
3. Individualistic Environment
4. Racial/Ethnic Similar Others
5. Racial/Ethnic Differences
6. Peace
7. Assimilation
8. Acculturation
9. Spirituality
10. Religion
11. Folk-Healers
12. Native Language
13. Second Language
14. Ethical Principles
15. Moral Principles
16. Appearance
17. Pigmentation Familiarity
18. Socialization
19. Isolation
20. Political Awareness
21. Social Class
22. Socioeconomic Status
23. Sexual Orientation
24. Personal Identity
25. Group Categorization
26. Conformity
27. Introspection/Autonomy
28. Gender Issues
29. Self-Awareness
30. Openness from Others
31. Healthy Identity
32. Passive Acceptance
33. Environmental Influence
34. Geographical Location
35. Climate
36. Pride in Self
37. Pride in Culture
38. Expressiveness of Culture

39. Personal Identification
40. Kinship Ties
41. Parental Ties
42. Familial Ties
43. Friendships
44. Contact with Religion-Religious Expression
45. Prefer Native Customs
46. Global Influence
47. Tradition/Heritage Influence
48. Vacation
49. Time-off to Visit Family/Friends
50. Retirement Benefits
51. Medical/Dental Benefits
52. Gender Support
53. Gender Similarity
54. Gender Differences
55. Immigration
56. Naturalization
57. Concerns with Visa
58. Employment Concerns
59. Job Hunting Skills
60. Balancing Competitive Marketability Skills
61. Returning to Country of Origin
62. Financial Issues
63. Discrimination
64. Professor Relations
65. Peer Relations
66. Contribute to Cultural Awareness
67. Contribution to U.S. Economy
68. Contribute to Family of Origin Economy
69. Enhance Academic Program's Diversity

Conclusions

International students play an important cultural and economic role in higher education; however, limited attention has been given to their career development. The ISCS assessment, presented in this paper, was developed to facilitate international students' career transitions by integrating Super's career archway with culture-specific variables. Utilizing the ISCS during career counseling can strengthen students' self-concept while assisting them with successful career transitions. Moreover, it provides an impetus for exploration of the many variables impacting career development of international students. As a new assessment instrument, the next research step for the ISCS is to further validate the instrument with a wide range of international students.

References

Bhandari, R., & Chow, P. (2007). *Open Doors 2007: Report on International Educational Exchange.* New York: Institute of International Education.

Brott, P. (2004). Constructivist assessment in career counseling. *Journal of Career Development, 30,* 189-200.

Lin, J. C. G., & Yi, J. K. (1997). Asian international students' adjustment: Issues and program suggestions. *College Student Journal, 31,* 473-479.

Mori, S. (2000). Addressing the mental health concerns of international students. *Journal of Counseling and Development, 78,* 137-144.

Obst, D., & Forster, J. (2005). Perceptions of European higher education country report: USA. In Academic Cooperation Association Secretariat (Ed.), *Perceptions of European higher education in third countries.* Retrieved from http://www.aca-secretariat.be/02projects/Perceptions.htm

Reynolds, A. L., & Constantine, M. G. (2007). Cultural adjustment difficulties and career development of international college students. *Journal of Career Assessment, 15,* 338-350.

Shih, S., & Brown, C. (2000). Taiwanese international students: Acculturation level and vocational identity. *Journal of Career Development, 27*(1), 35-47.

Shupe, E. (2007). Clashing cultures: A model of international student conflict. *Journal of Cross-Cultural Psychology, 38*, 750-771.

Singaravelu, H., White, L., & Bringaze, T. (2005). Factors influencing international students' career choice: A comparative study. *Journal of Career Development, 32*, 46-59.

Spencer-Rodgers, J. (2000). The vocational situation and country of orientation of international students. *Journal of Multicultural Counseling and Development, 28*, 32-49.

Super, D. E. (1990). A life-span, life-space approach to career development. In D. Brown & L. Brooks and Associates (Eds.), *Career choice and development* (2nd ed., pp. 197-261). San Francisco: Jossey-Bass.

Wadsworth, B., Hecht, M., & Jung, E. (2008). The role of identity gaps, discrimination, and acculturation in international students' educational satisfaction in American classrooms. *Communication Education, 57*, 64-87.

Ward, C., Leong, C. H, & Low, M. (2004). Personality and sojourner adjustment: An exploration of the Big Five and the cultural fit proposition. *Journal of Cross-Cultural Psychology, 35*, 137-151.

Wei, M., Heppner, P., Mallen, M., Ku, T., Liao, K., & Wu, T. (2007). Acculturative stress, perfectionism, years in the United States, and depression among Chinese international students. *Journal of Counseling Psychology, 54*, 385-394.

Yi, J., Giseala, J., & Kishimoto, Y. (2003). Utilization of counseling services by international students. *Journal of Instructional Psychology, 30*, 333-342.

Yoon, E., & Portman, T. (2004). Critical issues of literature on counseling international students. *Journal of Multicultural Counseling and Development, 32*, 33-44.

Using Career Counseling to Influence Minority Dropout Rates

Paper based on a program presented at the 2008 National Career Development Association Global Conference, July 9-11, 2008, Washington, DC.

Janet G. Froeschle

Dropout rates are high for all students; but among minority students, these numbers range from 50% for African Americans to 53% for those who are Hispanic (Orfield, Losen, Wald, & Swanson, 2004; Swanson, 2004). It has been suggested that a correlation exists between the high minority dropout rate and high stakes standardized testing as mandated by the *No Child Left Behind Act* (2002; McNeil, Coppola, & Raddigan, 2008; Walden & Kritsonis, 2008). It becomes crucial, therefore, that counselors advocate for change in policies and implement programs to assist minority children.

In order that counselors understand suggested reasons for high dropout rates and their implications, the following section will describe the *No Child Left Behind Act* (2002). Advocacy for specific improvements in the act are discussed followed by a specific program school counselors can implement to aid the career and academic development of at risk students.

No Child Left Behind and Advocacy

During the 1900s, education was a luxury only afforded by upper class families (Wise, 2008). By the 1960s, all children were being educated and the United States ranked first in the world in number of high school graduates. Since this time, however, the nation has dropped to 13th in the world when comparing number of high school graduates (Wise, 2008). It has also been noted that the make-up of the United States' population is gradually shifting from an Anglo majority population to one comprised of disadvantaged minority individuals (U.S. Census Bureau, 2004).

The *No Child Left Behind Act* (2002) was enacted with the intent of closing the achievement gap among Anglo and minority students and raising standards so all students could perform more competitively in the world market. To accomplish this, the *No Child Left Behind Act* (2002) requires that all schools administer annual standardized tests to measure student progress. By the year 2014, all students must be proficient in reading and math as measured by the aforementioned tests. Schools failing to achieve adequate yearly progress (AYP) in raising low-scoring students' results to proficiency face stringent penalties. Subgroups of students (i.e., economically disadvantaged students, students from major ethnic groups, and students with limited English proficiency) are reported upon by category. Despite the *No Child Left Behind Act*'s (2002) intent that these measures improve learning for all students, research now exists suggesting a connection between the minority dropout rate and this policy (McNeil, Coppola, & Raddigan, 2008).

Several reasons have been touted for this phenomenon, the first of which may be complacency. A Center on Education Policy report concluded that the historical gap between Anglo and minority students decreased (Kober, Chudowski, & Chudowski, 2008). While this is encouraging, it is important to note that most of the increases were among elementary children. The report also does not consider the number of high school students who dropout and consequently will not take standardized tests. Counselors must advocate that lawmakers consider consequences of policies on middle and high school students. While touting successes among elementary children, policy makers must be held accountable should they ignore minority dropout rates.

Second, dropout rates may have increased because minorities, who have traditionally performed below their peers on standardized tests, are now viewed as deficits to schools trying to attain 100% passing rates (McNeil, Coppola, & Raddigan, 2008). With many school administrators and teachers facing individual penalties for student failure (e.g., lack of tenure, lower pay, potential job loss), stakes for student test performance are high (McNeil, Coppola, & Raddigan, 2008). In an attempt to block low performing students from taking annual tests, educators are tempted to remove or retain large numbers of minority students so they cannot be reported in yearly results. The result is a large number of minority dropouts who may have finished school had a more accepting environment been established. Counselors must advocate that schools and students be rewarded for progress and success in addition to reaching criteria. Linn (2005) also suggests advocating for alternative measures of assessment in lieu of using only one particular test.

Finally, the high stakes environment leaves little time for the establishment of student/educator relationships. Students must experience a sense of belonging to the school and establish a relationship with at least one adult if they are to be successful (Stanley & Plucker, 2008). Those at risk of dropping out of school are particularly vulnerable in a hostile environment and need caring, accepting schools (Stanley & Plucker, 2008). Glasser (1999) further stressed the necessity of relationships by emphasizing the human's need for love and belonging. Secondary school counselors can therefore help offset negative aspects of the *No Child Left Behind Act* by facilitating relationships between teachers, mentors, and at risk minority students. The following program incorporates aspects of De Shazer's (1988) solution focused brief therapy and Glasser's (1999) reality therapy such that a caring environment is created and career maturity developed.

Description of Program

The program consists of four distinct components: mentorship, small group solution-focused counseling sessions, psychoeducational career lessons led by counselors and mentors, and implementation of solution-focused skills within the classroom. A description of each component along with program placement follows.

Program Placement

At risk secondary school students can be screened and placed into the program through teacher, parent, or principal recommendation due to failing grades, low state test scores, attendance, and/or behavior concerns. Students are placed into two groups. The first group consists of every student selected into the program while the second placement is into a small group of seven or eight students. In addition, mentors are matched to individual students based on similar interests, ethnicity, and gender.

Mentorship Component

Mentorship is especially helpful in establishing positive relationships in the school setting (Britner et al., 2006; Murray, 1997). Due to the aforementioned problems associated with the *No Child Left Behind Act* (2002), at risk students are often treated as school deficits. It is not surprising, therefore, that many at risk students report experiencing criticism and never feeling accepted (Page, 2006). Mentors can counter these attitudes through unconditional positive regard and encouragement (Murray, 1997).

Volunteer adult community mentors are assigned to and meet with each student weekly. Mentors should be selected based on their ability to pass a background check (per local or state district policy), willingness to attend training sessions, and commitment to meet weekly with students. Consistency of meetings is crucial since abandonment by a mentor can negatively influence at risk students (Murray, 1997). Mentors listen to student concerns and offer empathy, support, and advocacy while modeling good behaviors and decision making. For many at risk minority students, this may be the first time an adult has offered to listen without criticism, accept without condition, and instilled a rationale for perseverance. It is suggested that mentors consult with the school counselor at the conclusion of each student meeting. This enables school counselors to stay informed and assist mentors with any difficulties or issues not discussed in trainings. In addition, school counselors offer students an opportunity to discuss mentoring sessions before, during, or after small group counseling sessions.

Solution Focused Group Component

The small group concept uses solution focused brief therapy which allows students opportunities to share positive accomplishments, refocus thoughts on positive personal traits that led to past successes, exceptions to problems, and leadership skills (De Shazer, 1982; Metcalf, 1995). Solution focused brief therapy contends that students are able to create positive change by focusing on times when problems are not occurring (De Shazer, 1982; Littrell et al., 1995). By using solution focused techniques such as the miracle question, exception questions, complimenting, and scaling questions, these meetings focus on empowerment as opposed to victimization and thus may aid at risk students who need to overcome survival and social or emotional issues to attain career maturity.

Glasser (1999) indicates that humans want to be heard in order to fulfill a need for power. Small group sessions allow students freedom to share thoughts in an accepting environment. In addition, added peer support offers motivation to make positive changes and helps students rationalize behavior changes that lead to better academic achievement (Murray, 1997; Quane & Rankin, 2006). Weekly solution focused brief therapy sessions offer groups of seven or eight students the opportunity to change from a problem focus to a solution or positive focus.

The first session is an opportunity for students to become acquainted. Students bring pictures of family, pets, or fun events to the first meeting. After sharing these pictures with the group, students are asked the miracle question, "If a miracle happened and suddenly everything in your life became perfect, what would be different?" The group shares thoughts and is asked to think about this question over the next week. The following meeting consists of a more in depth discussion of this question and students mark their level of disturbance on a scale numbered from 1 (the problem is in total control) to 10 (the student is in total control).

At the beginning of each subsequent session, students are asked to write a list of improvements and share with the group. Rather than dwelling on negative issues, students are asked questions such as, "What is going better this week?" When a student mentions something that is not going well, other students are taught to point out exceptions. For example, a student might say, "My grades are terrible this week." Other students are asked to think of times when this is not true. Another student might say, "Your art teacher liked your drawing this week." The school counselor (group leader) would ask an exception question such as, "Name a time when you had a good grade and tell us what was different when it occurred?"

Next, the counselor asks a scaling question such as, "On a scale from 1-10, with the number 1 meaning the problem controls you and the number 10 indicating that you control the problem, where are you? What would it take for you to move up the scale just one number?" This question empowers students because it places control in their hands rather than within another person or entity. In this respect, Naylor's (1989) contention that effective dropout prevention programs help students resolve personal problems is imbedded into the session.

These sessions offer an accepting environment where student thoughts and ideas are valued. Naylor (1989) stated that the establishment of a caring positive environment was crucial in retaining at risk students. As a result, a sense of belonging to the group and consequently to school is an intentional byproduct of these sessions.

Solution Focused Strategies in the Classroom
Teachers are trained to focus on students' positive attributes

in lieu of simply correcting students when they misbehave or fail. This changes the focus of the classroom from one of denigration to that of encouragement. Teachers write down times when students are performing well or have shown improvement. These lists can be given to the school counselor to share with students in small group counseling sessions or teachers can share the list privately with students when they are demonstrating misbehavior. As a result, the classroom focus is changed from that of students who must overcome behavior or academic problems to one of detecting positive accomplishments. This is important for at risk minority students since Bennacer (2000) and Pierce (1994) found that a focus on punitive measures increased a student's probability of dropping out of school.

Psychoeducational Group Sessions

Psychoeducational sessions are used to teach social skills, disseminate career information that leads to goal setting, create a sense of belonging to the group, support among all members, and as opportunities to participate in fun activities. Training in social skills has been shown to improve students' classroom behaviors (Gresham, Van, & Cook, 2006) and possessing a career goal has been suggested as a protective factor that leads to healthy student development (Fleming, Woods, & Barkin, 2006). The *ASCA National Model* (2003) states that school counselors work with students on three domains: academic, personal/social, and career. As such, career information and development are important parts of the program.

Students meet as one large group once a month to discuss career information and goal setting, learn social skills, participate in fun activities, and create a sense of belonging. Every other month, a different guest speaker from the community presents information about personal career development and skills needed for job attainment. On alternating months, students participate in fun activities such as field trips (tours of university campuses or job sites are especially relevant), or games (volleyball, croquet, or any number of other activities students might select).

The result is a program intended to offset many of the

negative consequences of the *No Child Left Behind Act* (2002) while instilling career development. The program replaces feelings of failure with a positive career emphasis. Feelings of rejection, failure, and boredom can be replaced with empowerment as students develop close relationships, attain a rationale for educational endeavors, and manage personal issues.

Conclusion

School counselors can advocate for policy changes within the *No Child Left Behind Act* (2002) while implementing programs to both aid the educational endeavors and decrease the dropout rates of at risk minority students. The principles found in reality therapy (Glasser, 1999) and techniques from solution focused therapy (De Shazer, 1982, 1988) can be used to implement a strengths based approach to helping the career and academic development of students. Small group counseling sessions, psychoeducational career sessions, mentorship, and a solution focused intervention implemented by classroom teachers are program components that together form a school based career counseling program with the potential to reduce dropout rates among minority students. Advocacy for policy changes along with the implementation of this program will result in a better educated class of minority students with greater academic and career potential, maturity, and choices.

References

American School Counselor Association. (2003). *The ASCA national model: A framework for school counseling programs.* Alexandria, VA: Author.

Bennacer, H. (2000). How the sociological characteristics of the classroom affect academic achievement. *European Journal of Psychology of Education, 15*, 173-189.

Britner, P. A., Balcazar, F. E., Blechman, E. A., Blinn-Pike, L., & Larose, S. (2006). Mentoring special youth populations. *Journal of Community Psychology, 34*, 747-763.

De Shazer, S. (1982). *Patterns of brief family therapy.* New York: Guilford Press.

De Shazer, S. (1988). *Clues: Investigating solution in brief therapy.* New York: Norton.

Fleming, C., Woods, C., & Barkin, S. L. (2006). Career goals in the high risk adolescent. *Clinical Pediatrics, 45,* 757-764.

Glasser, W. (1999). *Choice theory: A new psychology of personal freedom.* New York: Harper Collins.

Gresham, F. M., Van, M. B., & Cook, F. M. (2006). Social skills training for teaching replacement behaviors: Remediating acquisition deficits in at-risk students. *Behavioral Disorders, 31,* 363-377.

Kober, N., Chudowsky, C., & Chudowsky, V. (2008). Has student achievement increased since 2002? State test score trends through 2006-2007. *Center on Education Policy.* Retrieved December 29, 2008, from http://www.cep-dc.org /document /docWindow.cfm?fuseaction=document.viewDocument&docu mentid=241&documentFormatId=3794

Linn, R. L. (2005). Fixing the NCLB accountability system. *Crest Policy Brief, 8,* 1-8.

Littrell, J., Malia, J., & Vanderwood, M. (1995). Single session brief counseling in a high school. *Journal of Counseling & Development, 73,* 451-458.

Metcalf, L. (1995). *Counseling toward solutions.* San Francisco: Jossey-Bass.

Murray, B. (1997, May). Unique mentor programs bolster students' careers. *APA Monitor, 50,* 50.

McNeil, L. M., Coppola, E., & Raddigan, J. (2008). Avoidable losses: High stakes accountability and the dropout crisis. *Education Policy Analysis Archives, 16,* 1-48.

Naylor, M. (1989). Retaining at-risk students in career and vocational education. *ERIC Clearinghouse on Adult Career and Vocational Education.* (ERIC Document Reproduction Service No. ED308400)

No Child Left Behind Act of 2001, Public Law 107-110, 107th Cong., 1st sess. (January 8, 2002). Codified at U. S. Code Title 20 Sec. 6301 et. seq. Retrieved July 20, 2008 at http://www.ed.gov/policy/elsec/leg/esea02/index.html

Orfield, G., Losen, D., Wald, J., & Swanson, C. B. (2004). Losing our future: How minority youth are being left behind by the graduation rate crisis. *Urban Institute.* Retrieved December 29, 2008, from http://www.urban.org/publications/ 410936.html

Page, B. (2006). *At risk students: Feeling their pain, understanding their plight, accepting their defense ploys.* Pittsburgh, PA: Educational Dynamics.

Pierce, C. (1994). Importance of classroom climate for at risk learners. Journal of *Educational Research, 88,* 37-42.

Quane, J. M., & Rankin, B. H. (2006). Does it pay to participate? Neighborhood based organizations and the social development of urban adolescents. *Children and Youth Services Review, 28,* 1229-1239.

Stanley, K. R., & Plucker, J. A. (2008). Improving high school graduation rates. *Center for Evaluation & Education Policy, 6,* 1-12.

Swanson, C. B. (2004). *Who graduates? Who doesn't? A statistical portrait of public high school graduation rates, Class of 2001.* Washington, DC: Urban Institute.

U.S. Census Bureau. (2004). *U.S. interim projections by age, sex, race, and Hispanic origin.* Washington, DC: Author.

Walden, L. M., & Kritsonis, W. A. (2008). The impact of the correlation between the no child left behind act's high stakes testing and the high drop-out rates of minority students. *National Journal for Publishing and Mentoring Doctoral Student Research, 5,* 1-6.

Wise, B. (2008). High school at the tipping point. *Educational Leadership, 65,* 8-13.

Article 3

White Male Identity Development and the World of Work, Using the Key Model

Paper based on a program presented at the 2008 National Career Development Association Global Conference, July 9-11, 2008, Washington, DC.

David A. Scott

The current economic conditions, along with the constant strain to live up to the masculine stereotype (e.g., no emotions, family provider), continue to be ripe for ongoing oppression and racism by White men in the workplace. As unemployment rises, White men are losing jobs, continuing to be asked to collaborate with people of color and women on projects, and finding it harder to secure employment. These conditions can lead to frustration and anger by White men who are becoming disillusioned by the American dream. There are several questions that can be asked to help support the need for a discussion about the world of work and White male identity development: (a) Is there racism and oppression in the workplace? (b) Are White men being asked to work with people of color and women? (c) Can productivity and the "bottom line" be hurt by racist and oppressive behaviors? The issue of racism and oppression becomes very relevant to company administrators when a discussion of how the profit margin can be affected by these behaviors.

Many times much of a person's identity is associated with their occupation. Roe and Lunneborg (1990) state that, "In our society, no single situation is potentially so capable of giving some satisfaction, at all levels of basic needs, as the occupation" (p. 6). We also know that high levels of unemployment are associated with increased rates of chemical dependency, interpersonal violence, suicide, criminal activity, and admissions to psychiatric facilities (Herr, Cramer, & Niles, 2004). The Key model (Scott & Robinson, 2001) was developed as a tool that counselors (including career counselors) could use to help them understand their clients. The Key model can help career counselors by exploring, with the client, their issues of oppression, and by understanding the possible type of identity development attitudes a White male may be experiencing at the time. The Key model can be used during diversity training to assist the counselor in having open dialogue discussions needed for possible changes in thinking and a reduction in oppressive behaviors in the workplace.

History of Theories

Most of the popular work on racial identity models has focused on people of color. The majority of Black and White racial identity development models have been developed over the past 30 years. The most notable White racial identity development models are works by Helms (1990, 1995) and Sue and Sue (1990). These models delineate a difference between one's race, socially constructed attitudes about race, and racial identity development. They also aid in the understanding of how people move from relatively low levels of awareness regarding their racial selves to a more sophisticated understanding of themselves and others as racial beings (Helms, 1984). Racial identities can be unlearned and replaced with more functional belief systems.

The critique of White racial identity development (WRID) models has been mostly focused around several main issues. Rowe, Bennett, and Atkinson (1994) contend that some WRID models assume that racial identity develops in response to an oppressive dominant society as do identity models for people of color. Many of these WRID models are framed exclusively in Black and White terms, explaining how White people develop an appreciation of other racial groups. Little is communicated about White identity itself. Myers et al. (1991) contend that most models are linear and do not account for the forward, backward, and stalled moments that characterize normal human development. Issues of possible class, age, and gender are not addressed in some models.

The Key Model

Although not a linear model, the Key model reflects the notion that the early phases of development involve minimal self-interrogation, whereas the higher levels of development typically involve a personal dilemma (dissonance with existing belief system) and its resolution, which leads to greater understanding of the self. The main goal, through discussion, counseling, and experience, is for White men to challenge the debilitating socialized notion that they are superior to others.

The use of types and phrases rather than stages is used to describe a set of attitudes that can be modified by real-life experiences. The Key model (Figure 1) is circular in nature (instead of linear) and suggests that movement can occur in multiple directions. Men may actually exhibit the characteristics of several stages, and it is thought that one stage may be more prominent than the others.

The Key model addresses the types of attitudes described by the basic levels of Maslow's (1968) hierarchy of needs, which includes shelter and food. These basic needs can create a false drive to oppress others for security and personal career advancement. Traditionally, White men, as well as other men, are socialized to equate self-worth with economic terms. They are taught to function at all costs and to be in control. These power issues are linked to the salience of their race and gender. In American culture people are ranked on their proximity to the normal referents of society: White, male, middle-class, Christian, heterosexual, and able-bodied persons (Robinson, 1999).

Figure 1

The Key model as a circular model. The "Self" can rotate between types and exhibit different attitudes toward different populations (race, religion, physical, socioeconomic).

Type 1: Noncontact Type

Attitudes in this phase include little or no knowledge of other races or of their own race. The White male is functioning at work as he is stereotypically expected to function. He is fine with operating under the status quo and will ignore, deny, or minimize the issues dealing with race and oppression. He maintains very traditional attitudes concerning gender. Low level encounters with women or people of color will not trigger enough dissonance to create change in his thinking. His hiring practices typically include hiring only white males for management or supervisory roles. He also exhibits little effort to collaborate with people of color or women on projects at work.

Implications for career counselors.

Career counselors can assist by first helping administrators identify White males that may be engaging in behaviors associated with this type. Having discussions with administrators about their concerns over the attitudes and behaviors of these men can help open the dialogue between management and staff. When working with the client, it is important to provide a safe environment that will enable the White male to begin to discuss issues related to oppression and racism. Using accusatory statements in the beginning sessions will only lead to the client shutting down emotionally and restricting comments to only what is required. A healthy exploration of the meaning of manhood may be beneficial during the counseling sessions. Career counselors need to also be aware of their own feelings toward White males who exhibit attitudes and behaviors of this type.

Type 2: The Claustrophobic Type

Just as the name implies, White men may feel very "closed in" by the shifting of workers from White to diverse new workers. He may begin to blame people of color and women for the loss of his job or his friend's job. The oppressive and racist behaviors become very evident as they struggle with issues related to power and control. This type is many times characterized by an increase in oppressive and racist behaviors in an attempt to control others and secure his place at work. Because of the possibility of never experiencing true dissonance and/or the inability to become aware of one's privilege, many White men may never leave Type 1 or Type 2.

Implications for career counselors.

Even though the client is exhibiting oppressive behaviors, his feelings of a possible job loss are real. As stated earlier, job loss can lead to mental health problems at home and work. Career counselors can have open discussions about the client's feelings of loss, anger, and hostility towards the misconception of the American dream, people of color, and women. These early discussions can also lead to the development of healthy and collaborative career aspirations. Providing the client with current facts (e.g., unemployment rate for minorities is double that of whites) and realistic reasons for the company's downsizing may be beneficial.

Type 3: Conscious Identity Type

This phase is typically started by a real-life precipitating event that creates dissonance between the client's belief system and reality. An example of the event could be that a person of color does better on a job project than his White co-workers. Events similar to this will require the White male to reevaluate his belief system and the importance of collaboration at work. This is a very critical time in that he is finally realizing that oppression and racism do play a role in his attitudes and behaviors at work. It is important for career counselors to be aware that the level of dissonance required will differ for each individual.

Implications for career counselors.

This is a crucial time for the client. They can return to, and continue to exhibit behaviors of, the Claustrophobic type or may move to the Empirical type. The career counselor can work with the client on these feelings of confusion and guilt. Counseling techniques that encourage the client to begin the introspection of his belief system are beneficial at this point. Providing emotional support is also critical at this time. Many of the client's White friends may still be operating in the Noncontact or Claustrophobic type and pressure the client to "stick together" instead of working with women or people of color.

Type 4: Empirical Type

The realization of the role of oppression and racism in the client's life are now evident. He sees that his attitudes and behaviors at work are considered oppressive and discriminatory. His old concept of the American dream is no longer valid. The White male begins to understand how his unearned privileges (white skin) have been used to his advantage and to the disadvantage of others. He understands that people of color and women are not responsible for his job difficulties or job loss. White males in this type may step aside on a project and let a person of color or a woman take the lead role.

Implications for career counselors.

Discussions about the definitions of manhood, being White, and working with people of color and women are valuable at this time. Career counselors can help the client appreciate the value of collaboration at work. Administrators could potentially see an increase in profits and productivity through having staff work together on projects. Human Resources could also see a drop in discriminatory behaviors by these clients. The career counselor can facilitate group discussions about reducing oppressive behaviors and the importance of collaboration. Career counselors will need to have resources available (various readings on identity development and diversity at work) to provide to the clients during their self-exploration.

Type 5: Optimal Type

The positive change in the White male's worldview will be evident at both work and home. Collaboration and diversity will be a top career priority at this point. The client understands that the struggle for power and control over others is no longer a viable or healthy option. They acknowledge that working with all people is truly advantageous for success at work and in life.

Implications for career counselors.

Career counselors can continue to help the client have insight in how to be an agent of change at work. Encourage the client to work at ending oppressive and racist behaviors in the workplace. The client understands the true meaning of valuing each person and listening to other's ideas and solutions to issues and projects at work. Career counselors can also encourage administrators to recognize the change in attitudes and collaboration of these White males. Career counselors can also help collect data on changes in productivity and work success by these White men who are working with people of color and women on various projects.

Conclusion

One of the main goals of the Key model in career counseling is to facilitate growth in White males by seeing them as whole beings (Scott & Robinson, 2001). Career counselors of all races and backgrounds will be called upon to assist clients who possess different worldviews. Successful career counseling will require an in-depth understanding of the client's experiences and perceptions which have contributed to his oppressive behaviors. It is critical that career counselors recognize and understand the types of attitudes White males struggle with at work. For most of their lives they have been taught to equate productivity and control with success and manhood at both work and home. These White men could face ridicule and be ostracized at work for going against society's stereotyped definition of manhood. Career counselors need to be mindful of how these dynamics will affect the direction of counseling. Thus the Key model can be one tool that career counselors use to help understand the multiple facets of identity development in White men. The Key model may also be useful when developing diversity training in the workplace.

References

Helms, J. E. (1990). *In Black and White racial identity theory.* Westport, CT: Praeger Press.

Helms, J. E. (1984). Toward a theoretical explanation of the effects of race on counseling: A Black and White model. *Journal of Counseling Psychologist*, 12, 153-165.

Helms, J. E. (1995). An update of White and people of color racial identity model. In J. G. Ponterotto, J. M. Casas, L. A. Suzuki, & C. M. Alexander (Eds.), *Handbook of multicultural counseling* (pp. 181-198). Thousand Oaks, CA: Sage.

Herr, E. L., Cramer, S. H., & Niles, S. G. (2004). *Career guidance and counseling through the lifespan: Systemic approaches* (6th ed.). Boston: Allyn & Bacon.

Maslow, A. H. (1968). *Toward a psychology of being.* New York: Van Nostrand Reinhold.

Myers, L. J., Speight, S. L., Highlen, P. S., Cox, C. I., Reynolds, A. L., Adams, E. M., & Hanley, P. (1991). Identity development and worldview: Toward an optimal conceptualization. *Journal of Counseling & Development*, 70, 54-63.

Robinson, T. L. (1999). The intersections of dominant discourses across race, gender, and other identities. *Journal of Counseling & Development*, 77, 73-79.

Roe, A., & Lunneborg, P. W. (1990). Personality development and career choice. In D. Brown & L. Brooks (Eds.), *Career choice and development* (pp. 6-9). San Francisco: Jossey-Bass.

Rowe, W., Bennett, S. K., & Atkinson, D. R. (1994). White racial identity models: A critique and alternative proposal. *The Counseling Psychologist*, 22, 129-145.

Scott, D. A., & Robinson, T. L. (2001). White male identity development: The Key model. *Journal of Counseling and Development, 79*, (4), 415-421.

Sue, D. W., & Sue, D. (1990). *Counseling the culturally different: Theory and practice.* New York: Wiley.

Section II

Client Characteristics and Needs

Article 4

Adapting Counseling Skills for Multicultural and Diverse Clients

Paper based on a program presented at the 2009 American Counseling Association Annual Conference and Exposition, March 19-23, Charlotte, North Carolina.

Ireon LeBeauf, Marlowe Smaby, and Cleborne Maddux

Multicultural counseling takes place when a counselor and client are from differing cultural groups. Because significant demographic changes are taking place in the United States, multiculturalism is becoming increasingly important. In fact, multiculturalism has been called the "fourth force" in helping (Pederson, 1991, as cited in Skovholt & Rivers, 2007, p. 15). The other forces include *psychodynamic, humanistic/existential*, and *behavioral* counseling theories and methods. Knowledge and skills related to all four of these forces are critical for understanding behavior in the counseling process and for effective counseling in a multicultural context. Therefore, seven divisions of the American Counseling Association (ACA) have endorsed the multicultural counseling competencies developed by the Association for Multicultural Counseling and Development (AMCD; Sue & Sue, 1999).

However, whether or not mental health practitioners in the therapeutic setting subscribe to, or even understand, the principles and dynamics of what it means to be culturally competent remains a largely unanswered question (Tackey, 2001). Counselor education faculty often urge students to celebrate diversity, but the average student is not equipped with knowledge of the components of the RESPECTFUL Counseling Cube (D'Andrea & Daniels, 2001). These include religion and spirituality (R), economic class background (E), sexual identity (S), psychological maturity (P), ethnic and racial identity (E), chronological stage (C), trauma (T), family background (F), unique physical characteristics (U), and geographical location (L).

The evolution of counseling skills training has moved from an ill-defined process to more clearly delineated approaches. Five pioneers have made important contributions to this evolution. These include (a) Carl Rogers, (b) Robert Carkhuff, (c) Norman Kagan, (d) Alan Ivey, and (e) Stanley Baker. These influential individuals were responsible for (a) *Person-Centered Therapy*, (b) *Human Resource Development*, (c) *Interpersonal Process Recall*, (d) *Microcounseling*, and (e) the *Meta-Analytic and Narrative Review Approach*, respectively. (The latter is based on a narrative and meta-analytic review of three of the other approaches.) Elements from the training approaches of the first four of these individuals and from Baker's meta-analysis have been used to develop the Skilled Counselor Training Model (Smaby & Maddux, in press).

The Skilled Counselor Training Model (SCTM)

The Skilled Counseling Training Model (SCTM) is a skills-based training program that promotes attainment of skills through the use of modeling, mastery, persuasion, arousal, and supervisory feedback (Smaby, Maddux, Torres-Rivera, & Zimmick, 1999). In the SCTM, skills are divided into three stages: *exploring*, *understanding*, and *acting* (Smaby et al., 1999). For each stage, the Model illustrates (a) a purpose, (b) two counseling *processes*, and (c) six counseling *skills*.

The Exploring Stage

The purpose of the exploring stage is to help clients determine where they are in relationship to the problems they are facing. The *attending* process is a component of this stage and includes *eye contact, body language,* and *verbal tracking.* The *questioning and reflecting* process, also a component of the exploring stage, includes *open-ended questioning, paraphrasing, and summarizing.* The exploring stage should be marked by high levels of client talk and minimal counselor interruption. During this stage, the counselor should communicate acceptance, empathy, and positive regard. At the conclusion of the exploring stage, clients should feel fully and completely supported to explore issues from their own viewpoints (Smaby & Maddux, in press).

The Understanding Stage

The purpose of the understanding stage is to help clients recognize where they are in relationship to where they want to be with regard to the problems they are facing. During this stage, the counselor should confront the client concerning inconsistencies in behavior and attitudes. The counseling process of *interchangeable empathy* includes the skills of *stating feelings and content, self disclosure,* and *asking for concrete and specific expressions.* The *additive empathy* process includes the skills of *immediacy; identifying general problem situations, actions taken, and feelings;* and *caring confrontation.* Thus, when the understanding stage concludes, clients should have a fresh perspective or be able to generate new viewpoints regarding their life challenges (Smaby & Maddux, in press).

The Acting Stage

The purpose of the acting stage is to help clients identify what they need to do to get to where they want to be with regard to problems. The *decision-making* process includes the skills of *deciding, choosing,* and *identifying consequences.* At this point, the counselor should define clients' situation as consisting of a choice to (a) change ineffective coping behaviors or (b) continue to allow these futile patterns to be problematic (deciding skill). The counselor should then outline the thoughts and feelings that previously prevented clients from implementing change (choosing) while exploring the positive values that are important to clients as a result of the decision (skill of identifying consequences). The *contracting* process includes the skills of *reaching agreements; setting deadlines; and reviewing goals and actions to determine outcomes.*

If the counselor has employed sound exploring stage and understanding stage skills, it is rare that clients will opt for no change, because it is obvious that this would be self-defeating. However, if clients do opt for no change, the counselor should revert back to previous stage skills and attempt to build a relationship that will result in positive client outcomes (Smaby & Maddux, in press).

This article will describe how to use the RESPECTFUL Cube and the Skilled Counselor Training Model (SCTM; Smaby & Maddux, in press) in multicultural counseling relationships.

Using the RESPECTFUL Cube to Assess Potential Conflicting Views Between a Counselor and a Client

The first step is to identify how a counselor's attitudes related to the 10 domains of the RESPECTFUL Cube can conflict with views of clients. This exercise is designed to help counselors become more aware of their own beliefs and biases about clients who are from diverse groups and backgrounds. In this exercise, counselors use the 10 domains of the RESPECTFUL Cube to evaluate themselves on each issue.

For each of the 10 domains or issues, counselors should write a short statement about their views and how these views could be a source of contention with clients who have different views of these issues. Counselors should then use these 10 written statements as a basis for planning to modify how they interact with clients who may hold differing views.

Adapting the SCTM Skills for Addressing the RESPECTFUL Cube Domains

The second step in this exercise is to adapt skills of the exploring, understanding, and acting stages to various domains of the RESPECTFUL Cube. The following section describes how exploring stage skills can be adapted for ethnic and racial identity when working with American Minority clients.

Adapting the Exploring Stage Skills to Clients From Different Ethnic/Racial (E) Backgrounds

Clients from various racial backgrounds may have different perceptions of the exploring stage skills of eye contact, body language, verbal tracking, open-ended questioning, paraphrasing, and summarizing. It is imperative that the counselor consider how these skills will affect rapport with diverse clientele.

When beginning to counsel American Minority clients (Asian-American, American-Indian, African-American, and Latino-American), it is important to assess the level of acculturation of the client. For example, if the level of acculturation is minimal, direct eye contact, demonstrative body language, and continuous verbal tracking may be perceived as impolite by Asian American clients. The counselor will need to maintain a heightened awareness of how these skills are affecting the counseling session and reduce the use of these skills accordingly (Smaby & Maddux, in press).

Native American clients who maintain strong ties to their tribal groups may perceive persistent eye contact, direct questions, repetitive paraphrasing and summarizing as being invasive and authoritative. Such clients may prefer more oblique and circular questioning, analogies, stories related to the issues or problems of concern, and the use of silence. It is also important for the culturally competent counselor to have a working knowledge of and respect for clients' tribal customs and/or belief systems (Smaby & Maddux, in press).

Like some other American Minority clients, African-American clients are likely to suffer from cultural mistrust of counselors. This cultural mistrust can often be traced to past racist and discriminatory practices. Clients who present cultural mistrust often appreciate an acknowledgement and acceptance of their frustration with the system. The counselor should also attempt to create an environment where African-American clients are able to express themselves freely without prejudice or judgment (LeBeauf, 2008).

Acculturation stress and economic issues often play a major role in contributing to mental health issues in Latino communities. When counseling Latino clients, it is important to recognize the profound impact that immigration laws and racial discrimination have had in Latino communities. Casual rather than persistent eye contact along with genuine empathy-based paraphrasing may also be helpful in building rapport with Latino clients. Also, recognizing the important roles of the nuclear and the extended family in counseling can be important to Latinos, who often consider themselves closely tied to family and community (Smaby & Maddux, in press).

Adapting the Understanding Stage Skills for Addressing Sexual Identity (S)

Issues of gender and sexual orientation are often overlooked by counselors in training. The understanding stage of the SCTM focuses on skills of stating feelings and content; self-disclosure; asking for concrete and specific expressions; immediacy; identifying general problem situation, action taken, and feelings; and confronting in a caring way (Smaby & Maddux, in press). The following examples are how the skills of the understanding stage of the SCTM can be useful in understanding issues of gender and sexual orientation in counseling.

Understanding Stage Skills With Females and Males

Distinctive communication styles characteristic of each gender should be considered. For instance, a female may find the understanding stage skills of stating feelings and content, self disclosure, and asking concrete questions to be blunt and lacking dimension. Females may prefer a conversational style of counseling that allows them to express more personal and emotional feelings. In contrast, males may find the use of these skills beneficial to their progress in session, but may struggle to identify their emotions. Also, the understanding stage skills of asking for concrete and specific expressions; immediacy; identifying problem situations, action taken, and feelings; and confronting in a caring way may be considered by males to be overly intrusive and emotionally charged (Smaby & Maddux, in press). In either case, the counselor needs to monitor clients' personal communication styles and adjust use of the understanding skills accordingly. If the counselor senses intimidation, withdrawal, or anxiety by the client, the counselor should provide ample time and space to allow clients to express themselves in a way that is comfortable.

Understanding Stage Skills With Lesbian, Gay, Bi-Sexual, or Transgender Clients

The use of understanding stage skills with Lesbian, Gay, Bisexual, Transgender or (LGBT) clients may be considered too intrusive or direct, and may result in clients feeling vulnerable or attacked. Culturally competent counselors using these skills should consider softening their delivery and tone. It is also important that counselors recognize that the mental health problems manifested by members of the LGBT community may not be due to LGBT identity itself (Smith, Foley, & Chaney, 2008). Counselors should also consider the dual discrimination of persons of color who are also members of the LGBT community and who experience challenges related to racism and heterosexism. In order to be effective in the therapeutic setting with LGBT clients, the counselor must consistently communicate genuine empathy and support.

Adapting Acting Stage Skills for Addressing Economic Class (E), Chronological Age (C) and Psychological Maturity (P)

Economic Class

Clients affected by poverty may be reluctant to participate in counseling. These clients often struggle with basic life needs and may view acting stage skills of deciding, choosing, and identifying consequences as impossible for them. Thus, clients with lower incomes may require assistance in obtaining housing, food, and healthcare. Once these lower-level needs are met they may be more able to focus on strategies to improve their psychological functioning (Smith et al., 2008). Conversely, clients with higher levels of income may find the skills in the acting stage helpful, but may also feel the need to design their own interventions. For example, in regard to contracting, clients may decide what steps are needed to improve a situation without suggestions from the counselor.

Chronological Age

Acting stage skills may be difficult for children who are age 2 years and under due to their more limited cognitive and emotional development. Exploring stage skills may be much more appropriate. However, acting stage skills can be adapted for use with children ages 2 to 7 years. This can be achieved by proposing tentative hypotheses regarding decision-making and contracting as a way to nurture the development of higher-order thinking and expanding viewpoints. Children between the ages of 7 and 11 years may be able to engage in acting stage skills if they are presented in a concrete fashion. However, like younger children, they will require suggestions and assistance in contracting and decision-making skills. Play therapy, art therapy, and media may be useful tools in working with children and adolescents in counseling. Counselors should also consult with parents and caregivers to assist young children in their counseling journey (Smaby & Maddux, in press).

Psychological Maturity

Psychological maturity as it relates to the acting stage skills are based on clients' stage of cognitive and emotional development. For example, in Kohlberg's theory, those whose moral reasoning is at stages one or two obey rules of behavior based upon their fear of punishment or trading favors. Children at this stage may not fully benefit from acting stage skills due to egocentricity. On the other hand, children who have progressed to moral reasoning levels at stages three and four (good boy/good girl or law and order) may be able to view perceptions of self and others as important to good relationships and rule-following as necessary and important for the betterment of all. A counselor can deliver acting stage skills by suggesting tentative hypotheses that can be confirmed or denied by children. Children at the highest level of Kohlberg's theory of moral reasoning (social contract or golden rule) may be able to initiate acting stage skills and the counselor should allow such children to use their higher levels of maturity as springboards for developing effective coping strategies (Smaby & Maddux, in press).

Summary and Conclusions

The RESPECTFUL Cube identifies 10 domains that act as cultural lenses through which counselors experience their clients. Thus, counselor educators need to help counselors-in-training to assess how differing views of these domains by diverse clients may affect the counseling process. Secondly, counselor educators need to help counselors-in-training learn to adapt the 18 counseling skills of the SCTM by using the RESPECTFUL Cube domains. These domains can be used as a guide to accommodate clients from diverse cultural groups. It is time for the counseling profession not only to recognize multicultural and diversity issues, but to develop systematic and practical approaches for helping counselors address and adapt counseling practices with culturally diverse clients.

References

D'Andrea, M., & Daniels, J. (2001). RESPECTFUL counseling: An integrative model for counselors. In D. Pope-Davis & H. Coleman (Eds.), *The interface of class, culture and gender in counseling* (pp.417-466). Thousand Oaks, CA: Sage.

LeBeauf, I. (2008). Racial disparities in new millennium schools: Implications for school counselors. [Electronic version]. *Journal of School Counseling, 6*(10). http://www.jsc.montana. edu/articles/v6n10.pdf

Skovholt, T. M., & Rivers, D. A. (2007). *Helping skills and strategies.* Denver, CO: Love Publishing.

Smaby, M. H., Maddux, C. D., Torres-Rivera, D., & Zimmick, R. (1999). A study of the effects of a skills-based versus a conventional group counseling training program. *Journal of Specialist in Group Work*, 24, 152-163.

Smaby, M. H., & Maddux, C. D. (in press.) *Counseling skills: Assessing mastery, transfer, and client outcomes.* Pacific, CA: Brooks Cole.

Smith, L., Foley, P. F., & Chaney, M. P. (2008). Addressing classism, ableism, and heterosexism within multicultural-social justice training. *Journal of Counseling and Development, 86*, 303-309.

Sue, D. W., & Sue, D. (1999). *Counseling the culturally different: Theory and practice* (2nded.). New York: John Wiley & Sons.

Tackey, N. D. (2001). Eliminating bias in performance management [Electronic version]. *British Journal of Administrative Management, 27*, 12-18.

Article 5

Children's Responses to Disaster From Moral and Ethical Reasoning Perspectives

Paper based on a program presented at the 2009 American Counseling Association Annual Conference and Exposition, March 19-23, Charlotte, North Carolina.

Vaughn S. Millner and Jean N. Clark

Hurricane Katrina, the most destructive and costly natural disaster in history, resulted in the largest displacement of individuals in U.S. history (FEMA, 2006a) and forced more than 270,000 people into shelters along the U.S. Gulf Coast. According to FEMA reports (FEMA, 2006b), 113,000 individuals in Alabama applied for federal and state assistance and about 40,000 in the state sought services at FEMA centers. Herein, we respectfully disclose the reactions of third-grade children in Mobile, Alabama to Hurricane Katrina one month following the storm. Children in Mobile represent families that experienced a wide range of losses as a result of the hurricane and thus offer a unique snapshot of children's cognitive processes following disaster.

The College of Education (COE) at the University of South Alabama (USA) partnered with the Mobile County District School system and other agencies immediately after the hurricane to facilitate comprehensive recovery efforts for the school system. This study's authors were intensely involved in the collaboration. Millner was the Chair of the COE Hurricane Katrina Disaster Task Force and Clark interrupted her sabbatical at USA to serve as a school counselor and resource point person in the school system. One of the first collaborative efforts between the Mobile County School System's Student Services System and COE was the co-sponsorship of a crisis intervention program for school counselors, social workers, nurses, and other social agents who work in the school system as well as school counselors from neighboring Mississippi counties.

The purpose of this study was to understand children's lived experiences following a major disaster. The findings could have immediate relevance for school professionals following a disaster.

Method

Procedure

Immediately following the presentation and one month subsequent to Hurricane Katrina, a school counselor used an intervention she learned from the previously described crisis intervention program. After soliciting the permission of teachers in five third grade elementary classrooms, she asked the children to write "Dear Katrina" letters as part of a language arts lesson in their unit on writing a friendly letter. The archival data was given to the authors two weeks following the activity. IRB approval was obtained to review retrospective data, and both student assent and parental/guardian consent forms were collected.

Participants

Of the 122 children who participated, 100% provided consent. Five children were excluded because their gender category was unspecified, resulting in a sample of 117 (53 females; 64 males).

Data Analyses

This work is approached from both a qualitative and quantitative perspective, an appropriate method for human development research (Yoshikowa, Weisner, Kalil, & Way, 2008). Data analyses took over 18 months. During this time, the authors maintained a research journal to monitor personal assumptions and blind spots. The data was coded and re-coded according to emerging themes. The study has ample process validity and reliability. The materials were analyzed by each researcher over 100 times over a span of 18 months.

Quantitative analysis added to the depth and breadth of identified qualitative themes. To analyze gender differences, chi square analyses were run on all variables greater than 15% frequency. An alpha level of .05 was set.

Results and Discussion

Piaget's Cognitive Theory of Development

From the outset of this analysis, Piaget's cognitive theory of development (1973) rose to the forefront. The first of Piaget's stages, the pre-operational stage, usually ends by about ages six or seven and is characterized by concepts such as egocentrism, i.e., maintaining the perspective of self (Siegel, Brodzinsky, & Golinkoff, 1981). One-fourth of the letters demonstrated egocentrism, e.g., *I hate you for destroying the second and third graders field trip* (Respondent 50).

The concrete operations stage, which appears at about ages six or seven, is basically a system of internalized actions which permits the child to do in his or her mind what previously could have been done only in a three-dimensional plane. In the concrete operational stage, children are learning vocabulary and forming concepts based on experience. Their descriptions bear this developmental process: *You are a big pimple planted on earth* (Respondent 10). Approximately 85% of the third graders in this study fell into the concrete operations stage using concrete descriptions to explain their reactions.

Moral Reasoning

Moral reasoning, the second major theme to emerge, relates to the ways individuals think about and justify their behavior (Kohlberg, 1984). Kohlberg (1966, 1984) classified moral reasoning into six stages that become increasingly less egocentric and more abstract over time and his theory focused primarily on justice. Kohlberg's stages are related to Piaget's cognitive development theory in that individuals cognitively struggle with moral issues and their reasoning changes in developmental sequence that allows them to eventually resolve moral conflicts more effectively.

During stages 1 and 2, the preconventional level, children's thinking is very concrete and self-focused. Forty-five percent of this study's children reflected self-interest, e.g., *Why did you take my power away so I couldn't play my playstation 2?* (Respondent 106). Another hallmark of stages 1 and 2 reasoning is the focus on obeying authority, and therefore rules, for the purpose of avoiding punishment. Nine percent of the children believed that the hurricane should be punished as suggested by the following: *How dare you turn off the power for almost a week! How would like it if tore some of your roof off?! You smashed a ton of cars. Can I come over and pumbel your yard?* (Respondent 55).

Stages 3 and 4 are found at the conventional level, embody interpersonal cooperation and include a "good boy-good girl" line of reasoning. Twenty percent of the children viewed the hurricane as "bad" or "mean." For example, *Don't you know how mean that was for you to do that? Very mean!* (Respondent 5).

Stage 5 is the social-order-maintaining orientation and involves respect for societal laws as a means to ensure societal order for all. Stage 6, the final stage, is the universal ethical principle orientation. This highest stage is defined by ethical principles of conscience and global reasoning that consider all human beings with respect and consideration. Seven children provided examples of what could be considered higher levels of moral reasoning. For example, one child wrote: *During the Hurricane several people lost there loved one's. I don't really hate the hurricane because hurricans are a part of life. I know that Katrina was for a resion. And I know that the world will be back together soon! P.S. Hopefully, It was for a reasian!* (Respondent 42).

Concern for others was a major theme of moral reasoning in

this study and is also applicable to Gilligan's (1977, 1982) theory of moral reasoning care. As another way to view the children's expressions of concern for others, Gilligan, unlike Kohlberg (1966, 1984), emphasized (a) focus on one's own needs, (b) focus on self-sacrifice associated with concern for others' needs, and (c) balance of one's own and others' needs. In this study, 78% of the children identified concern for others. Moreover, there was a statistical difference in the frequency of females' expressions of concern for others compared to those of males: females were more than one and one-half times more likely than males to express concern for others.

Empathy-Related Responses

The third theoretical body of research that emerged in our analyses was associated with expressions of empathy and sympathy. Empathy is the comprehension of another's emotions and the experience of a feeling similar to what the person might be feeling (Eisenberg, 2005). Empathy can occur vicariously, that is, by either direct or indirect exposure to another's situation. Sympathy, an emotional response in reaction to another's emotional state or condition, may or may not reflect the other's emotions accurately, but does involve concern for others or sadness (Eisenberg, Wentzel, & Harris, 1998).

Consideration of others reflects a higher level of moral reasoning. Empathic responses were reflected in 37% of the children's responses as demonstrated by the following: *Your not what we needed. Now were just sad and hurt! You killed thousands of people! Gas prices are higher, with people needing gas to be lower! It was $2.45, not it's $5.95! People need help and God. No family needs this, all we need to do is hope, pray, praise, love, help and think of others!* (Respondent 83).

Both empathy and sympathy are a result of cognitive perspective-taking and extend this process (Eisenberg et al., 1998). Reasoning about the rightness or wrongness of an action reflects various levels of cognitive and moral reasoning but becoming personally distressed through feeling empathy or sympathy is an added response. An empathic person can feel sorrow and concern for others that lead to feelings of personal distress (Batson, 1991). Eighteen percent of the children expressed empathy or sympathy coupled with distress as in the following: " . . .*you have killed thousands of people in Louisana and New Orleans. It is heartbearking to watch. You make me sick to my stomach!* (Respondent 119).

Altruism, a type of prosocial behavior, is considered the "essence of the prosocial personality" (Eisenberg et al. 1999, p. 360), i.e., voluntary behavior motivated by the desire to help others (Eisenberg, 1986). An example follows: *A lot of people lost their houses, boat and other stuf. I am glad that I was ok but others are no ok. Some people have lost everything . . . I am glad to give money, Clothing, food, and supplies to Hurricane Katrina victims* (Respondent 65). Eight children (6.8%) expressed some form of prosocial behavior.

Implications for School Counseling Professionals

The following insights gained from this study's results may help in applying the cognitive and moral perception of children to the coping skills and processing necessary during and after such crises. The respondents' letters are poignant, invaluable directions toward a better understanding of interventions needed for school-age children following a period of crisis and/or disaster. All involved in the health and safety of children, especially school counselors, need specific education about disaster or trauma.

The best preparation for any life experience is the presence of accessible personal resources such as those found in the family, the community, and in personal strengths (Brock, 2002). For children, these resources are often found within the school experience (Robinson, 2006). If the school counseling program is strong and based on tenets of the American School Counseling Association National Model (ASCA 2004, 2005), students have the opportunity to develop academic, personal, and social skills needed to face life experiences. The school counselor, in coordination with the classroom teacher, can offer opportunities for growth in the academic, career, and social-personal domains. For students who need more support in any area, the school counselor works with teachers and community, providing resources and referring children who need help outside the school. Through such referrals students may receive counseling, academic support, or mental health support from private social workers or licensed counselors, psychologists or psychiatrists, medical personnel, or counselors in government or social agencies in the community.

Interventions With Children

In the case of disaster, the first form of help involves physical safety. Sometimes in this stage, counselors are involved as volunteer workers, as agents of social institutes or rescue entities, or school personnel (Kennedy, 2005).

Once safety is established, screening for serious mental health issues is important. Schools can partner with local mental health agencies to help screen for potential post-traumatic stress disorders or other serious mental and emotional problems. One type of recommended treatment by mental health professionals is some form of cognitive behavioral treatment (Cook-Cottone, 2004; Goenjian, Karayan, & Pynoos, 1997; March, Amaya-Jackson, Murray, & Schulte, 1998; Perrin, Smith & Yule, 2000; Yule, 2001). Yule (2001) suggests that this combination intervention works because it desensitizes children to their "triggers" – whether these are thoughts, behaviors, images and memories, or socio-environmental circumstances. The treatment uncouples the cognitive pairing between the traumatic events and the cognitive memories attached to them (Cook-Cottone, 2004). As discussed earlier, these cognitive memories are often accompanied by specific affective and/or behavioral reactions.

For children not identified with severe trauma symptoms and who remain in the classroom, there are several alternatives and many can be incorporated in the school curriculum. It is helpful to remember that children understand, perceive, and express in concrete terms. Creative expression has been used effectively, along with verbal communication, in small group or individual situations. These activities often include writing activities such as the "Letter to Hurricane Katrina," drawing, or play therapy (Biswas, 1995; Maitra, Ramaswamy, & Sirur, 2002) and may be administered by a range of school counseling professionals trained in the use of helping children express and process their feelings and experiences (White, 2005).

The point where cognitive development and emotions intersect is the place where children try to process their feelings by merging them with thought. This is especially true when the child is recounting something in their past: "every operation of the memory of evocation includes a reorganization" (Piaget, 1973, p. 43). In essence, this means that every time a child retells a story, an event from their past, or memory of something they have seen or experienced in some way, they reframe it cognitively.

To summarize, the current research is a critical contribution to the body of literature related to helping children who experience disaster. The integral relation of thinking and perceiving, alongside the expression of emotion in a safe environment, demonstrates the best of counseling and classroom instruction.

References

American School Counseling Association (ASCA). (2004). The role of the professional school counselor. Retrieved May 17, 2005, from http://www.schoolcounselor.org/content.asp? contentid =240

American School Counseling Association (ASCA). (2005). *The ASCA model: A framework for school counseling programs* (2nd ed.). Alexandria, VA: Author.

Batson, C. D. (1991). The altruism question: *Toward a social-psychological answer.* Hillsdale, NJ: Erlbaum.

Biswas, I. M. (1995). *A study of children affected by disaster.* Bank Street College of Education Dissertation LC 33842849.

Brock, S. E. (2002). Identifying individuals at risk for psychological trauma. In S. E. Brock, P. J. Lazarus, Jr., & S. R. Jimerson (Eds.), *Best practices in school crisis prevention and intervention*, 367-383. NASP Publications, ED 461085.

Cook-Cottone, C. (2004). Childhood posttraumatic stress disorder: Diagnosis, treatment, and school reintegration. *School Psychology Review, 33*(1), 127-139.

Eisenberg, N. (1986). *Altruistic emotion, cognition and behavior.* Hillsdale, NJ: Erlbaum.

Eisenberg, N. (2005). The development of empathy-related responding. *Nebraska Symposium on Motivation, 51*, 73-117.

Eisenberg, N., Guthrie, I. K., Murphy, B. C., Shepard, S. A., Cumberland, A, & Carlo, G. (1999). Consistency and development of prosocial dispositions: A longitudinal study. *Child Development, 70*(6), 1360-1372.

Eisenberg, N., Wentzel, N.M., & Harris, J. D. (1998). The role of emotionality and regulation in empathy-related responding. *School Psychology Review, 27*(4), 506-521.

FEMA. (2006a, August 22). By the numbers – one year later: FEMA recovery update for Hurricane Katrina. U.S. Department of Homeland Security. Retrieved September 22, 2007 from http://www.fema.gov/news/newsrelease.fema?id=29109

FEMA. (2006b, August 24). One year after Hurricane Katrina, Recovering continues in Alabama. Fema Aid at $970 million. U.S. Department of Homeland Security. Retrieved September 22, 2007 from http://www.fema.gov/news/newsrelease.fema?id =29185

Gilligan, C. (1977). In a different voice: Women's conception of the self and morality. *Harvard Education Review, 47*, 481-517.

Gilligan, C. (1982). *In a different voice: Psychological theory and women's development.* Cambridge, MA: Harvard University Press.

Goenjian, A. K., Karayan, I., & Pynoos, R. S. (1997). Outcome of psychotherapy among early adolescents after trauma. *American Journal of Psychiatry, 154*, 536-542.

Kennedy, A. (2005). Returning to normal. Counseling Today Online. American Counseling Association. Retrieved March 4, 2008, from www.counseling.org/CounselingTodayArticles.aspx? AGuid=927c3cb2-0

Kohlberg, L. (1966). A cognitive-developmental analysis of children's sex-role concepts and attitudes. In E. E. Maccoby (Ed.), *The development of sex differences* (pp. 82-173). Stanford, CA: Stanford University Press.

Kohlberg, L. (1984). *Essays on moral development: The psychology of moral development* (Vol. 2). San Francisco: Harper & Row.

Maitra, S., Ramaswamy, S., & Sirur, S. (2002). Use of play and art forms with children in disaster: The Gujarat experience. *The Indian Journal of Social Work, 63*(2), 263-283.

March, J. S., Amaya-Jackson, L., Murray, C., & Schulte, A. (1998). Cognitive-behavioral psychotherapy for children and adolescents with posttraumatic stress disorder after a single-incident stressor. *Journal of the American Academy of Child and Adolescent Psychiatry, 37*, 585-593.

Perrin, S., Smith, P., & Yule, W. (2000). Practitioner review: The assessment and treatment of post-traumatic stress disorder in children and adolescents. *Journal of Child Psychology & Allied Disciplines, 41*, 277-289.

Piaget, J. (1973). *The child and reality: problems of genetic psychology.* Translated by Arnold Rosin. New York: Grossman Publishers.

Robinson, S. (2006). Keynote address. Transforming School Counseling Initiative. Education Trust Annual Meeting, Boca Raton, FL: June 1-4, 2006.

Siegel, I. E., Brodzinsky, D. M., & Golinkoff, R. M. (1981). *New directions in Piagetian theory and practice.* Hillsdale, NJ: Lawrence Erlbaum Associates.

White, P. (Ed). (2005). Review of Young children and trauma: *Intervention and treatment. International Journal of Emergency Mental Health, 7*(1), 87-88.

Yoshikawa, H., Weisner, T. S., Kalil, A., & Way, N. (2008). Mixing qualitative and quantitative research in developmental science: Uses and methodological choices. *Developmental Psychology, 44*(2), 344-354.

Yule, W. (2001). Posttraumatic stress disorder in the general population and in children. *Journal of Clinical Psychiatry, 62*, 23-28.

Article 6

Exploring Intimate Partner Communication in Military Couples: Implications for Counselors

Paper based on a program presented at the 2009 American Counseling Association Annual Conference and Exposition, March 19-23, Charlotte, North Carolina.

Jessica Brown and Brenda Hall

"Reunited once again, for the third time; I sat and reflected on our relationship, thinking about all we had been through. The past three years were a blur; now we can slow down. But what now; do we even know how to live outside of the whirlwind of the deployment/reunion cycle we had been caught up in throughout our existence together? I almost couldn't fathom the fact that I didn't know how to talk with my own husband; and he didn't know how to talk to me. Perhaps the most disconcerting part was that we had been through these tumultuous events; and it still wasn't enough to keep us together."

Jessica Brown, former military spouse

There are many casualties of war; marriage being one of them (Cohan, Cole, & Davila, 2005). Separation and the pressures of deployment create multiple problems and high levels of stress among military personnel and their significant others. For military couples, maintaining healthy marital relationships is a major concern. Although statistics on divorce in the military vary, there is evidence to suggest that the expectations of military life, including deployment, increase the risk that married couples will experience failed marriages. As reported by Skipp, Ephron, and Hastings (2006), divorces within the military doubled in 2004. There are documented risk factors for marriage instability in the military, such as long-term separation and post-traumatic stress syndrome (Cook, Thompson, Riggs, & Coyne, 2004). Couples in the military are vulnerable to the effects of living within the military and through the cycles of deployment.

One crucial aspect in determining how well couples deal with the stressors of deployment and maintain a healthy relationship is how well they communicate. As cited in the National Military Family Association Report on Cycles of Deployment (2005), "Communication among service members, families, the unit/command, and family support providers is essential in dealing with both the separation of deployment, and the preparation for the reunion with the service member" (p. 5). Providing opportunities for the ongoing exchange of information helps to answer important questions about the deployment process and allows couples to stay in touch throughout periods of separation. While there seems to be general agreement that communication is an important issue in marital satisfaction, there is little written in the literature specifically about how communication between partners changes or is affected by military life and deployment.

In order to effectively examine elements of communication amongst intimate military couples and how they are affected by military deployment, it is first important to note healthy elements of communication. Healthy communication is paramount in a successful and happy marriage (Karahan, 2007; Walsh, Baucom, Tyler, & Sayers, 1993). When marriages lack elements of healthy communication, conflict may arise (Karahan, 2007). Couples who possess basic communication skills have less marital conflict; suggesting the importance of certain communication skills or elements (Karahan, 2007; Sanford, 2003). These crucial communication elements include: self-disclosure, problem-solving, and warmth.

Self-Disclosure

Self-disclosure involves individuals making themselves known to another person by sharing personal information (Gladding, 2006). Bradford, Feeney, and Campbell (2002) state that self-disclosure serves as the crucial core of an intimate relationship. In addition, the amount of self-disclosure in a relationship can change the dynamics or nature of the relationship (Bradford et al., 2002). When one or both individuals in a relationship withdraw from sharing thoughts and feelings, intimacy is negatively affected.

In military couples, self-disclosure can be affected greatly by the stressors of deployment. Soldiers often remain silent about their experiences in Iraq and Afghanistan. This reflects an aspect of military culture that expects soldiers to remain strong and quiet. Sharing strong personal feelings or expressing emotions openly could be viewed as a sign of weakness. While this code of silence may be necessary during times of combat, it can destroy effective communication between intimate partners. Unfortunately, the consequences of not talking about traumatic events often result in serious mental health issues that further damage relationships among military couples. Research indicates that individuals involved in military deployment are at increased risk for developing post-traumatic stress disorder (PTSD; Basham, 2008; Drummet, Coleman, & Cable, 2003). Additionally, Dekel, Enoch, and Solomon (2008) found that individuals with symptoms of post-traumatic stress disorder self-disclose less to their partners, in turn affecting marital adjustment and satisfaction. Individuals with symptoms of PTSD may be less likely to disclose to their partners about traumatic events because it may trigger a flashback or force the individual to think about painful events or memories. It is especially damaging when the trauma of PTSD results in intimate partner violence. Research suggests that individuals with PTSD are at an increased risk to engage in intimate partner violence. Cattaneo and Goodman (2005) found that symptoms of post-traumatic stress disorder were predictors of intimate partner violence.

Fortunately there is evidence to support that appropriate self-disclosure of returning combat veterans to their partners can contribute to healthy communication. Graham, Huang, Clark, and Helgeson (2008) found that self-disclosing, even when the emotion or event is negative, is related to a positive outcome. This concept emphasizes the benefits of honest expression of difficult emotions such as confusion, doubt, frustration, and other feelings associated with negative experiences. Couples who are able to define their own personal guidelines for communicating and learn effective strategies for open, two-way communication can more effectively address the stressors associated with the cycle of deployment.

Problem-Solving

Another element of healthy communication is problem-solving, which involves the ability to negotiate solutions and to cope with problems as well as maintain effective conflict resolution. Problem solving has been linked to effective communication in married couples (Hahlweg, Markman, Thurmaier, Engl, & Eckert, 1998). On the other hand, according to Jackman-Cram, Dobson, and Martin (2006), poor problem-solving behavior can lead to increases in marital conflict. Often problem-solving requires effective conflict resolution, especially with high stress situations (Ronan, Dreer, Dollard, & Ronan, 2004), such as military deployment. If couples can learn effective problem-solving skills while communicating, they may better navigate through the various cycles of military deployment.

Deployment involves separation and reunification of partners (Rotter & Boveja, 1999), which entails a variety of situations and events involving problem-solving skills. When a couple separates for deployment, they must decide who will take on certain tasks while the other partner is deployed (Rotter & Boveja, 1999). Tasks taken on by the partner staying at home may include increased financial responsibility, house and car repairs, and parenting by oneself. In preparing for deployment, couples can implement plans in order to deal with situations that will arise during deployment. In order to create and implement the plans, effective communication is crucial. For example, partners can discuss and negotiate about who should be contacted to make vehicle and car repairs during deployment. In order for this process to go smoothly, the couple must be able to actively dialogue and negotiate between one another. Then a plan can be put in place for the spouse at home so that phone numbers are provided for repairs that the deployed spouse used to handle. Utilizing communication skills that result in shared decision-making helps both partners to feel connected and less resentful about responsibilities at home during deployment.

Since deployment requires that the spouse at home manages more of the household duties, couples must often renegotiate roles when the soldier returns home (Rotter & Boveja, 1999). Reuniting after deployment involves relinquishing and undertaking tasks on behalf of both the deployed partner and the partner on the home front. This can be an extremely stressful time and the potential for communication that involves withdrawal and anger between partners is high. The partner who remained at home may feel resentment and express anger and the soldier may withdraw. Or, the soldier and partner who remained at home may both express anger or withdraw. Couples who get caught in the anger and withdraw pattern are unable to effectively solve problems or address conflict; in fact, this type of communication only increases conflict. The process of reintegration can go more smoothly if the couples are effectively communicating using problem-solving. The couple must be able to communicate to each other how they feel about the roles each had during deployment and identify the tasks they wish to reclaim or relinquish upon return. In order to do this, the couple must be able to negotiate a solution together. The couple will then be able to resolve any feelings of resentment and identify what tasks and roles each partner will claim.

Warmth

Gladding (2006) defines warmth as a positive emotion as well as the ability to communicate caring, concern, and acceptance of others. Warmth in couple communication can also be described as positive affect which involves the display of immediacy behaviors (Guerrero & Andersen, 1991). When partners display these behaviors, they are communicating a sense of closeness to one another. These behaviors include eye contact, touch, body orientation, the use of positive facial expressions, tone of voice, and other non-verbal signals that communicate a sense of warmth. These behaviors are related to the degree of closeness a couple has in their relationship (Guerrero & Andersen, 1991).

Warmth is a healthy element of communication because it undermines hostility in a relationship. Hostility implies a lack of warmth (Rogge, Bradbury, Hahlweg, Engl, & Thurmaier, 2006). The importance of warmth is illustrated when discussing the increasing rate of intimate partner violence (IPV) among returning combat veterans and their partners. Fonseca et al. (2006) suggest that "IPV is a dysfunctional and maladaptive manner of responding to disagreements in an intimate relationship" (p. 627). Couples who engage in hostile behavior, and who communicate about problems using aggression are more apt to experience IPV. If deployed individuals and their partners displayed aspects of warmth when communicating, such as showing that they genuinely cared and accepted each other, there could be a possible decrease in hostile interactions when returning home. For example, most deployments are lengthy in nature, some lasting over a year. During deployment, it may not be necessary for the deployed partner to use immediacy behaviors or communicate a sense of warmth or closeness to individuals. The nature of combat entails killing, injury and death. These experiences may necessitate detachment from oneself and others in order to cope. When transitioning home, there may be transference of detachment and lack of ability to communicate warmth on the behalf of the individual that was deployed. With the element of warmth missing from communication, it is easier for the couple to grow apart. The more emotionally separate the couple becomes, the more likely hostile behaviors could replace immediacy behaviors. Additionally, increased hostility in communication could contribute to intimate partner violence among military couples.

Implications for Counseling

Military couples represent a diverse and growing client population for professional counselors. Soldiers from all branches of service, including Army, Navy, Air Force, Coast Guard, Marines, Reserves and National Guard, their spouses, and children account for one-third of the United States population (Rotter & Boveja, 1999). Currently, military personnel are more accessible for counseling as increased numbers reside in civilian communities. It is inaccurate to assume that the military takes care of its own and military personnel do not want or need additional help and support. As cited in Hoshmand and Hoshmand (2007), there has been a shift away from military community support toward local community resources. Additionally, there is growing evidence that dependents of soldiers use or would seek counseling services if they were available to them (National Military Family Association, 2006). Married couples represent an important population within the military. Exploring how communication relates to relationship stability is an important aspect in serving military partners and their families. Couples who utilize effective communication, especially through deployment, are more likely to maintain and strengthen their relationship, thus keeping their families together.

There are many ways that counselors can reach out to military couples and help to foster positive, healthy communication and relationships. Being aware of the unique circumstances of military life and the effects of stressors such as deployment is an important first step. Counselors can be instrumental in helping military couples understand healthy communication elements of self-disclosure, problem-solving, and warmth, as well as in assisting couples explore how the various phases of deployment affect their communication patterns, both individually and as partners.

Counselors provide an environment that supports honest and appropriate self-disclosure. Outside the confines of the military structure, counselors can encourage the sharing of thoughts and feelings without fear of consequences. With an emphasis on respect, understanding, and open expression, couples can learn to effectively listen, express honest feelings and negotiate through difficult decisions. Counselors can also help couples practice skills in expressing honest feelings while maintaining positive regard for each other. In this way, intimate partners learn to focus on their relationship and to express their confusion and doubt in ways that are less likely to result in hostility and withdrawal. One aspect of this involves helping military couples to identify how they want to communicate with each other as intimate partners separately from the expectations for silence that is pervasive in the military culture. As soldiers and their intimate partners learn skills to clearly define and redefine their personal guidelines for effective communication, they can better negotiate the demands of military life and avoid being pulled into negative patterns of interactions.

Giving partners an opportunity to share the fears and expectations of deployment can help ease the anticipation of separation. They can establish guidelines regarding how everyday duties will be handled during separation and anticipate how to resolve problems as they arise. Not only does this lead to a more positive deployment departure for the couple, it also sets a strong foundation for reconnecting and for addressing the types of negotiation that reunification requires.

According to Sanford (2003), when couples are having problem-solving conversations regarding highly difficult topics, they are likely to engage in negative communication, such as criticizing each other. Counselors can help the couple use effective problem-solving skills when engaging in difficult conversations. Counseling can help restore a sense of trust and reliance on each other as the major support in each other's lives. Practicing strategies that promote two-way communication allows both members of the couple to express their concerns and needs and to feel as if they are being heard and understood. This type of interaction is more likely to pull them together instead of tearing them apart; thus, reducing the risk of hostile engagement and possible IPV. Counselors can offer strategies, interventions and programs that emphasize healthy communication and assist these couples in maintaining strong, satisfying marital relationships.

References

Basham, K. (2008). Homecoming as safe haven or the new front: Attachment and detachment in military couples. *Clinical Social Work Journal, 36*(1), 83-96.

Bradford, S. A., Feeney, J. A., & Campbell, L. (2002). Links between attachment orientations and dispositional and diary-based measures of disclosure in dating couples: A study of actor and partner effects. *Personal Relationships, 9*, 491-506.

Cattaneo, L., & Goodman, L. (2005). Risk factors for reabuse in intimate partner violence: A cross-disciplinary critical review. *Trauma, Violence & Abuse, 6*(2), 141-175.

Cohan, C. L., Cole, S., & Davila, J. (2005). Marital transitions among Vietnam–era repatriated prisoners of war. *Journal of Social and Personal Relationships, 22*(6), 777-795.

Cook, J. M., Thompson, R., Riggs, D. S., & Coyne, J. C. (2004). Post-traumatic stress disorder and current relationship functioning among World War II ex-prisoners of war. *Journal of Family Psychology, 18*(1), 36-45.

Dekel, R., Enoch, G., & Soloman, Z. (2008). The contribution of captivity and post-traumatic stress disorder to marital adjustment of Israeli couples. *Journal of Social and Personal Relationships, 25*(3), 497-510.

Drummet, A. R., Coleman, M., & Cable, S. (2003). Military families under stress: Implications for family life education. *Family Relations, 52*(3), 279-287.

Fonseca, C. A., Schmaling, K. B., Stoever, C., Gutierrez, C., Blume, A. W., & Russell, M. L. (2006). Variables associated with intimate partner violence in a deploying military sample. *Military Medicine, 171*, 627-631.

Gladding, S. T. (2006). *The counseling dictionary: Concise definitions of frequently used terms* (2nd ed.) Upper Saddle River, New Jersey: Pearson Prentice Hall.

Graham, S. M., Huang, J. Y., Clark, M. S., & Helgeson, V. S. (2008). The positives of negative emotions: Willingness to express negative emotions promotes relationships. *Society for Personality and Social Psychology, Inc., 34*(3), 394-406.

Guerrero, L. K., & Andersen, P.A. (1991). The waxing and waning of relational intimacy: Touch as a function of relational stage, gender and touch avoidance. *Journal of Social and Personal Relationships, 8*, 147-165.

Hahlweg, K., Markman, H. J., Thurmaier, F., Engl, J., & Eckert, V. (1998). Prevention of marital distress: Results of a German prospective longitudinal study. *Journal of Family Psychology, 12*(4), 543-556.

Hoshmand, L. T., & Hoshmand, A. L. (2007). Support for military families and communities. *Journal of Community Psychology, 35*(2), 171-180.

Jackman-Cram, S., Dobson, K. S., & Martin, R. (2006). Marital problem-solving behavior in depression and marital distress. *Journal of Abnormal Psychology, 115*(2), 380-384.

Karahan, T. F. (2007). The effects of a couple communication program on passive conflict tendency among married couples. *Educational Sciences: Theory & Practice, 7*(2), 845-858.

National Military Family Association. (2005). *Report on the cycles of deployment.* Alexandria, VA: Author.

National Military Family Association. (2006). *Report on the cycles of deployment.* Alexandria, VA: Author.

Rogge, R., Bradbury, T., Hahlweg, K., Engl, J., & Thurmaier, F. (2006). Predicting marital distress and dissolution: Refining the two-factor hypothesis. *Journal of Family Psychology, 20*(1), 156-159.

Ronan, G., Dreer, L., Dollard, K., & Ronan, D. (2004). Violent couples: Coping and communication skills. *Journal of Family Violence, 19*(2), 131-137.

Rotter, J. C. & Boveja, M. E. (1999). Counseling military families. *The Family Journal: Counseling and Therapy for Couples and Families, 7*(4), 379-382.

Sanford, K. (2003). Problem–solving conversations in marriage: Does it matter what topics couples discuss? *Personal Relationships, 10*(1), 97-112.

Skipp, C., Ephron, D., & Hastings, M. (2006). Trouble at home. *Newsweek 10/23/2006, 148*(17), 48-49.

Walsh, V. L., Baucom, D. H., Tyler, S., & Sayers, S. L. (1993). Impact of message valence, focus, expressive style, and gender on communication patterns among martially distress couples. *Journal of Family Psychology, 7*(2), 163-175.

Homesickness in International College Students

Paper based on a program presented at the 2009 American Counseling Association Annual Conference and Exposition, March 19-23, Charlotte, North Carolina.

Karen Kegel

Overview

Homesickness is among the most frequently reported concerns of international college students in the United States (Yi, Giseala Lin, & Kishimoto, 2003). Leaving family, friends, and a home culture in pursuit of an academic opportunity abroad, international students frequently find themselves simultaneously grieving for missed persons and places, building new social networks, and adjusting to new cultural and environmental demands (Chen, 1999; Mori, 2000; Sandhu & Asrabadi, 1994). It is therefore not surprising that upwards of 30% of international college students report frequent feelings of homesickness (Rajapaksa & Dundes, 2002/2003).

Yet the nature of homesickness remains elusive. The research community still has not reached consensus on an exact definition (Stroebe, van Vliet, Hewstone, & Willis, 2002; Nijhof & Engels, 2007). Many conceptualizations include a missed home environment in addition to missed significant persons (Willis, Stroebe, & Hewstone, 2003). Problems assimilating new experiences and maladaptation to a new environment also feed homesickness (Bell

& Bromnick, 1998; Willis et al., 2003). Some researchers have encapsulated homesickness in five factors: missing family, missing friends, feeling lonely, adjustment problems, and home ruminations (Willis et al., 2003). Homesickness can also be considered a "mini-grief" whereby relocation and adjustment to college life may turn into significant stressors when resources and coping strategies are lacking (Stroebe et al., 2002).

Recently, homesickness has begun to be studied as one of several acculturative stressors impacting individuals who experience cross-cultural transitions (Wei et al., 2007). According to Duru and Poyrazli (2007), acculturative stress consists of mental and physical discomfort that ensues from experiencing a new culture. As with homesickness, loss of social support and important persons is regarded as integral to the experience of acculturative stress (Yeh & Inose, 2003). As a contributing factor, homesickness has been woven into scales developed to measure acculturative stress, such as the Acculturative Stress Scale for International Students (ASSIS; Yeh & Inose, 2003).

Intrapersonal Factors

That age and gender affect homesickness in international students has been inconsistently supported (Poyrazli & Lopez, 2007; Ye, 2005; Yeh & Inose, 2003). However, English fluency appears to be a critical factor. Self-reported English fluency was negatively related to acculturative stress in a diverse sample of international students in the United States (Yeh & Inose, 2003). English proficiency also significantly predicts international student homesickness (Duru & Poyrazli, 2007; Poyrazli & Lopez, 2007). Greenland and Brown (2005) suggest students' expectations of their language abilities may contribute to experienced acculturative stress. Furthermore, English skills were not a mediator between social support and acculturative stress in a study by Poyrazli, Kavanaugh, Baker, and Al-Timimi (2004), indicating its effect is independent and direct.

Few studies have examined how personality variables

influence homesickness in international students. In one study, higher neuroticism and higher openness to experience were related to significantly greater acculturative stress among Turkish students in the United States (Duru & Poyrazli, 2007). Maladaptive perfectionism also positively correlated with acculturative stress in a study of Chinese international students (Wei et al., 2007). Finally, Ward and Kennedy (1993) demonstrated an external locus of control was positively related to homesickness among New Zealander students studying abroad in 23 different countries.

There is evidence that emotional intelligence may play into the experience of homesickness. Yoo, Matsumoto, and LeRoux (2006) found that recognition of contempt in a laboratory exercise predicted increased homesickness—and that international students' emotion regulation abilities predicted homesickness after approximately 1.5 academic years. Using emotion regulation to control negative emotions from acculturative stress could help students better maintain cognitive skills needed in the new environment (Yoo et al., 2006).

Interpersonal Factors

Quality of interpersonal connections appears to matter more than quantity when it comes to international student homesickness. In contrast to previous research cited by Chen (1999), Rajapaksa and Dundes (2002/2003) discovered that aside from international students who reported having zero close friends, total number of friends does correlate with adjustment. Furthermore, number of total close friends was a poor predictor of international students' satisfaction with their social networks (Rajapaksa & Dundes, 2002/2003). On the other hand, social connectedness negatively correlates with both acculturative stress and homesickness among international students (Yeh & Inose, 2003; Duru & Poyrazli, 2007). Additionally, a moderate negative correlation has been established between acculturative stress and social support (Yeh & Inose, 2003). Mori (2000) avers that creating a support system of co-nationals is crucial for international students' well-being, but that often low numbers of home country students limits interaction.

Other evidence suggests it is interactions with host country nationals that truly make the difference in international students' experiences. In a study of New Zealander international students, a greater amount of host national interaction was associated with significantly less homesickness (Ward & Kennedy, 1993). Moreover, greater co-national interaction translated to significantly more experiences of homesickness (Ward & Kennedy, 1993). Along those lines, Poyrazli et al. (2004) found that international students in the Unites States who principally socialized with other international students had greater acculturative stress. Such students reported less social support overall as well as higher acculturative stress than students who interacted with Americans and non-Americans in a more balanced fashion (Poyrazli et al., 2004).

Though objective social circumstances have some predictive power for homesickness, expectations and interpretations of these circumstances may be more directly tied to homesickness. Constantine, Anderson, Berkel, Caldwell, and Utsey (2005) reported greater perceived social acceptance is associated with lower adjustment problems among international students. Another study revealed international students who were not satisfied with their social network were more likely to report feelings of homesickness (Rajapaksa & Dundes, 2002/2003). Furthermore, international students whose actual lived experiences measure short of their expectations report significantly more homesickness (McKinlay, Pattison, & Gross, 1996).

Environmental Effects

Successful or unsuccessful adjustment to a new university environment can help or hinder coping with homesickness (Willis et al., 2003). Lu (1990) contended that academic demands can endanger international students' resources, increasing vulnerability to stress. The hypothesis was supported by a study of Chinese international students in Britain, as perceived academic demands were associated with increased homesickness 2 months into their stay (Lu, 1990).

Studies have been split on how increased time in the United States affects acculturative stress in international students (Wilton & Constantine, 2003; Ying, 2005; Greenland & Brown, 2005; Ye, 2005; Wei et al., 2007). Longer residence was associated with significantly decreased levels of acculturative distress in two studies (Wilton & Constantine, 2003; Ying, 2005). However, a longitudinal study of Japanese international students at British universities showed acculturative stress increased significantly between 2 weeks and 8 months and plateaued thereafter (Greenland & Brown, 2005). Two other studies showed no correlation between length of United States residence and homesickness or acculturative stress (Ye, 2005; Wei et al., 2007). It thus appears that simple exposure to a host environment does not lessen the experience of homesickness.

Cultural Differences

In one study, region of home country accounted for 11.4% of the variance in acculturative stress scores of students from Asia, Central and Latin America, Africa, and Europe (Yeh & Inose, 2003). Data suggest too that the more differences between international students' home and host cultures, the more homesickness and acculturative stress experienced (Ye, 2005). Accordingly, Asian international students consistently report greater acculturative stress than European international students in the United States (Yeh & Inose, 2003; Poyrazli et al., 2004; Wei et al., 2007). One study of Chinese international students in Britain revealed a 94.9% rate of homesickness (Lu, 1990). The researcher maintains that stronger family connections in the Chinese culture may have contributed to this widespread homesickness (1990). Meanwhile, Ying (2005) found that of the factors impacting acculturative stress among Taiwanese students in America, homesickness accounted for most of the variance.

Despite those statistics, Asian international students may not be the regional group most at risk for homesickness. In a study of more than 320 international students at American universities, African students reported significantly more acculturative stress than either Asian or Latin American students (Constantine, Okazaki, & Utsey, 2004). African students also reported more depression and more self-concealment behaviors than the other groups (Constantine et al., 2004). Based on a qualitative study, Constantine et al. (2005) concluded that African international students' cultural backgrounds may place more value and emphasis on close interpersonal relationships than does American culture—and that possession of communal and interdependent self-concepts may engender homesickness.

Although Latin American international students reported less acculturative stress than their African peers in the study by Constantine et al. (2004), this group still reported significantly more acculturative stress than Asian international students. Latin American students also demonstrated higher levels of psychological distress compared with Asian students in a separate study (Wilton & Constantine, 2003). Yet Latin American international students have reported greater social self-efficacy than either their African or Asian international peers (Constantine et al., 2004). Underrepresentation on campus may help explain the relatively high rates of homesickness among African international students and the disparity between homesickness and social self-efficacy in Latin American international students (Constantine et al., 2004; Wilton & Constantine, 2003).

Homesickness and Distress

The negative effects of homesickness on psychological well-being have been well documented. Homesickness negatively impacts the academic performance of college students (Willis et al., 2003; Stroebe et al., 2002), and excessive acculturative stress can contribute to eating and sleeping problems, low energy, and headaches (Ye, 2005). Moreover, numerous studies have demonstrated a link between homesickness or acculturative stress and depression. Ying (2005), Constantine et al. (2004), and Wei et al. (2007) cite moderate to strong positive correlations between homesickness or acculturative stress and depression among Asian, African, and Latin American international students in the United States. In one study, acculturative stress was significantly related to depression scores even after accounting for English fluency, sex, and home region (Constantine et al., 2004). Alarmingly, extreme consequences of homesickness-fueled depression in college students have been documented, including suicide (Willis et al., 2003).

Interventions and Future Directions

Helping international students establish friendships in their host country has been a mainstay of acculturation interventions on college campuses (Rajapaksa & Dundes, 2002/2003). Rajapaksa and Dundes (2002/2003) advocate initiatives to improve the quality of social networks rather than boost the number of close friends. In so doing, counselors should assess the level of social support students have—and whether support is limited due to personal characteristics (e.g., shyness or language barriers) or environmental constraints (e.g., prejudice; Carr, Koyama, & Thiagarajan, 2003).

Many international students remain in groups of fellow nationals even though greater interaction with host country students is predictive of better cultural adjustment (Yeh & Inose, 2003). Therefore, peer programs connecting international students with host nation peers could be an effective strategy for countering homesickness (Yeh & Inose, 2003). In fact, informal peer-pairing programs that connect international students with host country students may be more productive than formal counseling interventions (Chen, 1999).

Tailoring acculturative interventions for different subgroups of international students may be of substantial benefit. For instance, because African international students use forbearance as a coping strategy, it is wise to offer informal outreach workshops providing education on the importance of seeking professional help when acculturative stress runs high (Constantine et al., 2005). In light of cultural collectivist traditions, counseling staff should tap the existing social supports of Asian and Latin American international students through peer counseling programs (Wilton & Constantine, 2003).

Given the prevalence of homesickness among international students and its demonstrated relationship with depression, it is essential that university counseling centers initiate alternative, culturally sensitive services for this population. Perhaps the biggest lead for researchers and counselors alike is the critical gap between students' interpersonal expectations for studying abroad and actual experiences. Establishing the precise influence of social expectations versus social reality might bring much-needed clarity to the true nature of homesickness among international students.

References

Bell, J., & Bromnick, R. (1998). Young people in transition: The relationship between homesickness and self-disclosure. *Journal of Adolescence, 21*, 745-748.

Carr, J. L., Koyama, M., & Thiagarajan, M. (2003). A women's support group for Asian international students. *Journal of American College Health, 52*, 131-134.

Chen, C. P. (1999). Common stressors among international college students: Research and counseling implications. *Journal of College Counseling, 2*, 49-65.

Constantine, M. G., Anderson, G. M., Berkel, L. A., Caldwell, L. D., & Utsey, S. O. (2005). Examining the cultural adjustment experiences of African international college students: A qualitative analysis. *Journal of Counseling Psychology, 52*, 57-66.

Constantine, M. G., Okazaki, S., & Utsey, S. O. (2004). Self-concealment, social self-efficacy, acculturative stress, and depression in African, Asian, and Latin American international college students. *American Journal of Orthopsychiatry, 74*, 230-241.

Duru, E., & Poyrazli, S. (2007). Personality dimensions, psychosocial-demographic variables, and English language competency in predicting level of acculturative stress among

Turkish international students. *International Journal of Stress Management, 14*, 99-110.

Greenland, K., & Brown, R. (2005). Acculturation and contact in Japanese students studying in the United Kingdom. *The Journal of Social Psychology, 145*, 373-389.

Lu, L. (1990). Adaptation to British universities: Homesickness and mental health of Chinese students. *Counselling Psychology Quarterly, 3*, 225-232.

McKinlay, N. J., Pattison, H. M., & Gross, H. (1996). An exploratory investigation of the effects of a cultural orientation programme on the psychological well-being of international university students. *Higher Education, 31*, 379-395.

Mori, S. (2000). Addressing the mental health concerns of international students. *Journal of Counseling and Development, 78*, 137-144.

Nijhof, K. S., & Engels, R. C. M. E. (2007). Parenting styles, coping strategies, and the expression of homesickness. *Journal of Adolescence, 30*, 709-720.

Poyrazli, S., Kavanaugh, P. R., Baker, A., & Al-Timimi, N. (2004). Social support and demographic correlates of acculturative stress in international students. *Journal of College Counseling, 7*, 73-82.

Poyrazli, S., & Lopez, M. D. (2007). An exploratory study of perceived discrimination and homesickness: A comparison of international students and American students. *The Journal of Psychology, 141*, 263-280.

Rajapaksa, S., & Dundes, L. (2002/2003). It's a long way home: International student adjustment to living in the United States. *College Student Retention, 4*, 15-28.

Sandhu, D. S., & Asrabadi, B. R. (1994). Development of an acculturative stress scale for international students: Preliminary findings. *Psychological Reports, 75*, 435-448.

Stroebe, M., van Vliet, T., Hewstone, M., & Willis, H. (2002). Homesickness among students in two cultures: Antecedents and consequences. *British Journal of Psychology, 93*, 147-168.

Ward, C., & Kennedy, A. (1993). Psychological and socio-cultural adjustment during cross-cultural transitions: A comparison of secondary students overseas and at home. *International Journal of Psychology, 28*, 129-147.

Wei, M., Heppner, P. P., Mallen, M. J., Ku, T. Y., Liao, K. Y. H., & Wu, T. F. (2007). Acculturative stress, perfectionism, years in the United States, and depression among Chinese international students. *Journal of Counseling Psychology, 54*, 385-394.

Willis, H., Stroebe, M., & Hewstone, M. (2003). Homesick blues. *The Psychologist, 16*, 526-528.

Wilton, L., & Constantine, M. G. (2003). Length of residence, cultural adjustment difficulties, and psychological distress symptoms in Asian and Latin American international college students. *Journal of College Counseling, 6*, 177-186.

Ye, J. (2005). Acculturative stress and use of the Internet among East Asian international students in the United States. *CyberPsychology and Behavior, 8*, 154-161.

Yeh, C. J., & Inose, M. (2003). International students' reported English fluency, social support satisfaction, and social connectedness as predictors of acculturative stress. *Counselling Psychology Quarterly, 16*(1), 15-28.

Yi, J. K., Giseala Lin, J. C., & Kishimoto, Y. (2003). Utilization of counseling services by international students. *Journal of Instructional Psychology, 30*, 333-342.

Ying, Y. W. (2005). Variation in acculturative stressors over time: A study of Taiwanese students in the United States. *International Journal of Intercultural Relations, 29*, 59-71.

Yoo, S. H., Matsumoto, D., & LeRoux, J. A. (2006). The influence of emotion recognition and emotion regulation on intercultural adjustment. *International Journal of Intercultural Relations, 30*, 345-363.

Article 8

The Imposter Phenomenon Among African American Women in U.S. Institutions of Higher Education: Implications for Counseling

Paper based on a program presented at the 2009 American Counseling Association Annual Conference and Exposition, March 19-23, Charlotte, North Carolina.

Frances K. Trotman

The literature on the counseling and psychotherapy of African American women is relatively new. This author has been examining the imposter phenomenon, i.e., an internal experience of intellectual phoniness (Clance & Imes, 1978), among high achieving African American women since the early 1980s (see Trotman, 1984). Counselors must be aware of this phenomenon and its antecedents if they are to effectively assist all women who may seek their expertise. Counselors must fully understand the pain and emotional distress often inflicted on and experienced by their African American female clients in academic careers. Johnetta B. Cole, first female President of Spelman College, giving the keynote address at Smith College, stated that

> In our country... all black folks are doomed to be intellectually inferior to all white folks. Thus, the last image that many Americans would have of an African American woman is that of an intellectual, an academic, a college president, a person of academy. (Cole, 1997)

The Imposter Phenomenon

Several years ago, the concept of the imposter phenomenon was used to attempt to explain some of the conflicts and turmoil plaguing many high achieving African American women. Black women in the United States have experienced the imposter phenomenon by virtue of being both black people in white America and women in a male-dominated culture. Indeed, "black women have been doubly victimized by scholarly neglect and racist assumptions. Belonging as they do to two groups which have traditionally been treated as inferiors by American society—blacks and women—they have been doubly invisible" (Lerner, 1973, p. xvii).

In an effort to decrease the cognitive dissonance caused by an attempt to reconcile the institution and maintenance of slavery in a land founded on principles of liberty and justice for all human beings, the dominant culture attempts to diminish its resultant guilt and discomfort by postulating that African Americans are not really human. "Dehumanization involves first forming an idea of another living person as a *'thing'* so as to sustain one's dehumanized conception of [her]" (Kovel, 1970, p. 36). The seemingly cyclical rise of the IQ controversy as support for the genetic inferiority of African Americans, despite its having been repeatedly debunked and repudiated (Trotman, 1977), is perhaps one of the most blatant attempts at dehumanization that periodically emerges from the hallowed halls of the academy.

One's self-concept must be affected and self-esteem is likely to suffer as a result of such damaging appraisals by the society into which the black girl child is born. The effects of the imposter phenomenon are particularly virulent for those African American women who have chosen careers in higher education.

The subtle and not-so-subtle attacks on the African American woman as a student, a professor, or an administrator in U.S. institutions of higher education can seem relentless. "The perception that African American women are incompetent pervades much of their career, forcing upon them the undeserved stress of providing a defense they should not need to give and fighting to prove merit when merit is unquestionably apparent" (Myers, 2002, p. 21-22).

Throughout the 20th century, obstacles to upward mobility and equal life chances have confronted African American women. No other racial or ethnic group in the United States has been as enslaved or faced such perpetual racial segregation and discrimination in all institutional domains. Certainly, in those institutions which pride themselves on intellectual superiority, the black woman may be inclined to feel a sense of 'intellectual phoniness' (Wilkinson, 2000).

Counseling Implications

Other volumes (Trotman, 1977, 1978, 1984, 2000, 2002a, 2002b, 2002c, 2002d, 2005, 2006) have explored various approaches and ramifications of counseling and psychotherapy with African American women. The salience of the race of the therapist, the importance of cultural and social class of the therapist, the effect of therapist attitudes, same sex versus opposite sex of therapist, and the importance of role models have been identified as significant in the counseling and psychotherapy process of black female clients.

Wechsler (1997) reminded us that all new groups that have entered white male-dominated, Christian-based higher education have always been met with suspicion and trepidation. The African American woman is not only relatively new to the academy, but also brings with her the added stigma of presumed intellectual inferiority and incompetence. Counselors must understand the antecedents and consequences in order to be able to empathize with her plight and not add to her burdens by questioning her perceptions. In the white male dominated ivory tower, how does the ebony woman manage to survive the constant assaults on her academic contributions, her intellectual capacity, and her humanity without doubting herself and feeling like the imposter that many in the academy seem to perceive?

Assaults on her self-esteem can be combated with authenticity and assertiveness. The African American woman must demand respect and say 'out loud' what she knows is true. Yet when African American women exhibit any level of assertiveness, they are frequently labeled as "loose cannons" or trouble-makers who are dealing too much in triviality, or 'playing the race card.' Misconceptions and stereotypes about race and sex lead to the treatment of and interaction with African American women as labels, thus mystifying the real persons behind the stigma and encouraging self-fulfilling prophecies crafted by the sex and race that hold power (Kawewe, 1997). Myers (2002) contends that "white males show much more favor toward white females and black males than toward black females. This is even truer when the female is outspoken, independent, and assertive" (p. 66).

Knowing the Client's Experiences

Counselors of the high achieving African American woman need to appreciate the experience of strong female role models, who from the very beginning were viewed as sources of labor valued for the amount of work they could perform, thus leading to the "black superwoman" image with its concomitant expectation that the black woman must "do all" and "be all," often ignoring her individual needs. Alice Walker underscores this subtle difference in emotional and intellectual outlook by pointing out that "white feminism teaches white women that they are capable, whereas my [Black] tradition assumes I'm capable" (as cited in Trotman, 1984, p. 36). Rather than exploit her strengths, counseling must help the black woman to get in touch with her challenges and particular needs.

Campus life for faculty of color teaching in predominantly white colleges and universities is often characterized in terms of multiple lenses of marginalities (Aguirre, 2000; Alfred, 2001; Essien, 2003; Harvey, 1991, 1994; Thomas & Hollenshead, 2001; Turner, 2003). Thompson and Louque (2005) reported that disrespect for African American faculty stemmed from some colleagues' lack of knowledge about black culture in general as well as a lack of respect for African Americans' academic contributions and their professional opinions. Hart (2006) noted that feminist voices are still silenced within the academic culture. Counselors must provide the proper environment for African American women to express their sadness, disappointment, pain, and rage by providing an understanding ear, and being knowledgeable about black culture in general and about the presumed incompetence that fosters the imposter phenomenon, so potentially devastating to African American women.

The research literature is consistent. All conclude that black women faculty are the most stressed, the least satisfied, almost the least represented, possibly the least supported, and the most overworked of all faculty in academe (Alexander, 1995; Benjamin, 1997; Graves, 1990; Gregory, 1995, Malveaux, 1998; Peterson, 1990). "What is not found is literature on satisfied, well-respected... black women faculty" (Cooper, 2006, p. 3). The experiences for many faculty of color at predominantly white colleges and universities have been described as negotiating "personal and psychological minefields" (Ruffins, 1997, p.21). Stanley (2006) reports that the literature contains a variety of terms and phrases that determine and reflect the overall experiences of faculty of color teaching in predominantly white colleges and universities, including: 'multiple marginality', 'otherness', 'living in two worlds', 'the academy's new cast', 'silenced voices', 'visible and invisible barriers', 'the color of teaching', and 'navigating between two worlds' (p. 3).

Interaction with other faculty is a key factor in career longevity and success, but it is important to note that the self-worth of African American women cannot be entirely dependent on white faculty. Self-worth and self-reliance must be internally generated, with help from support networks established in and out of the university setting (Atwater, 1995). Group counseling experiences with other African American women can also be extremely helpful (Trotman & Gallagher, 1987). It is in the black women's group that the black woman can experience a safe environment in which she can speak expressively and directly about issues of vital importance to her mental health, while developing and modeling her unique style in the intimacy and love of her black sisters.

Group Therapy and Other Approaches

A black women's group, such as the one described above, can provide a safe setting in which the black woman can begin to re-experience some of the painful and damaging incidents of childhood. Some of the results of racism involve only other black people and are therefore inappropriate for discussion outside "the family" of blacks. Racism as a shared experience of black women can be assumed, and there appears to be little need to discuss it in a black women's group. The black woman can explore her options, e.g., acquiescence versus assertiveness, as a reaction to racial oppression.

The roles that the black woman play can he enhanced, developed, and expanded through the role modeling of the group therapist and the other group members. As black women communicate honesty, sincerity, and love to each other, they also subtly and simultaneously identify the details and mechanisms of their successes, "thereby demystifying success and making it accessible to the [other] black female group members" (Trotman, 1984, p. 105).

It is critical that the black woman suffering the imposter phenomenon feels safe enough and understood enough to share her feelings of fraudulence. A group experience with other achieving black women who risk exploring the commonality of fraudulent feelings is particularly therapeutic in such cases.

Because of their added stressors (Patitu & Hinton, 2003) and unique experiences, and being subjected to the ethnocentrism of the dominant culture, minority group members need group experiences with each other in order to validate their perceptions, help to decrease stress, and prevent illness. American minorities continue to face a multitude of barriers to success in the academic workplace. Despite recent efforts in higher education to increase faculty diversity and to implement multicultural curriculum requirements in educational programs, many American minority groups are still largely underrepresented in academic faculty and administrative positions. Underrepresentation places an additional burden on minority faculty as they are expected to assume supplementary minority-related responsibilities while continuing to meet the same expectations set for White colleagues (Aguirre, 2000). Various forms of overt and covert prejudices have been identified in the literature, and numerous authors have made recommendations suggesting that change is required and support is necessary for minority academicians. Counseling and psychotherapy support groups should be available to minority group members in the Academy.

Minorities in academia must have the opportunity to meet with other minorities in a group designed to share experiences. Another important strategy is for black women to continue to write about their experiences with racism and sexism. In doing this and assessing similarities in experiences across the country, African American women are better prepared to demand both the institutional and the individual support necessary for changing racist and sexist practices (Smith, 2000).

References

Aguirre, A., Jr. (2000). *Women and minority faculty in the academic workplace: Recruitment, retention, and academic culture* (ASHE-ERIC Higher Education Rep. No. 27[6]). San Francisco, CA: Jossey-Bass.

Alexander, M. W. (1995). Black women in academia. In B. Guy-Sheftall (Ed.), *Words of fire: An anthology of African-American feminist thought* (Rev. ed.) (pp. 454-460). New York: The New Press.

Alfred, M. V. (2001). Reconceptualizing marginality from the margins: Perspectives of African-American tenured female faculty at white research university. *Western Journal of Black Studies, 25*(1), 1-11.

Atwater, M. (1995). African-American female faculty at predominantly white research universities: Routes to success and empowerment. *Innovative Higher Education, 19*(4), 237-240.

Benjamin, L. (1997). Black women in the academy: An overview. In L. Benjamin (Ed.), *Black women in the academy: Promises and perils* (pp. 1-7). Gainesville, FL: University Press of Florida.

Clance, P. R., & Imes, S. A. (1978). The imposter phenomenon in high achieving women: Dynamics and therapeutic intervention. *Psychotherapy: Theory, Research, and Practice, 15*, 241-247.

Cole, J. B. (1997). *Ten years at Spelman: Reflections on a special journey.* Keynote address presented at Otelia Cromwell Day Symposium at Smith College, North Hampton, MA.

Cooper, T. L. (2006). *The sista' network: African-American women faculty successfully negotiating the road to tenure.* Bolton, MA: Anker Pub.

Essien, V. (2003). Visible and invisible barriers to the incorporation of faculty of color in predominantly white law schools. *Journal of Black Studies, 34*(1), 87-100.

Graves, S. B. (1990). A case of double jeopardy? Black women in higher education. *Initiatives, 53*, 3-8.

Gregory, S. T. (1995). *Black women in the academy: The secrets of success and achievement.* New York: Doubleday.

Hart, J. (2006). Women and feminism in higher education scholarship: An analysis of three core journals. *Journal of Higher Education, 77*, 40-61.

Harvey, W. B. (1991). Faculty responsibility and tolerance. *Thought and Action, 7*(2), 115-136.

Harvey, W. B. (1994). African-American faculty in community colleges: Why they aren't there. In W. Harvey & J. Valadez, *New directions for community colleges: No. 87. Creating and maintaining a diverse faculty* (pp. 19-25). San Francisco: Jossey-Bass.

Kawewe, S. (1997). Black women in diverse academic settings: Gender and racial crimes of commission and omission in academia. In L. Benjamin (Ed.), *Black women in the academy: Promises and perils* (pp. 263-269). Tampa: University Press of Florida.

Kovel, J. (1970). *White racism: A psychohistory*. New York: Pantheon Books.

Lerner, G. (1973). *Black women in white America: A documentary history*. New York: Vintage.

Malveaux, J. (1998). Retaining master jugglers. *Black Issues in Higher Education, 15*(1), 40.

Myers, L. W. (2002). *A broken silence: Voices of African-American women in the academy*. Westport, CT: Bergin & Garvey.

Patitu, C., & Hinton, K. (2003). The experiences of African-American women faculty and administrators in higher education: Has anything changed? *New Directions for Student Services, 104*, 79-93.

Peterson, S. (1990). Challenges for black women faculty. *Initiatives, 53*(1), 33-36.

Ruffins, P. (1997). The fall of the house of tenure. *Black Issues in Higher Education, 14*(17), 18-26.

Smith, P. (2000). A menage to sapphire and her sisters in academia. *Women in Higher Education, 9*(2), 31.

Stanley, C. A. (2006). *Faculty of color: Teaching in predominantly white colleges and universities*. Bolton, MA: Anker Pub.

Thomas, G. D., & Hollenshead, C. (2001). Resisting from the margins: The coping strategies of black women and other women of color faculty members at a research university. *Journal of Negro Education, 70*(3), 166-175.

Thompson, G., & Louque, A. (2005). *Exposing the "culture of arrogance" in the academy*. Sterling, VA: Stylus.

Trotman, F. K. (1977). Race, IQ, and the middle-class. *Journal of Educational Psychology, 69*(3), 266-273.

Trotman, F. K. (1978). Race, IQ, and the rampant misrepresentations: A reply. *Journal of Educational Psychology, 70*, 478-481.

Trotman, F. K. (1984). Psychotherapy of Black women and the dual effects of racism and sexism. In C. M. Brody, *Women helping women* (pp. 96-108). New York: Spring Publications.

Trotman, F. K. (2000). Psychodynamic and feminist psychotherapy with African-American women: Some differences. In L. C. Jackson, & B. Greene (Eds.), *Psychotherapy with African American women: Innovations in psychodynamic perspectives and clinical applications* (pp. 251-274). New York: Guilford Press.

Trotman, F. K. (2002a). African-American mothering: Implications for feminist psychotherapy from a grandmother's perspective. *Women and Therapy: A Feminist Quarterly, 25*(1), 19-36.

Trotman, F. K. (2002b). Feminist psychotherapy with older African-American women. In F. K. Trotman, & C. M. Brody, *Psychotherapy and counseling with older women: Cross-cultural, family, and end-of-life issues* (pp. 144-160). New York: Springer Publications.

Trotman, F. K. (2002c). Old, African-American, and female: Political economic and historical contexts. In F. K. Trotman & C. M. Brody, *Psychotherapy and counseling with older women: Cross-cultural, family and end-of-life issues* (pp. 70-86). New York: Springer Publications.

Trotman, F. K. (2002d). Political and historical contexts of aging African-American women. *Journal of Women and Aging, 14*(3).

Trotman, F. K. (2004). *Factors affecting minority student's successes.* Proceedings of the 2nd Annual Convention of the Hawaii International Conference on Arts and Humanities. Honolulu, HI.

Trotman, F. K. (2005). *Psycho-political context of women's aging in African America.* Proceedings of Universidad de la Habana, Catedra de la Mujer, VI Taller Internacional, Mujeres en el Siglo XXI. Havana, Cuba.

Trotman, F. K. (2006, May). *Daughters of Africa getting old in the USA: Historical, economic, and political contexts of aging in african america.* Proceedings of the 32nd African Literature Association Annual Conference. Accra, Ghana.

Trotman, F. K., & Gallagher, A. H. (1987). Group therapy for Black women. In C. Brody (Ed.), *Women's therapy groups: Paradigms of feminist treatment* (pp. 118-131). New York: Springer Publications.

Turner, C. S. (2003). Incorporation and marginalization in the academy: From border toward center for faculty of color? *Journal of Black Studies, 34*(1), 112-125.

Wechsler, H. (1997). In academic Gresham's Law: Group repulsion as a theme in American Higher education. In L. Godchild & H. Wechsler (Eds.), *The history of higher education* (pp. 416-431). Needham Heights, AM: Pearson.

Wilkinson, D. (2000). Rethinking the concept of "minority": Task of social scientists and practitioners. *Journal of Sociology and Social Welfare, 17*(1), 115.

Article 9

Tears of Blood: Understanding and Creatively Intervening in the Grief of Miscarriage

Paper based on a program presented at the 2009 American Counseling Association Annual Conference and Exposition, March 19-23, Charlotte, North Carolina.

Kristin I. Douglas and Joy R. Fox

Imagine the excitement that comes with a long awaited pregnancy, only to have that joy and excitement shattered by a miscarriage. A pregnancy suddenly ended by miscarriage is, unfortunately, not an uncommon experience for women (Cosgrove, 2004; DeFrain, Millspaugh, & Xie, 1996; Swanson, Connor, Jolley, Pettinato, & Wang, 2007). Many facets of grief often accompany miscarriage loss including emotional turmoil, confusion, shock, disbelief, guilt, fear, depression, anger, stress, frustration, and disappointment. Challenging questions accompany miscarriage such as, "What happened?" "Did I do anything to cause this?" "Will I be able to get pregnant again and carry a baby to full-term?" or "Will the emotional hurt and pain that I feel right now ever end?" Western culture does not often deal well with death. Cultural and societal expectations accompanying grief and loss create challenges for women and families coping with a miscarriage loss (DeFrain, Millspaugh, & Xie, 1996). The stigma associated with grieving a miscarriage can complicate the grief experience (Layne, 2006). Therapists can better connect with and assist their grieving clients if they identify and understand factors that impact miscarriage loss, honor and validate loss experiences, and help support clients in the grieving process.

Grief Reactions to Perceived Unacknowledged Loss

Women who have a pregnancy end early often question themselves about their loss and wonder if they did something to cause the loss or if they could have done something to prevent the loss. General bereavement responses include numbness and shock, preoccupation with and longing for what was lost, disorganization and depression, and anxiety (Klier, Geller, & Ritsher, 2002). Additionally, miscarriage loss responses may include alarm, confusion, shattered hope; difficulty understanding or finding meaning; sadness, emptiness, guilt, no sense of control; anxiety, fear and vulnerability; longing for someone to share their story with; and wanting recognition, support and validation of the loss from others, especially health care providers (Swanson et al., 2007; Adolfsson, Larsson, Wijma, & Bertero, 2004).

Although some pregnancies are unwanted, symptoms of grief are still similar to those who have long awaited pregnancies (Zaccardi, Abbott, & Koziol-McLain, 1993). Overall, grief and loss symptoms are deeply felt regardless of gestational age at the time of the loss (Klier et al., 2002). Even the decision process on what to do with the fetal remains is an emotional minefield for women and their partners (Mansell, 2006). A small qualitative study by St. John, Cooke, and Goopy (2006) indicates that women who have had prior pregnancy loss experience complicated grieving when pregnant once again. The complicated grief experienced by women who have previously miscarried includes feelings of fear as to whether or not they can carry a baby to full-term, feelings of anger, self-blame or rejection, searching for a sense of belonging from others, and feeling they have forever been transformed by their former loss.

Although knowing general bereavement patterns may be helpful, therapists and medical care providers need to remember that each loss is a unique experience to the woman experiencing the loss and that the grieving process manifests differently in each woman. Grieving miscarriage loss is repeatedly described as a very powerful and meaningful loss worthy of acknowledgement and support, yet many women do not perceive their miscarriage loss experience as validated and acknowledged (Renner, Verdekal, Brier, & Fallucca, 2000; Swanson et al., 2007). Grief experiences may be further complicated by individuals who mean well, but say disturbing things such as "perhaps you will be able to get pregnant another time," or "something must have been wrong with the fetus so it is a good thing you had a miscarriage." These insensitive statements, whether true or not, can add to anger, frustration, feelings of isolation and rejection, as well as a further sense that their intense loss is not being acknowledged or honored.

Unacknowledged Grievers

As difficult as it is for women to find appropriate outlets for expressing their grief resulting from the experience of miscarriage, family members and other individuals find themselves marginalized or ignored in the grief process. The entire family unit is drawn into a closer experience of the pregnancy due to early home pregnancy tests, heartbeat monitors, and other advanced technology such as ultrasound (Krakovsky, 2006). As the couple and other family members become involved in naming the developing fetus and decorating the nursery, the baby becomes more real to each person and may cause heightened yearning for the lost baby after miscarriage (Krakovsky, 2006; Brin, 2004). The expectant father, grandparents, and other family members often experience significant grief after a miscarriage but get lost or forgotten in the process of caring for the woman who miscarried (Weener-Lin & Moro, 2004).

Increasingly, expectant fathers are more closely involved with the pregnancy and seem to feel a greater sense of loss following miscarriage (Krakovsky, 2006). Research, though still sparse, has begun to focus on the impact of miscarriage on men (Klier et al., 2002). The length of the pregnancy and the experience of seeing the ultrasound scan may contribute to more intense levels of grief in men (Puddifoot & Johnson, 1999). Although males may display less immediate 'active grief' following a miscarriage than women do, men seem to be more vulnerable to feelings of despair and difficulty in coping (Puddifoot & Johnson, 1999). Cumming et al. (2007) found that men experienced a reduction in anxiety six months following miscarriage, but measured higher in anxiety thirteen months following miscarriage. Men report experiencing self-blame, loss of identity, and the pressure to appear strong while hiding feelings of grief and anger (McCreight, 2004). In fact, a father may feel overlooked, ignored, or dismissed as he grieves the sudden termination of pregnancy (Staudacher, 1991).

Implications for Counselors

Counselors need to look beyond overt expressions of grief to recognize other equally valid forms of grief expression. Unfortunately, both grief theory and current counseling practice promote the general Western bias of valuing affective expression as more therapeutic than physical or cognitive means of expression (Martin & Doka, 2000). Martin and Doka have developed a model of a continuum of grief that provides a more inclusive view of the grief process. The model centers on three grieving styles:

1) Intuitive. Emotional/feeling; expresses grief openly; allows time to experience inner pain; may become physically exhausted or anxious; may experience prolonged periods of confusion and have problems concentrating; may benefit from a support group.

2) Instrumental. Physical/thinking; needs physical ways to express grief and may be reticent in expressing feeling; pushes aside feelings to cope with the present situation; uses humor to express feelings and manage anger; seeks solitude to reflect and to adapt to loss; may only express feelings in private.

3) Blended. Somewhere between Intuitive and Instrumental on the continuum.

The stage of bereavement may impact the nature of grief expression. For example, individuals may temporarily exhibit less affect and focus on performing a physical task while experiencing feelings of anger within their bereavement. Some individuals may cope with their grief through a blended style of emotional expression, cognitive approaches, and physical tasks throughout the grieving process.

Each of the three grief coping styles is not determined by gender and each reflects inherent strengths and weaknesses. As the lens of gender is blurred, the individual is more clearly understood. This view of grieving allows counselors to be more insightful and creative in assisting clients to discover their unique path of grief expression. Counselors may elect to share this information with clients through a web resource that focuses on loss, grief, and bereavement (Dyer, n.d.).

Healing Through Creative Grief Expression

Miscarriage loss is often a time of crisis for many women and healing from this loss can be challenging and difficult, especially when the loss is not acknowledged, and few, if any, grief rituals exist for those grieving miscarriage losses (Trepal, Semivan, & Caley-Bruce, 2005). Healing from an early pregnancy loss often involves understanding the nature of the attachment pertaining to the loss, identifying factors contributing to the loss, helping clients share feelings and exploring meaning pertaining to the loss, and honoring the loss by connecting with clients as they share their personal experiences and story associated with the loss (Fowler, 2007; Gilbert, 2002; Trepal et al., 2005). Creative interventions can also help clients connect with their loss, express emotions by giving voice to difficult and/or complicated feelings associated with the loss, and create or shape meaning in the loss (Buser, Buser, & Gladding, 2005).

Creative interventions used to process grief vary from music, dance, writing and poetry, art, crafts, play, videography, and storytelling (Buser et al., 2005; Trepal et al., 2005). Art (and accompanying writing) will be the intervention focused on here.

Gladding (2005) stated that visual arts help clients reframe personal experiences as they work through crises or developmental issues in a creative and therapeutic way. Ganim (as cited in Withrow, 2004) believes creative interventions, like art, tap into the emotional centers of the right side of the brain, whereas traditional talk therapy draws on the left side of the brain. Combining creative interventions with traditional talk-therapy engages both sides of the brain, integrating cognitive and affective processes, further aiding a more complete healing process (Ganim, as cited in Withrow, 2004).

One of the authors' personal journeys through miscarriage grief will be shared to provide an example of an art intervention that could be used with clients grieving a miscarriage loss. The art drawing method used emphasizes drawing feelings experienced at or around the time of each drawing. The idea was that the art naturally serves as a type of journal that houses various feelings and emotions associated with pregnancy, and/or loss. The assumption is that what needs to surface from the art will surface. The art serves as a form of emotional expression and food for processing. Art can stand alone or be accompanied by writing to further assist with processing emotions, the art experience itself, and the grief process. Although the art journal kept by the author included many various works of art and some writing to aid the healing process, three art examples of pastel chalk drawings will be shared here.

The first art piece, *Nurturing Babies Within*, was drawn not long after finding out about being pregnant. What emerged in this drawing were feelings associated with finding out about being pregnant, being excited about the pregnancy, doubt about being an adequate parent, and having a sense there might be multiple babies involved. Writing accompanying the art served as a place to further clarify feelings manifested in the art. Although the drawing is seen in black and white, the original drawing includes vibrant colors of pink, orange, and yellow with a periwinkle blue color for the sky in the background. The bright colors of the eggs symbolize hope and courage to face fears associated with moving forward with starting a family. The eggs symbolize the perceived beginning of multiple fetuses growing inside. Some black is used to accent the eggs growing out of the ground. The black is symbolic of challenges and adversity that accompany fears and inadequacies of becoming a mother (see Appendix A).

The second art piece, *Tear of Blood*, was drawn after the miscarriage occurred a couple of weeks later. Filling in the gaps from the first drawing to this one, the author found out she was pregnant with triplets. This drawing reflects great inner turmoil and sadness felt about the miscarriage loss. The drawing also represents wonderment of what happened, questions as to if the author did something to cause the miscarriage or did any of the "babies" survive, and attempts to make meaning of the miscarriage on a spiritual level. The actual written journal entry that corresponds with this writing further clarifies thoughts and feelings about the loss and emotional turmoil experienced at this time. Although the colors of the drawing cannot be seen here, the background colors are similar to Caucasian skin tones with very faint dark smudges surrounding the eye and the teardrop. The teardrop represents intense sadness about the loss. It is outlined in black, like the eye is, and filled with a deep red color symbolizing the finality of a miscarriage, shock of the blood expelled from the body during the miscarriage, and the intense sadness of the loss (see Appendix B).

The third art piece, *Three Peas in a Pod*, was drawn a month after the miscarriage and after a half a dozen more works. This piece is symbolic of peace of mind from feeling a degree of resolution on a spiritual level from receiving spiritual guidance, finding a degree of meaning in the loss, and turning the loss over to God. This was the first night of feeling any type of peace about the loss. The experiences triggered great spiritual discussions with my spouse and a further exploration of his perspective on the loss. It felt like a turning point to coping with the grief, intense sadness, anxiety, confusion and frustration that accompanied this loss (see Appendix C).

Summary of Art Experiences and Tips for Therapists

The author's experience with art journaling has been a profound and meaningful creative expression of grief leading to self-awareness, emotional release of great turmoil, a degree of peace with the loss, and hope for the future. This drawing process can easily be used with clients to process their early pregnancy loss or other loss experiences. Clients choose a topic that is meaningful to them to be represented in the art (i.e., let clients guide the work). Counselors then allow the process to foster clients' movement through grief. Let clients decide if they would like to use art as a one shot experience, as an ongoing journal, or if they want to use writing to accompany the art and enrich the experience. Counselors should be careful not to interpret the art and let clients share the meaning of their creative expression and grieving loss experiences.

References

Adolfsson, A., Larsson, P. G., Wijma, B., & Bertero, C. (2004). Guilt and emptiness: Women's experiences of miscarriage. *Health Care for Women International, 25*, 543-560.

Brin, D. J. (2004). The use of rituals in grieving for a miscarriage or stillbirth. *Women and Therapy, 27*(3/4), 123-132.

Buser, T. J., Buser, J. K., & Gladding, S. T. (2005). Good grief: The part of arts in healing loss and grief. *The Journal of Creativity in Mental Health, 1*(3/4), 173-183.

Cosgrove, L. (2004). The aftermath of pregnancy loss: A feminist critique of the literature and implications for treatment. *Women and Therapy, 27*(3/4), 107-122.

Cumming, G. P., Klein, S., Bolsover, D., Lee, A. J., Alexander, D. A., & Maclean, M. (2007).The emotional burden of miscarriage for women and their partners: Trajectories of anxiety and depression over 13 months. *BJOG: An International Journal of Obstetrics & Gynecology, 114*(9), 1138-1145.

DeFrain, J., Millspaugh, E., & Xie, X. (1996). The psychological effects of miscarriage: Implications for health professionals. *Families, Systems & Health, 14*(3), 331-346.

Dyer, K. A. (2008). *Loss, grief and bereavement.* Retrieved October 9, 2008, from http://www.squidoo.com/grief-loss-bereavement

Fowler, K. (2007). "So new, so new": Art and heart in women's grief memoirs. *Women's Studies, 36,* 525-549.

Gilbert, K. R. (2002). Taking narrative approach to grief research: Finding meaning in stories. *Death Studies, 26,* 223-239.

Gladding, S. T. (2005). *Counseling as an art: The creative arts in counseling* (3rd ed.). Alexandria, VA: American Counseling Association.

Klier, C. M., Geller, P. A., & Ritsher, J. B. (2002). Affective disorders in the aftermath of miscarriage: A comprehensive review. *Archives of Women's Mental Health, 5*(4), 1434-1816.

Krakovsky, M. (2006). Private loss visible. *Monitor on Psychology, 37*(8), 50-53.

Layne, L. (2006). Pregnancy loss, stigma, irony, and masculinities: Reflections on and future directions for research on religion in the global practice of IVF. *Culture, Medicine, and Psychiatry, 30,* 537-545.

Mansell, A. (2006). Early pregnancy loss. *Emergency Nurse, 4*(8), 26-28.

Martin, T., & Doka, K. (2000). *Men don't cry, Women do: Transcending gender stereotypes of grief.* Philadelphia: Taylor & Francis.

McCreight, B. S. (2004). A grief ignored: Narratives of pregnancy loss from a male perspective. *Sociology of Male Health & Illness, 26*(3), 326-350.

Puddifoot, J. E., & Johnson, M. P. (1999). Active grief, despair, and difficulty coping: some measured characteristics of male response following their partner's miscarriage. *Journal of Reproductive and Infant Psychology, 17,* 89-94.

Renner, C. H., Verdekal, S., Brier, S., & Fallucca, G. (2000). The meaning of miscarriage to others: Is it an unrecognized loss? *Journal of Personal and Interpersonal Loss, 5,* 65-76.

St. John, A., Cooke, M., & Goopy, S. (2006). Shrouds of silence: Three women's stories of prenatal loss. *The Australian Journal of Advanced Nursing, 23*(3), 8-12.

Staudacher, C. (1991). *Men and grief.* Oakland, CA: Harbinger Publications.

Swanson, K. M., Connor, S., Jolley, S. N., Pettinato, M., & Wang, T. (2007). Contexts and evolution of women's response to miscarriage during the first year of after loss. *Research in Nursing and Health, 30,* 2-16.

Trepal, H. C., Semivan, S. G., & Caley-Bruce, M. (2005). Miscarriage: A dream interrupted. *Journal of Creativity in Mental Health, 1*(3/4), 155-171.

Weener-Lin, A., & Moro, T. (2004). Unacknowledged and stigmatized losses. In F. Walsh & M. McGoldrick (Eds.), *Living beyond loss: Death in the family.* New York: WW Norton & Company.

Withrow, R. (2004). The use of color in art therapy. *Journal of Humanistic Counseling, Education, and Development, 43*(1), 33-40.

Zaccardi, R., Abbott, J., & Koziol-McLain, J. (1993). Loss and grief reactions after spontaneous miscarriage in the emergency department. *Annals of Emergency Medicine, 22*(5), 799-804.

Appendix A

Pastel drawing No. 1, *Nurturing Babies Within*

Appendix B

Pastel drawing No. 2, *Tear of Blood*
and corresponding journal entry

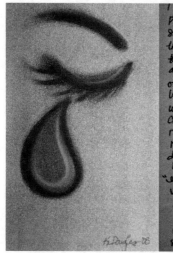

I can see this one of all pictures impacts me the most – its simple sincere + deep sadness – the blood represents not only tears but also loss of hope, dreams + a future. One, two, or three little ones that I have been waiting a lifetime for. Its been so hard for me to want to get to the point of having children + now am so excited + feel so ready. Lots of what its going through my mind + lots of "could I have done something different" going on in my mind. Lots of wishing I knew "exactly" what happened to them versus all the theories I have or have been taught. I believe God knows but I want to know too. Turning them over has been tough and just not sure if I am ready yet.

Appendix C

Pastel drawing No. 2, *Three Peas in a Pod*

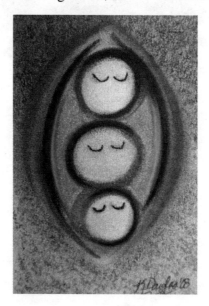

Section III

Counselor Education and Supervision

Application of the Transtheoretical Model Within the Integrative Developmental Model of Supervision

Paper based on a program presented at the 2007 Association for Counselor Education and Supervision Conference, October 11-14, Columbus, Ohio.

Dilani M. Perera-Diltz and Clancy J. Yeager

Behavioral Connections

Clinical supervision is indispensable for the development of new counselors (Bradley & Kottler, 2001) and even benefits more experienced counselors. Clinical supervision entails monitoring and directing services provided by another counselor or counselor trainee (Bradley & Kottler, 2001), referred to as supervisee, to promote professional functioning by facilitating the supervisee to reach higher levels of competence in both knowledge and skills (Bradley & Kottler, 2001).

Many models of clinical supervision are available to benefit a variety of styles of supervision (Bradley & Kottler, 2001). Depending on the model, the clinical supervisor may function in the roles of coach, teacher, consultant, counselor, and evaluator, and engage in challenging, stimulating, and/or encouraging the supervisee as needed to facilitate growth (Bradley & Kottler, 2001). The Integrated Developmental Model (IDM) developed by Carl D. Stoltenberg in the 1980s, based on human development theories (Stoltenberg, McNeil, & Delworth, 1998), tailors content and style of supervision to the developmental level of the supervisee. Supervision through IDM encourages progressive development leading to optimal functioning as counselors (Whiting, Bradley, & Planny, 2001).

The Transtheoretical Model (TTM) presented in the 1980s by James O. Prochaska and Carlo C. DiClemente (1994) is based on a similar progressive structure as IDM. TTM encourages meeting a client's level of readiness for change and facilitating the client to obtain goals through progressive movement through stages of change within a supportive environment (Prochaska & DiClemente, 1994). The authors propose using TTM concepts in supervision to facilitate a supervisee's acquisition of skills and knowledge. Although a discourse of neither IDM nor TTM is the intention of this paper, some components of both models are provided below to explain the proposed application of TTM within IDM.

Similarities between IDM and TTM promote the proposed application of TTM within IDM. Both models have an ecological, developmental, and positive focus. The complimentary nature of the two paradigms may enhance supervision by deepening the conceptualization of a supervisee within an IDM level and expanding available techniques to facilitate a supervisee's progress to the next IDM level. At the risk of oversimplification, the following sections provide a brief overview of the levels of IDM and applicable dimensions (i.e., processes and stages) of TTM.

The Three Levels of IDM for Supervisee Conceptualization

The IDM provides three developmental levels in which to conceptualize a supervisee. Once the level of a supervisee is determined, the supervisor operates from the corresponding environment (Stoltenberg & Delworth, 1987). A supervisee's level of development is assessed using three criteria (i.e., self- and other-awareness, motivation, and autonomy) which influence clinical practice (Stoltenberg & Delworth, 1987). Early supervision using IDM involves teaching, feedback, support, directives, and skill building within a trusting supervisory relationship. More advanced supervision includes correcting, clarifying, confronting, reflecting, and consulting (Stoltenberg et al., 1998).

An IDM level one supervisee requires skill and knowledge development as well as encouragement to demonstrate the newly learned trade. This supervisee is self-focused (Stoltenberg & Delworth, 1987) and experiences performance anxiety related to application of newly learned skills and to evaluation by the supervisor. Thus clients with less complex issues are best suited for the level one counselor. A highly structured and supportive supervisory environment is ideal for such a supervisee's development. In this hierarchical supervisory relationship the supervisor acts as teacher, evaluator, and coach; provides education; guides case conceptualization; and directs decision-making pertaining to skill application (Stoltenberg & Delworth, 1987). The goal is to move this anxious and dependent supervisee toward confidence and independence through experience and self-awareness (Stoltenberg & Delworth, 1987).

A level two supervisee is less self-focused but fluctuates between autonomy and dependence in decision-making (Stoltenberg et al., 1998). This supervisee requires more challenging clients to address the lack of experience and to promote advancement of skills (Stoltenberg et al., 1998). The supervisor, functioning in all five roles stated elsewhere, reduces structure in the supervisory environment to accommodate the supervisee's need for autonomy, promotes alternative case conceptualization, focuses on personal development more than skill improvement, and emphasizes counseling within a cohesive theory to facilitate appropriate independence and to maintain motivation (Stoltenberg et al., 1998).

A level three supervisee is an experienced counselor who demonstrates appropriate self- and other-awareness, motivation, and autonomy (Stoltenberg et al., 1998). Complex issues of personal development, transference and counter-transference, parallel processing, and client and counselor resistance as well as defensiveness are central topics of supervision (Stoltenberg et al., 1998). The supervisor acting as a consultant and the supervisee structuring supervision as needed are suitable. The goal is to encourage the supervisee to progress toward becoming a master counselor (Stoltenberg et al., 1998).

At times, assessment of the level at which a supervisee is functioning does not by itself provide adequate insight to facilitate growth in a timely manner. At such times, TTM provides a useful framework for enhanced conceptualization and timely movement of a supervisee within each IDM level.

Core Dimensions of TTM

The TTM's core dimensions are derived from empirical evidence based on how people change with or without professional assistance (Prochaska & Norcross, 2007). There are five stages through which a person progresses when engaging in change (Prochaska & DiClemente, 1994). Precontemplation is defined by lack of awareness of the problem and lack of motivation to change. Contemplation brings some awareness but rarely a need to rectify the problem (Prochaska & DiClemente, 1994). Preparation is marked by small cognitive and behavioral changes (Prochaska & DiClemente, 1994). Action involves further cognitive and behavioral changes. Finally, maintenance involves active preservation of changes made at previous stages to avoid a relapse (Prochaska & DiClemente, 1994). These five stages are both hierarchical and spiral, with a person moving through each stage more than once (Prochaska & DiClemente, 1994).

There are 10 empirically supported processes (Prochaska & Norcross, 2007) or activities that people utilize to alter feeling, thinking, and/or behaving within the above stages. These processes are: consciousness-raising, catharsis/dramatic relief, self-reevaluation, environmental re-evaluation, self-liberation, social liberation, counter-conditioning, stimulus control, contingency management, and helping relationships (Prochaska & Norcross, 2007). Some of these processes are more beneficial in facilitating progress through some stages than others (Prochaska & Norcross, 2007). Precontemplators who use very few change processes benefit mostly by consciousness-raising and dramatic relief (Prochaska &

Norcross, 2007). Contemplators, who readily engage in consciousness-raising, benefit from self and environmental re-evaluation (Prochaska & Norcross, 2007). Those in preparation stage, engaging in alternative healthier behaviors and thought processes, benefit from self and social liberation (Prochaska & Norcross, 2007). Those in action stage who need to move beyond a cognitive foundation benefit from counter-conditioning, contingency management, and stimulus control processes (Prochaska & Norcross, 2007).

Proposed Application of TTM Within IDM

Assuming that supervision is a cooperative attempt between a supervisor and a supervisee to facilitate learning and mastery (Prochaska & DiClemente, 1994), the following application of TTM within each level of IDM is proposed. For simplification of explanation, the authors present the progress of a novice counselor through all levels of IDM.

A level one counselor at precontemplation stage is unaware of self-focus related to performance anxiety and its effects on service provision. Such a supervisee, for example, would discuss the application of a technique without the awareness of the appropriateness and effectiveness of the technique for a client. Although self-focus is common at this stage, the goal is to move from self-focus to other-focus to become an effective counselor. To facilitate this cognitive shift a supervisor could use consciousness-raising (e.g., observations, interpretations, and confrontations) and dramatic relief (Prochaska & Norcross, 2007).

Precontemplators could be further conceptualized through four categories labeled the reluctant, the rebellious, the resigned, and the rationalizing (DiClemente, 1991). The reluctant supervisee is not fully conscious of the problematic nature of the behavior (DiClemente, 1991), thus consciousness-raising in a sensitive manner and utilizing dramatic relief is effective. The rebellious has a heavy investment in the problem behavior and prefers to make his or her own decisions (DiClemente, 1991). Providing choices and paradoxical strategies when consciousness-raising will shift the energy of rebellion into contemplation (DiClemente, 1991). The resigned is overwhelmed by the problem and has given up on the possibility of change (DiClemente, 1991). Instilling hope and exploring barriers to change in consciousness-raising and in dramatic relief processes will facilitate movement to contemplation. Finally, the rationalizing appears to have all possible solutions (DiClemente, 1991). Consciousness-raising through reflection and empathy are the best interventions for this group (DiClemente, 1991). Appropriate application of processes will facilitate the movement of the precontemplative supervisee to contemplation stage.

A neophyte counselor at contemplation stage with awareness of self-focus and anxiety, but not ready or able to remedy it, will benefit from self and environmental re-evaluation processes. Within a non-threatening, warm, and respectful supervisory environment (DiClemente, 1991), facilitating assessment of personal values, effects of supervisee's conduct on the client (Prochaska & Norcross, 2007), application of new skills, and good decision-making (DiClemente, 1991) will move the supervisee to preparation stage.

A level one supervisee in preparation stage has begun some changes in thinking and behavior. A supervisor acts as teacher, coach, and counselor providing knowledge, skills, support, and encouragement and thus empowers the supervisee to believe in his or her abilities as a counselor. Such self-liberating processes (Prochaska & Norcross, 2007) influence cognitive and behavioral changes (DiClemente, 1991) facilitating movement to action stage.

A supervisee in action stage continues to address performance anxiety and begins to shift to other-focus. This supervisee is very likely to demonstrate independence in decision-making similar to what is expected from an IDM level two supervisee. For instance, the supervisee may seek supervision regarding client conceptualization, but show hesitance in accepting feedback due to the need to be self-sufficient. It is essential that counter-conditioning, contingency management, and stimulus control processes are utilized during this stage to facilitate the supervisee's growth without relapse into initial anxieties and self-focus.

Shift to maintenance stage is indicated by significant progress in diminishing anxiety and self-focus, in augmenting client conceptualization, and in maintaining appropriate changes. The supervisor's task is to monitor overconfidence while supporting the progress of the supervisee. Planning for challenges ahead is appropriate for this stage (Stoltenberg & Delworth, 1987). Once in maintenance stage, a supervisee acts as in IDM level two.

Following is a similar conceptualization using TTM within IDM level two. The main goal of level two is to facilitate true and appropriate autonomy in the supervisee (Stoltenberg & Delworth, 1987). Providing the supervisee with more complex cases and consciousness-raising regarding personal abilities or inabilities mobilizes the supervisee from precontemplation to contemplation. Creating appropriate and sufficient anxiety pertaining to abilities (Stoltenberg & Delworth, 1987) and engaging in dramatic relief will also influence change. In contemplation stage, engaging the supervisee in self and environmental re-evaluation facilitates re-examination of personal values (Prochaska & Norcross, 2007) and the impact of the supervisee's current counseling strategies on the client, thus facilitating movement to preparation stage. In preparation stage, engaging the supervisee in self-liberation activities facilitates transition to action stage. In action stage, applying contingency management, counter-conditioning, and stimulus control facilitates progress to maintenance stage.

Similar to the above discourse, a supervisee's development can be conceptualized using TTM within IDM level three. The goal of this level is to facilitate increased independence and application of a superior level of skills, techniques, and client conceptualization (Stoltenberg & Delworth, 1987). Using appropriate processes at appropriate stages as described in the above paragraphs, a supervisor facilitates a supervisee's professional growth through stages. Once a supervisee reaches TTM maintenance stage within IDM level three, the supervisee will demonstrate appropriate ability to make and maintain changes related to professional advancement to promote client welfare. The supervisory relationship at this point will

Table 1: *The Application of TTM Within Each Level of IDM.*

IDM Levels / Stages of Change	Level One	Level Two	Level Three	Processes
Precontemplation	Unaware of self-focus and performance anxiety.	Unaware of the struggle for autonomy	Unaware of personal abilities and overly dependent on supervisor.	Consciousness-Raising
Contemplation	Aware of self-focus and performance anxiety but unsure of the ways to change	Aware of excessive and insufficient confidence but not sure of how or what to change	Aware of lack confidence in personal abilities and unnecessary dependence on the supervisor	Self Re-evaluation Environmental Re-evaluation
Preparation	Initiates small cognitive and behavioral changes to address self-focus and performance anxiety.	Initiates small cognitive and behavioral changes to address excessive or insufficient confidence.	Initiates changes to facilitate self-confidence and conditional dependence on supervisor.	Self Liberation
Action	Continues changes to move to other focus and reduction of performance anxiety	Manages or eliminates excessive or insufficient confidence in skills and knowledge.	Continues changes to facilitate self-confidence and conditional dependence	Contingency Management, Counter-conditioning and Stimulus Control
Maintenance	Takes steps to prevent retreat to self-focus and performance anxiety.	Takes steps to maintain changes made in action stage.	Takes steps to maintain changes achieved in action stage.	

resemble and perhaps function as peer consultation (Stoltenberg et al., 1998). Conceptualizations using IDM levels and TTM stages and processes are presented in Table 1.

Vignettes of the Application of TTM Within IDM

Brian was a doctoral student new to sex offender assessment and treatment and somewhat anxious and uncertain. The supervisor began the process by assessing Brian's awareness of self and others, motivation, and autonomy. The supervisor determined that Brian had a fairly well developed sense of awareness of others, appropriate insight into his anxiety, and a high level of motivation although still at IDM level one. Using TTM, he determined that Brian was in contemplation stage. Hence the supervisor provided Brian opportunities to engage in educational experiences to learn skills specific to working with people who had committed sex offenses. Concurrently, the supervisor engaged Brian in self and environmental re-evaluation for Brian to gain more insight related to his values and how his counseling skills affected his new client population. When Brian indicated readiness (i.e., preparation stage), the supervisor facilitated further opportunities for Brian to educate himself. Once the supervisor determined that Brian had gained sufficient knowledge and skills in the treatment of people who committed sex offenses and had begun utilizing his new skills in treatment which indicated action stage, the supervisor helped Brian with contingency management, counter-conditioning, and stimulus control. Brian agreed to monitor and manage anxiety and uncertainties when novel situations in treatment arose.

Another clinician, James, a licensed professional counselor, had worked for about two years with clients who committed sex offenses. James had confidence in his skills and was able to function independently, working with clients presenting with complex issues. The supervisor, who determined that James was in IDM level two requested that he complete a sex offender assessment tool independently to which request James demonstrated hesitance. Using TTM, the supervisor was able to conceptualize James at preparation stage related to his abilities, and engaged James in self-liberation processes facilitating James' movement to action stage. Once James was comfortable to administer sex offender assessment tools the supervisor allocated more responsibilities to James, such as leading a specialized psycho-educational program for low-risk offenders. In addition, the supervisor mobilized contingency management, counter-conditioning, and stimulus control to prevent James relapsing back to being a less confident clinician in a more dependent supervision relationship.

The third clinician, Ann, was a licensed independent social worker who had worked for eight years assessing and treating people who committed sex offences. The supervisor assessed Ann with superior knowledge and skills in the field and with a high level of awareness, motivation, and autonomy. Ann demonstrated ability to seek supervision when needed and to provide the necessary structure for it. However, at times, Ann demonstrated doubts regarding her abilities. Using TTM, the supervisor conceptualized Ann at preparation stage and worked on self-liberation to move Ann to action stage as well as on contingency management, counter-transference, and stimulus control to move toward maintenance of change. With time the relationship between the supervisor and Ann resembled more one of mutuality and consultation typical of IDM level three supervision.

Limitations and Challenges of Using TTM Within IDM

Although utilizing TTM within IDM facilitates enhanced conceptualization and processes to mobilize supervisees through personal and professional development, like the colors of a rainbow, IDM levels and TTM stages are not clearly distinct or discreet and overlap and blur together, as evident in case vignettes. In addition, although evidence based on how people change with or without outside intervention should apply to supervision as well, there is a lack of empirical evidence directly related to using TTM by itself or within levels of IDM for supervision. Furthermore, TTM has been criticized for its lack of deep exploration of issues, lack of providing insight, and focusing on change processes typical to western society (Prochaska & Norcross, 2007).

Conclusion

Application of TTM within IDM levels may facilitate timely and satisfactory supervisory experience. Although such application appears well suited because both models are based on a philosophy that is progressive and developmental in nature, the explanation of these processes tends to oversimplify the complex issues of human development and supervision. It is hoped that this paper would initialize interest in clinical and research application of TTM within IDM.

References

Bradley J. L., & Kottler, J. A. (2001). Overview of counselor supervision. In J. L. Bradley & N. Ladany (Eds.), *Counselor supervision: Principles, process, and practice* (3rd ed., pp. 3-21). Philadelphia: Brunner-Routledge.

DiClemente, C. C. (1991). Motivational interviewing and stages of change. In W. R. Miller & S. Rollnick (Eds.), *Motivational interviewing: Preparing people to change addictive behaviors* (pp. 191- 206). New York: Guilford.

Prochaska, J. O., & DiClemente, C. C. (1994). *The transtheoretical approach: Crossing traditional boundaries of therapy* (pp. 150-162). Malabar, FL: Krieger.

Prochaska, J. O., & Norcross, J. C. (2007). *Systems of psychotherapy: A transthoeretical analysis* (6th ed., pp. 507-539). Belmont, CA: Brooks/Cole.

Stoltenberg, C., & Delworth, U. (1987). *Supervising counselors and therapists: A developmental approach.* San Francisco: Jossey-Bass.

Stoltenberg, C., McNeill, B., & Delworth, U. (1998). *IDM supervision: An integrated developmental model for supervising counselors and therapists.* San Francisco: Jossey-Bass.

Whiting, P. P., Bradley, L. J., & Planny, K. J. (2001). Supervision-based developmental models of counselor supervision. In J. L. Bradley & N. Ladany (Eds.), *Counselor supervision: Principles, process, and practice* (3rd ed., pp. 125-146). Philadelphia: Brunner-Routledge.

Article 11

Connecting Counselors Around the World: Enhancing Counselor Training Through Cultural and Global Initiatives

Paper based on a program presented at the 2009 American Counseling Association Annual Conference and Exposition, March 19-23, Charlotte, North Carolina.

David D. Hof, Julie A. Dinsmore, Catherine M. Hock, Thomas R. Scofield, and Michael A. Bishop

Over the last several decades, there has been a rapid increase in racial and ethnic minorities in the United States due to immigration as well as growth domestically within non-White groups (U.S. Census Bureau, 2000). This growth has led to a heightened awareness in the counseling profession that counselors need to adjust their practice in order to meet the individual and systemic needs of clients from these groups. Both the American Counseling Association (2005) and the American Psychological Association (2002) have deemed it unethical to serve diverse clients without having developed multicultural competence. More specifically, the standards for the preparation of counselors, developed by the Council for the Accreditation of Counseling and Related Educational Programs (CACREP) emphasize the importance of the advocacy role of counselors by stating that programs should include "counselors' roles in social justice, advocacy and conflict resolution, cultural self-awareness, the nature of biases, prejudices, processes of intentional

115

and unintentional oppression and discrimination, and other culturally supported behaviors that are detrimental to the growth of the human spirit, mind, or body" (CACREP, 2001). Attitudes, knowledge, and skills that constitute multicultural counseling competence have been identified, which in turn have delineated domains of learning that counselor training programs should incorporate into their curriculum (Arredondo et al., 1996; Lewis, Arnold, House, & Toporek, 2003; Sue, Arredondo, & McDavis, 1992).

Most counselor training programs have designated a course focusing on diversity issues in counseling as the primary way to build multicultural competence in trainees (Atkinson, Brown, & Casas, 1996; Brown, 2004; Dinsmore & England, 1996). These courses have been shown to focus heavily on facilitating students' cultural identity exploration and imparting knowledge of non-dominant cultural groups in the U.S., and often do not address skill development (Priester et al., 2008). More specifically, these courses generally do not help trainees develop the expertise in systems intervention needed to act as advocates and address sociopolitical forces and systemic barriers impacting client mental health (Constantine, Hage, Kindaichi, & Bryant, 2007; Ponterotto & Casas, 1991; Sue & Sue, 2008). Additionally, they do little to promote a global perspective that would enhance trainee understanding of issues specific to immigrant and refugee clients (Chung, Bemak, Ortiz, & Sandoval-Perez, 2008) and the broader implications of governmental policy decisions for these clients.

These findings suggest that counselor training programs must move beyond the curriculum in the designated multicultural courses and provide opportunities for trainees to engage globally and domestically with diversity. One way to do this is to develop a variety of extracurricular and curricular experiential activities that focus on skill development and the advocacy role in counseling. These types of activities have been shown to better support trainee development of the attitudes, knowledge, and skills necessary to respond to the challenges that accompany a rapidly diversifying client base and community context (Kim & Lyons, 2003). This article details initiatives developed by the Department of Counseling & School Psychology (CSP) at the University of Nebraska at Kearney (UNK) that focus on skill development in clinical practice, research, and advocacy and provide trainees with hands-on experience with both global and domestic diversity. Over the past decade, the area in which the university is located has experienced a rapid increase in the non-White refugee and immigrant population that has resulted in a 960% increase in non-English or limited English speakers (U. S. Census Bureau, 2000).

Extracurricular Immersion Experiences

Outreach to the Immigrant Latino Population

Faculty in the CSP department assisted in developing a grant-funded program that has played a significant role in increasing enrollment of Latino students on campus by 266% since 2000 (University of Nebraska at Kearney, 2008). Several initiatives connected to this grant program have provided counseling trainees with hands-on clinical and advocacy experience with recently arrived Latino immigrant populations.

Cultural Unity Conference

Annually, this conference draws 300 Latino and multiracial high school students to UNK to introduce them to the campus, discuss the benefits of higher education, and provide information on resources that may help them access a college education. Most of these students are immigrants and/or potential first-time college attendees in their families. During the conference, students and faculty from the CSP department facilitate growth groups that help participants explore their fears and discuss the individual and systemic barriers that are impacting their readiness for, or access to, further education. Participants also brainstorm interventions to meet those needs.

Grief Groups

The CSP department collaborates with the Office of Multicultural Affairs to provide counseling support for students who access their office and for members of the Latino sorority and fraternity on campus. Individual and group counseling services have been provided, an example of which are grief groups offered in response to the death of a Latino student well known among the Latino campus community.

Justice for All Conference

The Kent Estes Justice for All Conference (JFA) is a statewide training event focused on advocating for underserved populations that was developed by the department's Upsilon Nu Kappa Chapter of Chi Sigma Iota. The annual student-led conference is intended to empower members of the educational and mental health communities to respond to the reality of social injustice through professional and client advocacy. Community counselors, school psychologists, school counselors, social workers, educators, students, faculty and other mental health practitioners throughout the state engage in a day of active learning and interdisciplinary collaboration via discussion, lecture, group learning and experiential activities. Attendees receive training on specific social advocacy strategies such as collaborating with other professionals to advance mental health services to marginalized groups, practice their new knowledge on site, and develop advocacy plans that utilize these skills in their schools or agencies. Over the past six years, the conference has provided training to approximately 600 students, faculty, and practicing professionals to address a broad spectrum of advocacy topics such as immigrant populations, non-dominant sexual orientation, cognitive disabilities, social class, underrepresented racial/cultural groups, elderly, survivors of domestic violence and sexual assault, bullying, and infant/toddler mental health. Outcome research conducted on the implementation of the advocacy plans developed at the conference shows the positive impact of this training event on putting advocacy into action (Hof, Scofield, & Dinsmore, 2006).

Professional Development Workshops

The department offers six professional development workshops per year, designed to make in-depth training on important issues available to both students and practicing professionals. At least one of these workshops each year is devoted to an advocacy issue, such as cyber-bullying or legal and ethical issues impacting children and adolescents. Students may apply credit earned for workshop attendance to the elective course requirement on their degree program. If students take this option, they are required to create an individual learning project that focuses on application of the workshop content. Approximately 400 students, faculty, and practitioners attend these training workshops annually.

Pine Ridge Reservation

This annual immersion experience for students and faculty on the Pine Ridge Indian Reservation emphasizes cultural exchange, in-depth experience with indigenous helping traditions, and a clearer understanding of the barriers to effective mental health services for American Indians. Students and faculty have participated in a Sundance, Purification Ceremony (Sweat) and other cultural experiences that helped them gain valuable insights into the Lakota Sioux culture, concrete ideas on the nature of advocacy actions needed to support American Indian clients, and relationships that have led to collaborative training initiatives for mental health professionals.

International Collaborative Research Initiative

The International Collaborative Research Initiative focuses on exploring the counselor role globally through cooperative teaching and research exchanges between the CSP department at UNK and the department's international counterparts. Over the past several years, the CSP department has partnered with Black Hills State University to exchange faculty and students with the psychology department at Vytautas Magnus University in Lithuania. This international experience has provided teaching activities and discussions in both the U.S. and Lithuania centered around effective mental health practice and social interventions to support clients. Through these opportunities, counseling trainees develop a global perspective and clinical skills. Another unique opportunity afforded trainees by this international partnership are interactive real-time video research symposiums between U.S. and Lithuanian students who present and discuss their current research projects. Another aspect of this international collaboration is co-ownership by the CSP department at UNK and Vytautas Magnus University of an international research journal focusing on issues in counseling and psychology. In addition to the program in Lithuania, the CSP department maintains a connection with an international research journal published by Chulalongkorn University in Thailand.

Immersion Experiences Within the Curriculum

The extracurricular opportunities available to students are augmented by required immersion and advocacy activities that are part of four of the counselor education program core courses. These activities are designed not only to increase student awareness and knowledge of social justice issues (e.g., racism, oppression, discrimination, stereotyping), but to also develop skills in the emerging counselor role of client advocacy in institutional and community settings.

Organization and Practice Course

Students are introduced to the ACA-endorsed advocacy competencies (Lewis et al., 2003) and then required to design Service Learning Projects for their communities that focus on one of the following: (a) Direct Community Services-Preventative education, (b) Direct Client Services-Outreach and counseling to vulnerable populations, (c) Indirect Community Services-Design of more responsive social environments and/or systemic change through public policy initiatives, or (d) Indirect Client Services-Creation of new helping networks, provision of consultation and advocacy services to people and agencies. Students, in small cooperative groups, identify an underrepresented population for which they will provide service and they then work collaboratively to develop an advocacy plan. By repeatedly examining competency building activities from increasingly more complex perspectives, the students not only learn about specific concepts, but also have the opportunity to consider how those concepts work together to create a comprehensive service delivery effort for a focal client population within their respective communities.

Consultation Course

Advocacy skill development in this course focuses on environmental or systemic change interventions within the school setting. Each student identifies an advocacy need for an underrepresented group within his or her school and designs and implements an advocacy plan to address that need.

Seminar in Professional Issues & Ethics

Students are required to research advocacy issues in a community or school setting and develop a needs assessment instrument based on their findings. In addition, discussion of ethics vignettes includes an exploration of the advocacy implications of each vignette.

Multicultural Counseling Course

Students develop two Multicultural Action Plans, the first being an interview with a member of a non-dominant group and the second an immersion experience, in order to gain a clearer understanding of the worldview and socio-political experiences of individuals within that group, including individual and/or institutional barriers that have had a negative impact, and to then develop implications for counseling practice.

Professional Orientation Course

Students are expected to become involved in one social justice issue that interests them and to document that involvement. Their plans can be highly individual and can take place on a community, department, college, university, state, national, or international level. Examples include using the www.care2.com website to sign up for information from a particular issue/interest group, sign petitions, write letters to government officials, and keep up to date on relevant news; joining a professional organization and signing up for a listserv such as the one sponsored by Counselors for Social Justice, a division of ACA, posting on the listserv, and keeping up to date on relevant issues; or getting involved in a local or community project where you spend time for a particular cause.

A sample of the types of advocacy plans and experiences emerging from these various course requirements include the development of the following: an ELL literacy project, a shelter for abused women and children, a homeless shelter, access to counseling services for an incarcerated population, a GLBT Community Center, a GLBT youth support group at a local YMCA, parity in university financial support for student organizations serving non-White students, a Daycare Program for the elderly, after-school enrichment and support programs for at-risk children, and ELL services within a school.

Conclusion

The initiatives described in this article focus on developing counselor expertise in the areas of domestic and global diversity. They emphasize multicultural skill development and competence in implementing client advocacy at both the individual and systemic levels. Change through these initiatives is not accomplished through individual didactic learning, but experientially through partnering and interacting with colleagues, both here and abroad, as well as with members of a number of marginalized client groups. In addition to extending the scope of the counselor education program, the activities impact a significant number of practicing professionals annually by providing training related to their workplace and client caseloads. The uniqueness of these activities is the opportunity for participants to practice skill development and implement practical advocacy initiatives. Hopefully, the ideas presented here will provide direction for other counselor education programs on ways they can help their trainees develop not just attitudes and knowledge related to global and domestic diversity, but skill at interacting with members of non-dominant groups and competence at developing and implementing the advocacy initiatives needed to more effectively meet the needs of their diverse clients.

References

American Counseling Association. (2005). *ACA code of ethics.* Alexandria, VA: Author.

American Psychological Association. (2002). *Ethical principles of psychologists and code of conduct.* Retrieved September 11, 2008, from http://www.apa.org/ethics/code2002.html

Arredondo, P., Toporek, R., Brown, S. P., Jones, J., Locke, D. C., Sanchez, I., et al. (1996). Operationalization of the multicultural counseling competencies. *Journal of Multicultural Counseling & Development, 24*, 42-78.

Atkinson, D. R., Brown, M. T., & Casas, J. T. (1996). Achieving ethnic parity in counseling psychology. *The Counseling Psychologist, 24*(2), 230-258.

Brown, E. L. (2004). What precipitates change in cultural diversity awareness during a multicultural course: The message or the method. *Journal of Teacher Education, 55*(4), 325-340.

Chung, R. C., Bemak, F., Ortiz, D., & Sandoval-Perez, P. A. (2008). Promoting the mental health of immigrants: A multicultural/social justice perspective. *Journal of Counseling & Development, 86*, 310-317.

Constantine, M. G., Hage, S. M., Kindaichi, M. M., & Bryant, R. M. (2007). Social justice and multicultural issues: Implications for the practice and training of counselors and counseling psychologists. *Journal of Counseling & Development, 85*, 24-29.

Council for the Accreditation of Counseling and Related Educational Programs. (2001). *2001 Standards.* Retrieved September 11, 2008, from http://www.cacrep.org/2001Standards.html

Dinsmore, J. A., & England, J. T. (1996). A study of multicultural counseling training at CACREP-accredited counselor education programs. *Counselor Education & Supervision, 36*(1), 58-77.

Hof, D. D., Scofield, T. R., & Dinsmore, J. A. (2006). Social advocacy: Assessing the impact of training on the development and implementation of advocacy plans. In G. R. Walz, J. C. Bleuer, & R. K. Yep (Eds.), *Vistas: Compelling perspectives on counseling 2006* (pp. 211-213). Alexandria, VA: American Counseling Association.

Kim, B. S., & Lyons, H. Z. (2003). Experiential activities in multicultural counseling competence training. *Journal of Counseling & Development, 81*, 400-408.

Lewis, J., Arnold, M., House, R., & Toporek, R. (2003, March). *Advocacy competencies.* Retrieved September 11, 2008, from http://www.counseling.org/Counselors/

Ponterotto, J. G., & Casas, J. M. (1991). *Handbook of racial/ethnic minority counseling research.* Springfield, IL: Charles C. Thomas.

Priester, P. E., Jones, J. E., Jackson-Bailey, C. M., Jana-Masri, A., Jordan, E. X., & Metz, A. J. (2008). An analysis of content and instructional strategies in multicultural counseling courses. *Journal of Multicultural Counseling & Development, 36*(1), 29-39.

Sue, D. W., Arredondo, P., & McDavis, R. J. (1992). Multicultural counseling competencies and standards: A call to the profession. *Journal of Counseling & Development, 70*, 477-486.

Sue, D. W., & Sue, D. (2008). *Counseling the culturally diverse: Theory and practice.* New York: John Wiley & Sons.

University of Nebraska at Kearney. (2008). *UNK factbook.* Retrieved September 25, 2008, from http://aaunk.unk.edu/factbook

U. S. Census Bureau. (2000). *CensusScope.* Retrieved September 25, 2008, from www.censusscope.org

Article 12

Critical Issues in Implementing the New CACREP Standards for Disaster, Trauma, and Crisis Counseling

Paper based on a program presented at the 2009 American Counseling Association Annual Conference and Exposition, March 19-23, Charlotte, North Carolina.

Jane M. Webber and J. Barry Mascari

After September 11, 2001, increasing attention has focused on the counselor's role in disaster and trauma response (Smith, 2005; Uhernik, 2008; Webber, Mascari, Dubi, & Gentry, 2006). The American Counseling Association (ACA) partnered with the American Red Cross to provide disaster mental health specialists after 9/11 and subsequent hurricane relief efforts, and thousands of counselors volunteered for deployment. During this time counselors and organizations of trauma professionals raised concerns over the depth and quality of counselors' disaster response preparation.

During the standards review process in 2006, the Council for Accreditation for Counseling and Related Standards (CACREP) received a federal grant to study the need for counselor training in emergency preparedness and response (Beckett, 2008). During the draft review period, feedback solicited from counseling professionals indicated strong support for CACREP's initiative. The 2009 CACREP Standards (CACREP, 2008) provide competencies for crisis, disaster, and trauma response that are infused in both core counseling and program specific curricula (Table 1). These standards represent a major shift from basic counselor training requirements to an infusion of disaster and trauma competencies across counselor preparation. Carolyn Beckett (2008), Project Manager for the Department of Health and Human Services grant, cited the importance of the new standards:

> The emergency preparedness language incorporated into the third draft of the standards, in alignment with the National Response Framework, reflected the knowledge and skills counselors have utilized during recent community, regional and national emergencies, including university shootings, bridge collapses, uncontrolled wildfires, hurricane devastation and terrorist attacks. (p. 1, 8)

This article discusses the relevance of the new counselor standards to professional training and practice, describes organizations providing certification, accreditation, and resources, and identifies issues requiring consideration when implementing the new CACREP standards.

The Call for Standards: Progress

Howard Smith (2005), an American Red Cross Disaster Mental Health Trainer, was one of the early counselors to caution, "Providing mental health services in a disaster environment requires an additional set of skills that are noticeably lacking in counselor education programs" (p. 37). Webber and Mascari (2005) advised that a critical lesson learned from September 11th and its aftermath was the need for readily available appropriately trained disaster mental health volunteers. Webber, Mascari, Dubi, and Gentry (2006) addressed nine issues related to trauma counseling and laid the foundation for trauma initiatives with counselors in the ACA Trauma Interest Network who shared similar concerns. Two critical issues called for the inclusion of crisis and trauma training in counselor education programs and the development of training models and curriculum.

Green Cross Academy, the Association of Traumatic Stress Specialists (ASTSS), and other private organizations offer accreditation or certification for mental health professionals. However, none has been universally adopted as the standard in the field, making the establishment of counselor preparation standards even more critical. The American Red Cross requires licensure as a mental health professional for Disaster Mental Health Services training and work. *The Uniform Emergency Volunteer Health Care Practitioners Act* (National Conference of Commissioners on Uniform State Law, 2006) also requires licensure; however, based on their national certification, National Certified Counselors and Certified Rehabilitation Counselors are authorized to provide services.

With CACREP's new standards and the State of New Jersey's Disaster Response Crisis Counselor (DRCC) certification, the counseling profession has made substantial progress toward the establishment of a common credential. Charles Figley, founder of Green Cross Academy and the International Society for Traumatic Stress Studies (ISTSS), provided further evidence of the counseling profession's pioneering effort to establish training standards. In a keynote address at the January 2008 conference of the American Association of State Counseling Boards (AASCB) in New Orleans, Figley (2008) praised the standards and pronounced them as the cutting edge. After reviewing Draft 3 of the 2009 CACREP Standards, Figley announced that, based on the new standards, professionals graduating from a CACREP accredited program would be automatically certified by Green Cross.

After September 11th, the State of New Jersey Mental Health Services Disaster and Terrorism Branch partnered with the Mental Health Association in New Jersey and the Certification Board, Inc. to establish the DRCC credential in 2007 (New Jersey Department of Human Services [NJDHS], 2008). Training requirements for the DRCC are organized on a four-tiered curriculum with specific skills and competencies. All levels require Incident Management Command System (ICS-100), National Incident Management (NIMS-700), and courses in disaster mental health, psychological first aid, ethics in crisis response, and cultural diversity. Advanced coursework is required in grief, trauma, crisis response, and family and group work for Level I licensed mental health professionals, and for team leaders (NJ Disaster Mental Health, 2007).

As of August 2008, more than 540 DRCCs have been approved, and 980 applicants are working toward certification (NJDHS, 2008). Future plans anticipate issuing standardized identification badges to allow DRCCs to travel during states of emergency, and providing advanced continuing education to keep counselors current with outcome based practices.

Implications of the CACREP Standards for Counselor Educators

Counselor educators and professionals unfamiliar with this growing specialty will need to be well versed in the theory and practice of traumatology, crisis intervention, and emergency preparedness in order to infuse new standards into program objectives and syllabi. Six general guidelines are presented to assist counselor educators and professionals in insuring compliance with the new standards.

Know the Organizations and Government Agencies and Their Purposes

Numerous organizations and government agencies provide services, accreditation, certification, and training resources for emergency preparedness; and disaster, crisis, and trauma response. Prominent organizations are described in this section with the website address, major publications, and the mission or purpose quoted from the website.

American Red Cross (ARC). The American Red Cross provides immediate response each year to more than 70,000 disasters, primarily fires. Courses are offered in all aspects of emergency preparedness and response. "Disaster Mental Health Services staff are licensed mental health professionals trained to recognize the emotional impact of a disaster on those affected—both victims and workers" (*Disaster Services*, n.d.). They are required to complete the course Foundations of Disaster Mental Health "to provide for and respond to the psychological needs of people across the continuum of disaster preparedness, response, and recovery" (*Foundations*, 2005). Publications: Many available in several languages such as *Facing Fear: Helping Young People Deal with Terrorism and Tragic Events; Disaster Preparedness for People with Disabilities*. http://www. redcross.org/

Association of Traumatic Stress Specialists (ATSS). With members worldwide, ATSS is "dedicated to excellence in training, education and experience to ensure that victims of crime, abuse, war, terrorism and disasters receive the most compassionate and effective care as possible" (*Mission*, n.d.). ATSS provides a comprehensive international certification program; a certified sponsor consults with the applicant throughout the process. Certified Trauma Specialist requires 2,000 hours of experience specific to trauma; 240 hours of core courses and trauma-specific training; and 50 hours of the applicant's own counseling "to recognize and address those areas which may compromise or enhance the counselor's ability to provide assistance to trauma victims" (*Certifications*, n.d.). Publication: *International Journal of Emergency Mental Health*. http://www.atss.info/

Federal Emergency Management Agency (FEMA). Under Homeland Security, FEMA is the government agency responsible for managing all phases of disasters from intervention through recovery. Online and certified on-site courses in trauma and disaster are offered including Incident Command System (ICS 100) and National Incident Management System (NIMS 700), often required for participation in state or federal disaster mental health response. Many publications, such as *Are You Ready: An In-Depth Guide to Citizen Preparedness*. www.fema.gov

Green Cross Academy of Traumatology. The mission of

Green Cross is to "to accredit training sites throughout the world, to certify traumatologists throughout the world, and to deploy traumatologists when and where requested throughout the world" through the Green Cross Assistance Program. Training and certification include Core/Clinical Traumatologist, Field Traumatologist, and Certified Compassion Fatigue Specialist. No publications listed. www.greencross.org

International Society for Traumatic Stress Studies (ISTSS). ISTSS is an "international multidisciplinary, professional membership organization that promotes advancement and exchange of knowledge about severe stress and trauma. This knowledge includes understanding the scope and consequences of traumatic exposure, preventing traumatic events and ameliorating their consequences, and advocating for the field of traumatic stress" (*What Is ISTSS*, n.d.). Members are active through Special Interest Groups and the annual conference; ISTSS does not credential individuals. Publications: *The Journal of Traumatic Stress, Effective Treatments for PTSD: Practice Guidelines from ISTSS, Childhood Trauma Remembered.* www.istss.org

National Voluntary Organizations Active in Disaster (National VOAD). In this forum, national, state, and local organizations share knowledge and resources about the disaster cycle to help communities and disaster survivors. The National Response Framework designated National VOAD and the American Red Cross to represent nongovernmental organizations at FEMA's National Response Coordinating Center during disaster response. Publications: *Disaster Recovery Case Management Standards, Long-Term Recovery Manual.* http://www.nvoad.org/

New Jersey Disaster Response Crisis Counselor Certification (DRCC). The state-sponsored DRCC certification's purpose is to develop a workforce of trained disaster mental health responders "who follow best practice models of intervention" (NJDHS, 2008). Extensive coursework insures "uniformity of screening for competencies necessary for effective crisis counseling, as well as providing a standardized training curriculum for all mental health responders" (NJDHS). Publication: *New Jersey Crisis Counselor.* www.njdisasterresponsecrisiscounselor.org

Understand the Major Principles of Disaster Response, Trauma Counseling, and Crisis Intervention, and Their Differences

Considerable trauma-related research has been conducted since 9/11. New terms separate victims' and providers' experiences into more specific diagnosable and treatable conditions beyond Post-Traumatic Stress Disorder (Figley & Nash, 2007; Uhernik, 2008; Webber, Mascari, Dubi, & Gentry, 2006). New disaster and trauma concepts have emerged such as combat stress injury, psychological first aid (PFA), ICS (Incident Command System), psychological debriefing (PD), critical incident stress debriefing (CISD), critical incident stress management (CISM), vicarious traumatization, compassion fatigue, and compassion satisfaction. This list provides an initial vocabulary to begin expanding curriculum.

Insure That Students Understand Their Ethical Responsibility to Practice Disaster Response and Trauma Counseling Only to the Extent of Their Competence

At the 2007 Argosy University Symposium, *Trauma, Tragedy and Crisis*, Figley (2007) addressed the needs of massive numbers of veterans suffering from a variety of mental health disorders who will return from Iraq and Afghanistan. Figley cautioned that untrained professionals, while well meaning, could potentially do more harm than good in treating combat veterans. Students must be aware of the ethical and legal responsibilities of licensed professional counselors to practice within their scope of competence.

In addressing ethical considerations in crisis work, Sommers-Flanagan and Sommers-Flanagan (2008) assigned special emphasis to the use of evidence-based practices. Counseling students may benefit from competency-based statements in their curricula that specifically address the ethics of using evidence-based techniques and competencies.

Develop Knowledge and Practice Competencies in Disaster Response, Trauma Counseling, and Crisis Intervention If You Plan to Teach This Specialty in Classes

In addition to theoretical knowledge, counselor educators can develop skills through specialized training experiences, conferences, and additional certifications. Field experiences with multidisciplinary emergency response teams include emergency drills, disaster simulations, tabletop exercises, and volunteering for actual disaster response.

Establish Relationships With Credentialed Disaster and Trauma Specialists With Field Experience Who Are Willing to Be Guest Trainers for Specialized Course Components

Many practicing disaster specialists and traumatologists are willing to share their expertise by teaching topics calling for the demonstration and practice of techniques. Counselor educators can build a network of specialists available for class presentations.

Recognize That Disaster and Trauma Counseling Is a Growing Specialty That Needs Research and Study to Insure Outcome Based Practices

Since 9/11, effective emergency preparedness and disaster response have been the subject of investigation and study. Researchers are developing tools to collect data after disasters, assess survivors' needs at various stages of recovery, match needs to treatment strategies, and evaluate treatment effectiveness. Counselor educators can engage in research and encourage thesis and dissertation students to investigate issues related to disaster response and trauma counseling.

Continuing to Move Forward

An ancient Japanese proverb tells us that the journey of a thousand miles begins with one step. The adoption of the 2009 CACREP standards is a major step on the journey toward preparing competent counseling graduates to provide disaster and trauma mental health services. While the task of developing and validating model curricula and training practices for disaster and trauma competencies is a work in progress, the counseling profession is in the lead in setting standards.

References

Council for Accreditation of Counseling and Related Educational Programs. (2008). *2009 Standards.* Retrieved October 2, 2008, from http://www.cacrep.org/2009standards.html

Beckett, C. (2008, Spring). CACREP'S emergency preparedness efforts commended. *The CACREP Connection*, 1, 8.

Certifications. (n.d.). Association of Traumatic Stress Specialists Web Site. Retrieved October 2, 2008, from http://www.atss.info/docs/ATSS-CTS-app.pdf

Disaster services. (n.d.). American Red Cross Web Site. Retrieved October 2, 2008, from http://www.redcross.org/services/disaster/0,1082,0_319_,00.html

Figley, C. (2008, January). Paper presented at the annual meeting of the American Association of State Counseling Boards. New Orleans, LA.

Figley, C. (2007, May). Paper presented at the Argosy University Symposium on Trauma, Tragedy and Crisis. Sarasota, FL.

Figley, C., & Nash, W. (2007). Introduction: For those who bear the battle. In C. Figley & W. Nash (Eds.), *Combat stress injury* (pp. 1-8). New York: Routledge.

Foundations of disaster mental health fact sheet ARC 3077-4. (2005, December). Washington, DC: American Red Cross.

Mission. (n.d.) Association of Traumatic Stress Specialists Web. Retrieved October 2, 2008, from http://www.atss.info/

National Conference of Commissioners on Uniform State Law. (2006). *The Uniform Emergency Volunteer Health Practitioners Act.* Retrieved October 4, 2008, from http://www.uevhpa.org/DesktopDefault.aspx?tabindex=1&tabid=55

New Jersey Department of Human Services. (2008, Summer-Fall). Department news and notes: DRCC credentialing update. New *Jersey Crisis Counselor.* Retrieved October 4, 2008, from http://www.disastermentalhealthNJ.com/newsletter_summer_2 008.htm

New Jersey Disaster Mental Health. (2007). Certification levels. Retrieved October 4, 2008, from www.njdisasterresponse crisiscounselor.org

Smith, H. (2005). The American Red Cross: How to be part of the solution, rather than part of the problem. In J. Webber, D. D. Bass, & R. Yep (Eds.), *Terrorism, trauma, and tragedies: A counselor's guide for preparing and responding* (pp. 37-38). Alexandria, VA: American Counseling Association Foundation.

Sommers-Flanagan, R., & Sommers-Flanagan, J. (2008). Advanced ethical considerations in the use of evidenced-based practice and in crisis/humanitarian work. In G. R. Walz, J. C. Bleuer, & R. Yep (Eds.), *VISTAS: Compelling perspectives in counseling 2008* (pp. 259-269). Alexandria, VA: American Counseling Association.

Uhernik, J. (2008). The counselor and the disaster response team: An emerging role. In G. R. Walz, J. C. Bleuer, & R. Yep (Eds.), *VISTAS: Compelling perspectives in counseling 2008* (pp. 313-321). Alexandria, VA: American Counseling Association.

Webber, J., Mascari, J. B., Dubi, M., & Gentry, E. (2006). Moving forward: Issues in trauma response and treatment. In G. R. Walz, J. C. Bleuer, & R. Yep (Eds.), *VISTAS: Compelling perspectives in counseling 2006.*

Webber, J., & Mascari, J. B. (2005). September eleventh: Lessons learned. In J. Webber, D. D. Bass, & R. Yep (Eds.), *Terrorism, trauma, and tragedies: A counselor's guide for preparing and responding.* Alexandria, VA: American Counseling Association Foundation.

What Is ISTSS. (n.d.) International Society for Traumatic Stress Studies Web Site. Retrieved October 2, 2008, from www.istss.org/what/index.cfm

Table 1: Emergency Preparedness and Response Language included in the 2009 CACREP Standards (CACREP, 2008)

G. Common core curricular experiences and demonstrated knowledge in each of the eight common core curricular areas are required of all students in the program.

1. PROFESSIONAL ORIENTATION AND ETHICAL PRACTICE—studies that provide an understanding of all of the following aspects of professional functioning:

b. professional roles, functions, and relationships with other human service providers, including strategies for interagency/interorganization collaboration and communications;

c. counselors' roles and responsibilities as members of an interdisciplinary emergency management response team during a local, regional, or national crisis, disaster or other trauma-causing event;

d. self-care strategies appropriate to the counselor role;

3. HUMAN GROWTH AND DEVELOPMENT—studies that provide an understanding of the nature and needs of persons at all developmental levels and in multicultural contexts, including all of the following:

c. effects of crises, disasters, and other trauma-causing events on persons of all ages;

d. theories and models of individual, cultural, couple, family, and community resilience;

f. human behavior, including an understanding of developmental crises, disability, psychopathology, and situational and environmental factors that affect both normal and abnormal behavior;

5. HELPING RELATIONSHIPS—studies that provide an understanding of the counseling process in a multicultural society, including all of the following:

g. crisis intervention and suicide prevention models, including the use of psychological first aid strategies.

Addiction Counseling

Understands the impact of crises, disasters, and other trauma-causing events on persons with addictions.

Understands the operation of an emergency management system within addiction agencies and in the community.

Understands the principles of intervention for persons with addictions during times of crises, disasters, and other trauma-causing events.

Career Counseling

Understands the impact of crises, emergencies, and disasters on a person's career planning and development.

Clinical Mental Health Counseling

Understands the impact of crises, disasters, and other trauma-causing events on people.

Understands the operation of an emergency management system within clinical mental health agencies and in the community.

Understands the principles of crisis intervention for people during crises, disasters, and other trauma-causing events.

Understands appropriate use of diagnosis during a crisis, disaster, or other trauma-causing event.

Differentiates between diagnosis and developmentally appropriate reactions during crises, disasters, and other trauma-causing events.

Marriage, Couple and Family Counseling

Understands the impact of crises, disasters, and other trauma-causing events on marriages, couples, families, and households

Understands the impact of addiction, trauma, psychopharmacology, physical and mental health, wellness, and illness on marriage, couple, and family functioning

School Counseling

Understands the operation of the school emergency management plan and the roles and responsibilities of the school counselor during crises, disasters, and other trauma-causing events.

Understands the potential impact of crises, emergencies, and disasters on students, educators, and schools, and knows the skills needed for crisis intervention.

Knows school and community collaboration models for crisis/disaster preparedness and response.

Student Affairs and College Counseling

Understands the impact of crises, disasters, and other trauma-causing events on people in the postsecondary education community.

Understands the operation of the institution's emergency management plan and the roles of student affairs professionals and counselors in postsecondary education during crises, disasters, and other trauma-causing events.

Demonstrates an understanding of the psychological impact of crises, disasters, and other trauma-causing events on students, faculty, and institutions.

Understands the principles of intervention for people in the learning community during times of crises and disasters in postsecondary education.

Demonstrates skills in helping postsecondary students cope with personal and interpersonal problems, as well as skills in crisis intervention in response to personal, educational, and community crises.

Doctoral Standards

Theories pertaining to the principles and practice of counseling, career development, group work, systems, consultation, and crises, disasters, and other trauma causing events.

Understands the effectiveness of models and treatment strategies of crises, disasters, and other trauma-causing events.

Understands models, leadership roles, and strategies for responding to community, national, and international crises and disasters.

Article 13

Ethics Beyond the Obvious: Psychologically Based Ethics Instruction

Paper based on a program presented at the 2009 American Counseling Association Annual Conference and Exposition, March 19-23, Charlotte, North Carolina.

Cecile Brennan

Substantive instruction in ethics is a requirement of state licensing boards and professional organizations. This fact reflects the importance the profession gives to instructing students and refreshing practitioners about the ethical dimension of their work. The counseling profession's focus on teaching ethics is paralleled by similar requirements in other professions: law, medicine, and business come most readily to mind (Robinson, Dixon, Preece, & Moodley, 2007). The near universality of some form of ethics instruction highlights both the importance of ethics and the realization that appropriate, in this case ethical, behavior does not come naturally: our first instinct may not be the best.

In the counseling field there is a remarkable consistency in what is taught and how it is taught (Hill, 2004). Ethics texts tend to cover essentially the same material and are organized in a similar fashion, focusing on ethical codes and legal responsibilities, as well as on the importance of processing ethical questions and ethical quandaries by means of a decision-making model. Research focusing on the content of ethics courses concludes that most courses are divided into three areas: decision-making models, principle ethics, and the standards of care (Hill, 2004). Common themes were found throughout ethics curricula, indicating that an identifiable "core curriculum" exists in the discipline.

The focus of the content areas is on what students need to know to be in compliance with ethical standards and how they ought to engage in a decision-making process when confronted with an ethical dilemma. While focusing on the mechanics of ethical practice is necessary and important, it is not sufficient for a thorough training of professionals. Nor has it proven to be consistently successful in training ethical counselors (Neukrug, Milliken, & Walden, 2001; Phelan, 2007; Rapisarda & Britton, 2007; Zibert, Engels, Kern, & Durodoye, 1998). In addition, it presumes that ethical lapses result from a lack of knowledge or from a hasty and ill-conceived response to an ethical dilemma, one that was not informed by an adequate decision-making model. What this approach neglects is a sufficient focus on the whole person of the ethical decision-maker.

The Need for Psychologically Based Ethics Instruction

Ironically, in a field that acknowledges the role of unconscious motivation and defense mechanisms employed to ward off conflicts and unacceptable emotions, ethics instruction operates as if an individual who is expected to adhere to standards of ethical practice is a rational and unconflicted human being who will calmly and assuredly put aside self-interest and personal experience in order to make ethically informed decisions. In order to account for the psychological blind spots which contribute to ethical violations, we must turn to a consideration of the personal psychology of the counselor.

Not surprisingly, when attention is turned to the personal psychology of the counselor, certain themes begin to emerge. First, once we eliminate those breaches of ethics that arise out of a truly disordered personality, such as an individual with antisocial personality disorder, we are left with situations which give credence to Freud's classical image of the psyche as an iceberg. In this image, the psyche is portrayed as an iceberg with only a small tip (i.e., consciousness) appearing above the surface. This tip represents the conscious good intentions of the majority of counselors. However, an old adage says, "The road to hell is paved with good intentions." What rests below this tip are preconscious and unconscious needs, wants, and motivations. It is this churning unconscious that is not accounted for by ethics instruction that is intellectual, based essentially on the conscious mind.

The philosopher and ethicist Sissela Bok discusses the effect of the unconscious on ethics and decision making when she refers to the lies we tell to, and the secrets we keep from, ourselves (Bok, 1982). In her work she assigns many ethical lapses to the fact that self-interest overpowers moral principles and rules. It feels desirable, and so we do it. It fulfills our unconscious and is not allowed to enter fully our consciousness. So actions are taken before reflection reaches the level of our conscious mind where actions would be tempered by ethical codes. This activity of the unconscious mind has been termed 'ethical fading' by the business ethicists Tenbrunsel and Messick (2004). These authors argue that psychological processes cause ethical principles to fade, to recede into the background. Their work builds on the work of Messick and Bazerman (1996) who held that psychological tendencies create unethical behavior. The key, then, to preventing ethical lapses is to find some way of locating and then defusing these unconscious mechanisms. What is needed is a method that can be incorporated into a classroom or lecture setting which takes into account the individual psychology of a particular person, and the general tendency of people to deceive themselves in identifiable ways.

In order to create a psychologically based ethics curriculum, it is useful to review what is known about educational approaches that have a strong track record of success with adult learners. The literature on adult learners emphasizes the need for adults to be active participants in the learning process (Knowles, Holton, & Swanson, 2005; Merriam, Caffarella, & Baumgartner, 2006). Adults need to feel in charge of the process and assured as to the relevancy of what they are being asked to do. The learning process itself must be seen as relevant: clearly practical, arising out of the lived experience of the learners, constructed from lived as well as intellectual experience. What is clearly called for is a constructivist approach, one that puts the learner in the driver's seat. In this case, the goal is to have individuals examine their own psyches in order to determine where and how ethical violations are likely to occur. In essence, participants are encouraged to deconstruct, take apart, and analyze their own personal psychology.

What follows are initial attempts to create a curriculum which leads participants through the process of examining their personal psychology and then identifying areas of potential ethical lapse. As this curriculum has been piloted, it has proven most successful when conducted in a small group setting. It is possible to have a large group, but the group should ideally break down into smaller groups so the participants can benefit by sharing the process with others. This is important because often an issue that one person is not yet prepared to share, or perhaps even to consider in a conscious way, is raised by another participant.

Identifying the Counselor's Personal Psychology

The first step is to have participants identify past developmental themes. They are asked to apply two adjectives or phrases to each of three earlier periods: infancy through preschool, childhood, and adolescence. After they have completed this exercise, at least 10 to 15 minutes should be allowed for its completion, the results should be shared with the group. Responses might include: For the infancy/preschool period — loved, tantrum-filled, frustrated, nurtured, frightened; For childhood — bullied, ignored, dreamy, contented, shy; For adolescence — sad, wild child, angry, confused, in love. At this point the group processing is focused on listening to the experience of another, helping each person to connect with a present felt sense of that younger self.

The next step is for the same process to be conducted

focusing on present developmental themes. Here participants are asked to apply two adjectives/phrases to each of the following common aspects of adulthood: personal/intimate identity, professional identity, and social identity. Some responses have been: Personal/intimate identity — fragmented, confusing, contented, squared away; Professional identity — comfortable, don't think of myself that way, constraining; Social identity — fun-loving, reserved, supportive friend, a giver. Again, all responses should be processed with the group.

These two steps are meant to reacquaint the participants with the themes of their lives, both past and present. Obviously, these are not the only ways to begin to access the self-statements and subconscious motivations that drive behavior. This approach is meant to exemplify the kind of investigation which must occur, because until these currents within are identified, they can cause a good deal of damage. If an individual is unaware, or only partially aware, that she sees herself as a fun-loving, thrill-seeking, free spirit, or a neglected, shy, yet caring person, the force of these currents can result in inappropriate actions being taken in personal life, but more importantly from a counseling ethics perspective, also in professional life.

After reviewing developmental processes, uncovering and examining issues or topics that emotionally involve the counselor should occur. The first step in this process is to identify the "hot" issues, those events that arouse passion by inducing either sadness or anger—producing tears or raising blood pressure.

For instance, participants may be asked: "What events or issues arouse your passion? What kinds of people raise your blood pressure? What kinds of clients make you sad or make you feel incompetent?" By responding to these prompts, individuals are led to consider the clients and circumstances that "push their buttons." Responses to these questions have included the following: "I can't stand working with men who mistreat women." "Rich people whining annoys me." "I can't work with people who hold extreme religious views." Finally, participants might be asked: "Based on what you have discovered about yourself, what kinds of clients are most likely to raise a red flag or most likely to place you in an ethically risky situation?" Here again, the goal is to assist the participants in gaining some useful information about themselves. In this case the information gained focuses on the kinds of clients and client issues that are most emotionally inciting for the counselor.

Participants may next consider the exact opposite kind of client and circumstance: those clients and situations which leave the counselor cold and unmoved. In this case the following questions are asked: "What kinds of events or issues leave you cold, uncaring, without any passion? What kinds of clients induce boredom, lethargy, lack of concern or interest?" Responses to these questions include: "Women who complain about the men in their life without being willing to do anything about it." "People who repeat the same story each week." "Clients who do not feel alive if they are not complaining." At the end of this process, participants are asked once again to consider, based on what they have learned about themselves, what specific kind of client is most likely to leave them bored and unresponsive, disengaged from their role as helper and facilitator.

Following this brief examination of personal psychology, attention is turned to the mechanisms of ethical violation. This section of the curriculum presents to participants two of the more common psychic mechanisms which may result in a developmental theme or emotional issue being inappropriately expressed in a counseling setting outside the awareness of the clinician.

Identifying Mechanisms of Ethical Violations

The first of these mechanisms is the already familiar concept of countertransference. Countertransference refers to feelings the counselor has for the client that are triggered by the counselor's past history rather than being an accurate reading of the client (Frosh, 2003). For instance, if the counselor had a difficult adolescence during which she made decisions which negatively impacted her life, she might overly react to a teen client's normative rebellion against family rules. Countertransference is felt to be ubiquitous during the counseling session. Neither good nor bad, what is important is for the counselor to recognize when countertransference is occurring. Unfortunately, this can be a very difficult task since one of the hallmarks of countertransference is that it is, almost by definition, beneath one's awareness. If left out of awareness, countertransference can negatively affect the counseling process. The counselor is not responding to the client in front of her; rather she is responding to her own projection onto the client.

The second mechanism to be discussed here is the defense mechanism of splitting. Splitting occurs when an individual is confronted with two competing desires (Freud, 1989). The psychic conflict created results in the individual splitting off this conflict. Metaphorically speaking, it is placed into a corner of the mind: visible, but only if looked at directly. An example is the married minister who is not able to fully enjoy sexual relations with his wife because he feels it would be lustful and sinful. He splits off these desires and puts them out of his conscious awareness. Away from his wife, he meets a young attractive woman and without making a fully conscious decision, he finds himself having sexual relations with her. The split off part has emerged.

Whenever these mechanisms become active during a counseling session, it is imperative that the counselor recognizes their activation. However, this is difficult to accomplish since the aim of the psyche is to keep their emergence unconscious. Instructing counselors to continually introspect about their emotions and actions within the counseling session will assist in this process. Shea (1998) has developed a model which describes how the counselor must shift among attentional vantage points during sessions. One of these vantage points requires the counselor to shift attention inward in order to be able to identify and assess any changes in his own psychic equilibrium. While obviously not foolproof, this approach reduces the likelihood that the counselor will unknowingly fall victim to unconscious impulses.

Developing Ethical Violation Equations

The three components of a psychological and experiential approach to ethics instruction are now in place. First, developmental themes are identified; second, issues that either arouse passion or produce withdrawal and lack of interest are described; finally, instruction in countertransference and splitting is provided in order to enable the clinician to identify these both if they emerge in the counseling setting. Putting these three components together is the next important step in the development of a curriculum which aims to develop individuals who are operating from a realization that ethical action must finally arrive from the core of an ethical individual. A metaphor to help visualize how these components work together is the ethical violation equation:

Developmental Theme + Hot Issue + Countertransference = Possible Violation
Developmental Theme + Cold Issue + Countertransference = Possible Violation
Developmental Theme + Hot Issue + Splitting = Possible Violation
Developmental Theme + Cold Issue + Splitting = Possible Violation

At this point, counselors who worked through the curriculum have had an opportunity to evaluate themselves in terms of each component of the violation equation. Putting all of the components together allows them, in advance of a specific incident, to foresee their potential vulnerability in a counseling setting. For instance, if I know that one of my developmental themes is a feeling of having been uncared for and abandoned emotionally as a child, which has lead me to develop an identity as a caring person who would never abandon anyone, and I know that children who are feeling abandoned or neglected arouse a great deal of sympathy from me, when a child climbs onto my lap and says "I wish you were my Mommy. You would take care of me," I am in great danger of responding to the youngster's transference with a countertransference action of my own: buying the child a toy she has wanted, taking the child to McDonald's, allowing the child to spend the weekend with my family. On the other hand, if one of my developmental issues is the feeling of rejection I experienced by the "in crowd" during my school years, and my present social identity is as a reserved, loner-type person who has difficulty in social gatherings, when I have as a client an attractive, socially gregarious man who is clearly enjoying my company, there is a high potential for splitting. My needy high school self emerges and I find myself in Starbucks having coffee and sharing personal stories with my client.

Conclusion

These are only two of myriads of possible examples. What is important is for participants to work through each component by plugging in issues specific to themselves. While not absolutely guaranteeing that a violation will not occur, the old adage "Forewarned is forearmed" is apt here. Counselors who have formally worked through their own issues and potential areas of lapse, are in a much stronger position to avoid committing ethical violations. When this experimental, psychologically based approach is combined with the knowledge based approach of the traditional ethics course, a truly comprehensive curriculum has been developed, one that will hopefully reduce the number of ethical violations.

References

Bok, S. (1982). *Secrets: On the ethics of concealment and revelation.* New York: Pantheon Books.

Freud, S. (1989). *An outline of psychoanalysis.* New York: W. W. Norton. (Original work published in 1940).

Frosh, S. (2003). *Key concepts in psychoanalysis.* New York: New York University Press.

Hill, A. L. (2004). Ethics education: Recommendations for an evolving discipline. *Counseling and Values, 48*(3), 183-203.

Knowles, M., Holton, E. F., & Swanson, R. A. (2005). *The adult learner, sixth edition: The definitive classic in adult education and human resource development.* Burlington, MA: Butterworth-Heinemann.

Merriam, S. B., Caffarella, R. S., & Baumgartner, L. M. (2006). *Learning in adulthood: A comprehensive guide.* San Francisco: Jossey-Bass.

Messick, D. M., & Bazerman, M. H. (1996). Ethical leadership and the psychology of decision making. *Sloan Management Review, 37*(2), 9-22.

Neukrug, E., Milliken, T., & Walden, S. (2001). Ethical complaints made against credentialed counselors: An updated survey of state licensing boards. *Counselor Education & Supervision, 41,* 57-70.

Phelan, J. E. (2007). Membership expulsions for ethical violations from major counseling, psychology, and social work organizations in the United States: A 10-year analysis. *Psychological Reports, 101,* 145-152.

Rapisarda, C. A., & Britton, P. J. (2007). Sanctioned supervision: Voices from the experts. *Journal of Mental Health Counseling, 29*(1), 81-92.

Robinson, S., Dixon, R., Preece, C., & Moodley, K. (2007). *Engineering, business & professional ethics.* Burlington, MA: Butterworth-Heinemann.

Shea, S. C. (1998). *Psychiatric interviewing and the art of understanding,* (2nd ed.) Philadelphia: W.B. Saunders Co.

Tenbrunsel, A. E., & Messick, D. M. (2004). Ethical fading: The role of self-deception in unethical behavior. *Social Justice Research, 17*(2), 223-236.

Zibert, J., Engels, D. W., Kern, C. W., & Durodoye, B. A. (1998). Ethical knowledge of counselors. *Counseling & Values, 43*(1), 34-49.

Article 14

A Framework for Remediation Plans for Counseling Trainees

Paper based on a program presented at the 2009 American Counseling Association Annual Conference and Exposition, March 19-23, Charlotte, North Carolina.

Roxane L. Dufrene and Kathryn L. Henderson

Remediation of counselors-in-training presents a critical issue to supervisors working with trainees during master's-level and post-master's clinical work. Counselor trainees with inabilities in professional issues, clinical skills, and/or documentation skills create situations that should be addressed by supervisors and counselor educators. Identifying and implementing useful supervision strategies with trainees struggling with these inabilities can be challenging. The purpose of this article is to provide a procedural framework to develop and implement an Individual Remediation Plan (IRP) which includes a process for monitoring, intervening, and remediating trainees' development.

Guidance from the literature related to remediation is not robust; there is a lack of empirical research, especially in the counseling field. Multiple models for gatekeeping and dismissing students from counselor education programs can be found (Baldo, Softas-Nall, & Shaw, 1997; Bemak, Epp, & Keys, 1999; Frame & Stevens-Smith, 1995; Kerl, Garcia, McCullough, & Maxwell, 2002; Lamb, Cochran, & Jackson, 1991; Lamb et al., 1987; Lumadue &

Duffey, 1999; McAdams & Foster, 2007; McAdams, Foster, & Ward, 2007; Wilkerson, 2006). However, the focus is on dismissing students from counseling programs using the gatekeeping process, rather than remediation. These models include steps where remediation should occur but do not provide details on how exactly the remediation process unfolds. Based on the literature, it is apparent that remediation is considered a part of the overall gatekeeping process.

From a legal perspective, procedures and documentation help address due process doctrine that must be met (Baldo et al., 1997; Frame & Stevens-Smith, 1995; Jackson-Cherry, 2006; Kerl et al., 2002; Lamb et al., 1987; Lumadue & Duffey, 1999; McAdams & Foster, 2007; McAdams et al., 2007) in addition to addressing the directive to document in the *ACA Code of Ethics* (2005). Supervisors have an ethical mandate to evaluate and obtain remedial assistance for trainees as noted in section F.5 of the *ACA Code of Ethics*. But few guidelines are provided on how to implement this mandate. The Code stipulates that supervisors should remediate trainees who are presenting with inabilities (F.5.b). However, the *Code* does not specify the details or extent of remediation procedures necessary to work with trainees' inabilities. Similarly, the *Ethical Guidelines for Counseling Supervisors* (1993) from the Association for Counselor Education and Supervision (ACES) requires that supervisors provide remedial assistance. In addition, the *Guidelines* maintain that supervisors should screen trainees from programs or employment and should refuse to endorse such trainees, as does the *ACA Code* (F.5.b, F.5.d). Also mirroring the *ACA Code*, ACES instructs supervisors to provide trainees with opportunities that will resolve any problems, allowing trainees to continue with their professional development.

Considering the recent landmark court case experienced by faculty and students at The College of William and Mary (*Plaintiff v. Rector and Board of Visitors of The College of William and Mary*, 2005), counselor education programs are imbued with specific responsibilities and obligations that must be considered when working with student challenges during clinical work (McAdams et al., 2007). The *ACA Code* separately addresses counselor educators' and supervisors' roles in evaluation and remediation of students in Section F.9. The *Code* requires that counselor educators and supervisors "are aware of and address the inability of some students to achieve counseling competencies that might impede performance" (p. 16). This section also contains the directive to help trainees secure remedial assistance and to document any decisions to dismiss or refer trainees for assistance. Ethical guidelines suggest that remediation should be attempted *before* dismissal from training programs or post-master's supervision experiences.

Occurrences of trainees requiring remediation often happen during clinical experiences in graduate programs (Kerl et al., 2002; Lamb et al., 1987; McAdams & Foster, 2007; McAdams et al., 2007). The need for remediation can also occur during post-graduate clinical work. Supervision during trainees' clinical work is an integral part of the remediation process. Bernard and Goodyear (2004) broadly defined supervision as an experienced professional mentoring and providing direction, training, feedback, and evaluation to novice supervisees. With this perspective, supervision is designed to improve trainees' clinical skills, monitor client welfare, and provide opportunities for professional development. However, supervision and trainees' professional development are not always straightforward processes. Therefore, it may be difficult for supervisors to address trainees' inabilities that can occur during clinical work. When trainees' inabilities are recognized during clinical work, remediation is important. An explicit definition of remediation could not be found in the literature or the ethical codes. Considering this, remediation is defined as a documented, procedural process that addresses observed inabilities in trainees' performance with the intent to provide trainees with specific means to remedy their inabilities.

Individual Remediation Plan (IRP)

A particular challenge of trainees needing remediation is the subjective nature of the circumstances that call for remedial assistance. As supervisors, we must evaluate and remediate when necessary. The last phrase, 'when necessary,' is what can prove decisive to the decision to initiate remediation. When does remediation become necessary? What does remediation entail and encompass? During our experience implementing remediation plans with master's-level trainees, a procedure was developed to initiate remediation and implement carefully documented plans in a systematic fashion to address trainees' needs. For an individual trainee, remediation is initiated after customary educational techniques and supervision procedures have not worked. The process begins with a discussion between the trainee's supervisors and/or clinical faculty coordinator. A decision is reached collaboratively among the faculty and supervisors of the trainee to formally begin the documentation process and pursue remediation. During a master's level trainee's development, other counselor educators are consulted throughout the remediation process. The supervisors included in this stage of the process might include the faculty coordinator in the role of the university supervisor, another faculty member, possibly a doctoral student assigned as a university supervisor, in addition to the on-site supervisor.

As a result of the collaborative decision of the faculty and supervisors, an IRP would be developed and written by the university supervisor. A review of the trainee's inabilities determines what is included in the IRP. A meeting is arranged with the faculty clinical coordinator, supervisors, and the trainee. At the meeting, the purpose of remediation would be discussed and the plan would be reviewed with the opportunity for collaboration with the trainee. Collaboration with the trainee is important in encouraging the trainee to be invested in the process and facilitate the remediation in a positive direction. Collaboration also incorporates procedural due process doctrine, allowing the trainee the opportunity to respond to the decision to remediate (Baldo et al., 1997; Frame & Stevens-Smith, 1995; Jackson-Cherry, 2006; Kerl et al., 2002; Lumadue & Duffey, 1999; Lamb et al., 1987; McAdams & Foster, 2007; McAdams et al., 2007). After the meeting, the IRP would be revised as necessary. The first meeting with the trainee, faculty coordinator, and/or supervisors also incorporates informed consent through the use of the IRP as a step-by-step objective guide to both the supervisors and the trainee of what will be expected of the trainee. Confidentiality is not implied between the trainee and supervisors at any point in the remediation process, highlighting the importance of communication between all supervisors and faculty involved. The IRP serves as basic documentation of the remediation process; the final document is not static, rather it is used on a consistent basis for the entirety of the remediation process. The following sections provide a description of the IRP.

IRP Framework

The framework of an IRP includes three elements: a) professionalism of the trainee, b) counseling skills of the trainee, and c) documentation of clinical work by the trainee (see Table 1). We have found that each of these three elements have consistently arisen within various remediation plans we have developed. These elements can encompass an array of challenges and inabilities that a trainee experiences. As found by Li, Trusty, Lampe, and Lin (2008), and in accordance with our experience, the most consistent indicators of trainee inabilities are interpersonal skills, receiving feedback, and inappropriate boundaries. The first element of the IRP, professionalism, encompasses these indicators.

The IRP is developed for an individual trainee, customized to the trainee's inabilities and contextual situation. A review of the trainee's inabilities determines which of the three elements will be included in the IRP; not all elements are always included in the IRP, only the ones that are necessitated by the trainee's inabilities. Specific inabilities within each of the three elements should be addressed in the IRP as well as areas that necessitate flexibility depending on the trainee's progress. Under each of the three elements chosen for inclusion in the IRP, specific directives addressing each inability of the trainee are listed with a Likert scale. The trainee is assessed on each item in the plan according to the scale.

Element 1 - Professionalism of the Trainee

The first element of the IRP, professionalism, is tailored to the trainee's observed challenges related to interpersonal demeanor, procedural compliance, and developing a professional counselor identity. The interpersonal demeanor of the trainee involves the trainee's responses to communication between the trainee and one or more supervisors, other professionals, and/or clients. Specific items included in the IRP addressing this part of the first element might include the trainee: displaying receptivity and implementing feedback; demonstrating appropriate boundaries with clients, peers, supervisors, and faculty; examining personal issues; and being willing to attend personal counseling. Procedural compliance might include items such as: demonstrates knowledge of rules and regulations for the clinical setting, abides by the rules and regulations of both the university as well as the site, and attends supervision meetings on time. Professional counselor identity might include items that address the trainee's understanding of the ethical code and awareness of the different roles within the chosen specialty/emphasis area, for example, mental health, college, or school counseling.

Element 2 - Technical Counseling Skills of the Trainee

The second element of the IRP is aimed at the trainee's inabilities related to technical counseling skill acquisition and demonstration of those skills. Items included in this element of the IRP may address the trainee's inabilities in basic counseling skills. One option in addressing this element is to use an attachment to the IRP of an existing rating scale used to assess basic counseling skills as additional documentation. This additional documentation would be used weekly by the university supervisor when reviewing tapes of client sessions. Other items under this element might include using advanced counseling skills, such as a theoretical orientation, case conceptualization, and awareness of transference and countertransference.

Element 3 - Documentation by the Trainee

The third element, documentation by the trainee, assesses a trainee's inabilities in completing and submitting formal documents required for clinical work. Logs for direct and indirect hours, evaluations of supervisors by the trainee, and/or evaluations of the trainee by supervisors are examples of specific items that assess the trainee's ability to complete and submit formal paperwork required as part of his or her clinical experience. Meeting due dates or accurately completing these documents can also be items included in this element.

Table 1: Item Examples Within Each Element of the Individual Remediation Plan (IRP)

Professionalism	Counseling Skills	Documentation
Interpersonal Demeanor 1. Receptive to feedback from supervisor. 2. Open to self-examination. 3. Exhibits appropriate boundaries with clients, peers, colleagues, supervisors, and faculty. *Procedural Compliance* 1. Knowledgeable of site and university rules and procedures. 2. Attends supervision on time weekly. 3. Participates in required staffing and meetings. *Professional Identity* 1. Identifies appropriate counselor roles in specialty area. 2. Demonstrates ethical behavior.	1. Demonstrates basic counseling skills. 2. Consults with other professionals and coordinates services related to clients. 3. Demonstrates advanced counseling skills. 4. Demonstrates his or her theoretical orientation. 5. Able to conceptualize client cases.	1. Completes and submits application for clinical work. 2. Completes and submits logs on time. 3. Completes and submits evaluations on time. 4. Completes and submits audio/video tapes of counseling sessions. 5. Takes notes during supervision. 6. Writes client case notes.

An IRP is approached from a positive stance by developing constructive and specific choices for the trainee to succeed. The plan is effective for a specific time frame delineated in the introduction of the document, for example, from the time the plan is initiated until the end of the current semester. At the end of the articulated time frame, the outcome of the remediation process is assessed, with the specification that obtaining the total hours required by a counseling program or a licensure board is a minimum, and the plan subsequently may require additional clinical hours. The IRP serves as a concrete, tangible, and facilitative roadmap for a process that oftentimes seems vague and ambiguous. Having defined requirements can help ease trainee anxiety and counteract catastrophizing. The language used in the IRP is from the perspective of what the trainee will do, not what the trainee will not do. The IRP is completed weekly by the university supervisor and signed by all parties in attendance at each supervision session. Formal notes of each supervision session are also maintained by the university supervisor. A standardized supervision form (Vernon, 2007) is used each supervision session to document what topics were discussed and what each party is expected to accomplish for the next supervision session. The notes can be collaboratively written at the end of the session with the trainee. Audio or videotaping supervision sessions are also used as a form of documentation and a processing tool for both the supervisor and trainee.

Summary

Counselor educators and supervisors have an important responsibility to remediate both the professionalism and skill development of trainees experiencing challenges. Remediation is a fairly new process in supervision, with few documented resources for procedures and techniques that address both the supervisors' and the trainee's concerns. We have presented an IRP framework which allows supervisors and the trainee to collaborate during the remediation process. This framework provides objective guidelines to address trainee inabilities through specifically articulated expectations. Using the IRP as a three-element framework, faculty and supervisors can assist trainees to resolve inabilities in professionalism, counseling skills, and documentation. The IRP is proactive in nature, encouraging collaboration between faculty, supervisors, and the trainee. The IRP also provides an important record articulating clear requirements and responsibilities of a trainee which is documented with signatures of the faculty, supervisors, and the trainee. Thus, an IRP can provide a systematic way of incorporating documentation practices for faculty and/or supervisors, whether a trainee is a master's level or post-master's level. We have found the IRP to be beneficial during a trainee's clinical work; the IRP could also be used early in a trainee's didactic experiences as well as providing additional procedural documentation to a counselor education program's dismissal policy.

References

American Counseling Association. (2005). *ACA code of ethics.* Alexandria, VA: Author.

Association for Counselor Education and Supervision. (1993). Ethical guidelines for counseling supervisors. Retrieved September 14, 2008, from http://www.acesonline.net/documents.asp

Baldo, T. D., Softas-Nall, B. C., & Shaw, S. F. (1997). Student review and retention in counselor education: An alternative to Frame and Stevens-Smith. *Counselor Education & Supervision, 36,* 245-253.

Bemak, F., Epp, L., R., & Keys, S. G. (1999). Impaired graduate students: A process model of graduate program monitoring and intervention. *International Journal for the Advancement of Counselling, 21*(1), 19-30.

Bernard, J. M., & Goodyear, R. K. (2004). *Fundamentals of clinical supervision* (3rd ed.). Boston: Pearson.

Frame, M. W., & Stevens-Smith, P. (1995). Out of harm's way: Enhancing monitoring and dismissal processes in counselor education programs. *Counselor Education & Supervision, 35,* 118-129.

Jackson-Cherry, L. R. (2006). Protecting our gatekeepers? Hard lessons learned from the dismissal of a graduate counseling student. In G. R. Walz, J. C. Bleuer, & R. K. Yep (Eds.), *Vistas: Compelling perspectives on counseling 2006* (pp. 157-160). Alexandria, VA: American Counseling Association.

Kerl, S. B., Garcia, J. L., McCullough, C. S., & Maxwell, M. E. (2002). Systematic evaluation of professional performance: Legally supported procedure and process. *Counselor Education & Supervision, 41,* 321-332.

Lamb, D. H., Presser, N. R., Pfost, K. S., Baum, M. C., Jackson, V. R., & Jarvis, P. A. (1987). Confronting professional impairment during the internship: Identification, due process, and remediation. *Professional Psychology: Research and Practice, 18,* 597-603.

Lamb, D. H., Cochran, D. J., & Jackson, V. R. (1991). Training and organizational issues associated with identifying and responding to intern impairment. *Professional Psychology: Research and Practice, 22,* 291-296.

Li, C., Trusty, J., Lampe, R., & Lin, Y. (2008, September 2). Remediation and termination of impaired students in CACREP-accredited counseling programs. Retrieved October 2, 2008, from the Connexions Web site: http://cnx.org/content/m 17376/1.2/

Lumadue, C. A., & Duffey, T. H. (1999). The role of graduate programs as gatekeepers: A model for evaluating student counselor competence. *Counselor Education & Supervision, 39,* 101-109.

McAdams, C. R., III, & Foster, V. A. (2007). A guide to just and fair remediation of counseling students with professional performance deficiencies. *Counselor Education & Supervision, 47,* 2-13.

McAdams, C. R., III, Foster, V. A., & Ward, T. J. (2007). Remediation and dismissal policies in counselor education: Lessons learned from a challenge in federal court. *Counselor Education & Supervision, 46*, 212-229.

Vernon, D. (2007, October). *Training school counselors to be supervisors.* Paper presented at the meeting of the Association for Counselor Educators and Supervisors, Columbus, OH.

Wilkerson, K. (2006). Impaired students: Applying the therapeutic process model to graduate training programs. *Counselor Education & Supervision, 45*, 207-217.

Article 15

Managing Diversity in the Counselor Education Classroom

Paper based on a program presented at the 2007 Association for Counselor Education and Supervision Conference, October 11-14, Columbus, Ohio.

Devika Dibya Choudhuri

Introduction

Classrooms are complex sites of intersecting diversity that can often leave counselor educators feeling overwhelmed with the differing calls on their attention. Thinking of classroom diversity as focusing on what counseling students bring in terms of their race and ethnicity, gender, socioeconomic status, age, religious and spiritual affiliation, disability status, or sexual orientation, is overwhelming enough. However, to grasp the systemic interplays of diversity, we also need to factor in other dimensions. Of these, particularly salient aspects are the diversity of identities and experience we bring as counselor educators into the classroom, the culture of the counseling field, the topic areas of the course content, as well as the interactions that students have with their peers. Another issue that all educators become increasingly concerned with is handling and managing conflicts in the classroom that may well arise from the intersections of any or all of these areas. An asset that counselor educators bring to this endeavor are their skills in managing and working with groups.

On the other hand, our preoccupation with coverage of content as well as discomfort with conflict can lead us to overlook or refuse to attend to these issues.

Culture

Conceptualizing culture subjectively might be useful in terms of pedagogical process. According to Triandis (1972), a system of cultural knowledge can be defined as a given group's distinctive way of perceiving and understanding its social environment. People who share related basic life experiences thus develop similar and integrated cognitive and emotional structures. Within such a definition, cultural conflict occurs due to the internal and interactional tensions that arise when systems of cultural knowledge confront each other, particularly when the interpretation of cultural patterns is not available to others. In other words, cultural conflict arises when we are making the correspondence error (Gilbert & Malone, 1995) of overemphasizing personality-based explanations for people's behaviors and under-emphasizing cultural and situational explanations. For instance, when an African American man argues with a European American woman, the woman may feel intimidated (due to her sociocultural gender and racial socialization), perceive the interaction as a fight, and respond by trying to move the argument to safer impersonal grounds (gender socialization towards relationship and away from conflict). Meanwhile, the man is experiencing the woman as typically uncaring (based on his racial experience) about the issues and distancing, so he increases the force and passion of his arguments (cultural communication expression). The dance of misunderstanding goes on as each seeks to communicate with the other in culturally comfortable ways, but end up miscommunicating in profound ways that may well lead to each making personality-based explanations of the other such as "He's out-of-control and scary" or "She's shallow and there's no point trying to talk to her."

Different cultural systems take different positions on a series of value continuums, first identified in a major work by Kluckhohn and Strodtbeck (1961). Table 1 depicts these four major dimensions and the continuums along which cultures line up. These dimensions become particularly important in terms of relationship and communication in the classroom, as culture is present in everyday activities and pedagogical decisions.

Table 1: Value Continuums

Authority Dimension	
	Egalitarian . . . . .Heirarchical
	Informal . . . . .Formal
Relational Dimension	
	Independence . . . . .Interdependence
	Competition .Cooperation
	Individualism . . . . .Collectivism
	Low Context . . . . .High Context
Activity Dimension	
	Doing . . . . .Being
Temporal Dimension	
	Limited . . . . .Abundant
	Evolving . . . . .Historical

Expectations from students and the instructor about how authority is manifested in the classroom and how hierarchical or formal it is need to be negotiated. How do you introduce yourself to your students? Is it alright for different students to address you differently? Are learning and related activities presented competitively or cooperatively? For instance, grading on a curve is a competitive function while group projects require cooperation. Are individuals required to be independent to demonstrate competence or interdependent? In other words, do we value those who do their work together, or do we suspect collusion? Is classroom interaction and participation in learning activities (high context) valued as much as written work (low context)? Are assignments time-limited or evolving in process and content? As the counselor educator, your decision making on these educational questions and concerns interacts with the cultural norms of the field, which privileges certain values on the continuum over others.

Counseling Culture

One aspect of being the educator in this context is that one's membership in the profession means that one speaks from insider status. In other words, as counselor educators, we are immersed in the culture of our field, and are actively transmitting it. This means that our teaching can never be innocent. It is important to move away from this naiveté and critically reflect on the paradigmatic assumptions that we bring to the endeavor of counselor education. Just as we encourage students to identify their personal theories of human nature and change as preparatory to understanding theories of personality and counseling, we must interrogate our own theories of pedagogy and understand the positions from which we teach.

Cultural capital, first developed as a concept by Bourdieu (1986), refers to the knowledge and experiences that a person brings that can allow them greater ease and therefore adeptness in a certain setting leading to greater success. In the classroom context, students who have cultural capital are often similar to the YAVIS client popularized by Schofield (1964), in being young, attractive, verbal, intelligent, and successful, as well as often being European American, middle or upper middle class in origin, able-bodied, heterosexual, and Christian. They demonstrate the embodied form of cultural capital by their status social identities, as well as the institutionalized form of capital of academic knowledge through being adept at the forms of writing papers, carrying out research, and communicating effectively.

Sue and Sue (2003) point out some of the major characteristics of counseling that therapists expect from their clients such as openness or psychological mindedness, and verbal, behavioral, and emotional expressiveness and articulateness. What we want from our clients, we are delighted to get from our students. The counseling student, who self-reflects openly, applying theories and ideas to themselves, sharing their understanding and insights in class and journals, tells us in subtext that we are successful educators. However, we need to notice that diverse students may have different preparation, assumptions, understandings, and expectations of the process. Even though most counselor educators may have left behind the banking model of education (Freire, 1996), many of our students may still believe in it. Much education in the public school system is through such methods and students who did not have well trained teachers in well funded classrooms in school, may well have experienced only the methods that relied on students maintaining a receptive and submissive demeanor. The challenge and open articulation of difficulties that we welcome might be extremely difficult for a student who has been taught that such confrontation is threatening and that disclosing incomprehension is divulging lack of intelligence.

An example of such a pedagogical practice that may hold different meanings for those with different cultural capital is the use of circles, where everyone sits facing each other. While the counselor educator and some students may indeed find this format egalitarian and welcoming, for students who come from marginalized groups, the circle may be painful rather than reassuring. It can be experienced as forced self-disclosure rather than an opportunity to be heard. The implicit pressure to participate can be mortifying rather than liberating if the requisite trust and safety in the instructor has not been built (Brookfield, 1995). This example is not used to imply that circles should not be used, but rather that their use should be understood as being complicated and being perceived differently by different students.

Pedagogical Preparation

As the counselor educator, it is helpful to consciously reflect on and attend to issues in planning and delivery. Start with selecting textbooks that attend to and raise these issues, or if you do not have choices about it, incorporate diversity in discussing topic areas, where you can highlight presence or absence. Ponder the philosophical choices between a stand alone chapter on multicultural issues versus addressing multicultural issues through a section in every chapter. One choice highlights its importance for students but presents it as a separate issue, while in the other choice, its integration confirms its constant presence but students may not consider it important and merely a pro forma nod to correctness. You can supplement textbooks with additional readings that directly address, critique, or challenge the topic areas from multiple vantage points (Derek Bok Center, 2006).

Similar to the explicitness we value in gaining informed consent in counseling, address issues of respect and acknowledgement of diversity in your syllabus, and early on in the course lay down ground rules for difficult class discussions. Be careful here as you acknowledge that some rules may be for your benefit as the instructor and not necessarily culturally congruent for all. For instance, asking that people speak one at a time and focus on the topic rather than the person, are helpful guidelines in defusing tension, but also leave students who feel passionate and personal about topic areas at a loss for ways to engage.

Depending on the course content, one may have less or more time to focus on process. For instance, a counseling skills course would need to be able to actively use the skills being acquired to be able to engage in difficult conversations. An informational piece on cultural styles of communication could then be tied in to diversity discussions through interpretation and self-reflection communication styles (Choudhuri, 2007). In covering theories of counseling, the discussions may focus more externally on the applicability of various theories and interventions with different populations, and less on the experience of the students themselves. As the counselor educator, you need to constantly make moment-by-moment decisions on whether to stay with your teaching plan and topic coverage or discard it in favor of greater exploration of the specific discussion occurring in the classroom. It is helpful to reflect on your decision making and to examine whether factors such as rigid expectation of content coverage, discomfort with spontaneous discussions, unease with emotion-laden process, or specific ideas on what it is important for counselors-in-training to know are overly influencing your choices.

You can generate constructive dialogue through setting clear goals and expectations, as well as by modeling through your own participation and process. If your discussion topics focus on issues of diversity, the message that you welcome dialogue on such issues will be clearer. Use and model the skills of accurate listening and reflection when discussions arise, to encourage the conversation. Be genuine and authentic in your responses, but notice that you need to summarize the student voices first, paying careful attention to include multiple perspectives. Creating a space for constructive conversations is based on structuring safety but also on encouraging risk taking. Inevitably, when one encourages students to take risks, the instructor will not be in complete control. In essence, the first risk is yours as the educator, to invite in uncertainty and unknown process. The more you are willing to take such risks and can model coping and surviving ambiguity, the greater the chances that students will follow through. On the other hand, understand that risk taking is differential across diverse students. What is easy for one student to disclose may be immensely difficult for another. It is important to value and legitimize the risk-taking rather than the content of the disclosure.

Many people, focused on the conflict potential of cross-cultural conversations, end up avoiding the discussion altogether. You can increase the safety of such conversations by attending to timing and establishing context. For instance, using humor about a cross-cultural issue may be well-received later in a class when students and instructor have greater comfort and trust with each other, while early on, students often observe the instructor for cues on how such issues will be processed. If you misstep, and note offense taken, strive to publicly acknowledge the gaffe and, if time permits, to process all reactions. Your humility will model for your students that it is okay to be wrong.

If conflict does occur, instructors can use various de-escalation strategies such as gentle reminders of ground rules (own your opinions, speak for yourself rather than as a representative of a whole group), the technique of wait and respond (note the issue and state that you will look into it and then respond), inviting additional research, acknowledgement, linking, as well as process interpretations and deflections to the larger issue. Some specific techniques include time outs, where the conversation is interrupted, the conflict explicitly acknowledged, everyone invited to take a break to regain their emotional balance, and then the conversation restarted with instructions on how to proceed. In tying the process to counseling content, it is helpful to remind students about the interconnections between identity and experience and perception. In one minute journals, everyone is invited to journal for a couple of minutes. Here, everyone in the class gets an opportunity to voice their opinion in relatively safe writing, which they can then share from in smaller groups. The journaling can be free form, or structured, asking students to focus specifically on describing their affect, cognitions, and sensations, and then describe their judgments and assumptions.

Not all issues need to be processed in the classroom. Some merely need to be interrupted and stopped. For instance, intentionally hateful and discriminatory speech or behavior needs to be addressed immediately, and the person responsible informed that it is unacceptable. One can process the issue with the student one-on-one in privacy after the class or during an appointment. At the same time, it is important to protect the lone outlier, whether attacked or attacker, from being mobbed by other students. Every student will watch the instructor's reaction and response with concerns about their own safety.

Instructors can use diverse case studies and examples in multiple ways and in degrees of complexity. These can range from developing case studies that focus in on diverse cultures to simply using a variety of names in random examples. Thus in a developmental course, instead of Bobby or Tim beginning to understand Kant's categorical imperative on the playground, it could be Juanita and Wei-Fan. The essential concern doesn't change but it acknowledges that there are a wider set of actors in the world. Be careful however that such usage is not biased (Amoja Three Rivers, 1990). In other words, don't always use examples such as Benita Washington when discussing poverty and Ling Lu in examples of submissiveness (Bailey & Toro-Morn, 2001). Case studies that use diverse examples should be culturally applicable and coherent, meaning that the cultures referenced are those that students may well interact with, and that the behavior described is neither stereotypical nor outlandish.

Additionally, instructors can vary teaching strategies to accommodate different learning styles as well as different aspects of comfort. These include having random small group discussions, finding ways to solicit participation from every member of the class, get written anonymous feedback on specific questions about classroom environment, using guest speakers to bring in diverse voices and experiences into the classroom context, assigning group as well as individual projects, so that every student regardless of their cultural system has some area where they can participate and learn comfortably.

In the counselor education process, it is vital for students beginning to perceive themselves as the tool of their chosen profession to develop a counseling identity and stance that is flexible and authentic. The being of the counselor then becomes more central to the endeavor than performance as a counselor. To engage in a counseling relationship with others, students must become adept in extending themselves while understanding implicit boundaries, both their own as well as those of others. An essential component of such understanding is becoming as aware of the failure of good intentions to encompass all differences as it is the success of being able to build a relationship from the starting point of difference rather than commonality. All that happens in counselor education classrooms, conflict and harmony, discussion and silence, understanding and disagreement, becomes grist for the mill when related to the point of constantly circling from process to content and connecting it to counseling.

After all the discussions of difference, exhortations of caution, and advice on sensitivity contained in this paper, it is important to remember that the desired goal in counselor education classrooms is not the erasure or silencing of cultures leading to some pasteurized and processed environment that will be "conflict-free", but a fruitful and engaged conversation that may at times be passionate, argumentative, or even hostile, but that expands the knowledge and understanding of all parties present and is ultimately much more stimulating.

References

Amoja Three Rivers. (1990). *Cultural etiquette: A guide for the well-intentioned.* Indian Valley, VA: Market Wimmin Press.

Bailey, A., & Toro-Morn, M. (2001). *Classroom etiquette: A guide for the well-intentioned instructor.* Retrieved September 16, 2008, from http://www.teachtech.ilstu.edu/additional/tips/Class Etiquette.php

Bourdieu, P. (1986). Forms of capital. In J. G. Richardson (Ed.), *Handbook for theory and research for the sociology of education* (pp.46-58). Westport, CT: Greenwood Press.

Brookfield, S. (1995). *Becoming a critically reflective teacher.* San Francisco: Jossey-Bass.

Choudhuri, D. D. (2007). *Fostering parallels of relationship and meaning making towards transformative learning. Proceedings of the 7th International Transformative Learning Conference.* Albuquerque, NM: University of New Mexico Press.

Derek Bok Center for Teaching and Learning. (2006). *Tips for teachers: Teaching in racially diverse classrooms.* Retrieved September 12, 2007, from http://isites.harvard.edu/fs/html/icb.topic58474/TF Trace.html

Freire, P. (1996). *Pedagogy of the oppressed* (M. B. Ramos, Trans.). New York: Penguin Books.

Gilbert, D. T., & Malone, P. S. (1995). The correspondence bias. *Psychological Bulletin, 117*(1), 21-38.

Kluckhohn, F. R., & Strodtbeck, F. L. (1961). *Variations in value orientations.* Evanston, IL: Row, Patterson & Company.

Schofield, W. (1964). *Psychotherapy: The purchase of friendship.* Englewood Cliffs, NJ: Prentice-Hall.

Sue, D. W., & Sue, D. (2003). *Counseling the culturally diverse* (4th ed.). New York: John Wiley & Sons.

Triandis, H. C. (1972). *The analysis of subjective culture.* New York: Wiley-Interscience.

Article 16

The Role of an Interpreter: Unique Dynamics in Teaching and Supervision

Paper based on a program presented at the 2007 Association for Counselor Education and Supervision Conference, October 11-14, Columbus, Ohio.

Brooks Bastian Hanks, Nicole R. Hill,
and Carrie Alexander-Albritton

The Western Interstate Commission for Higher Education (WICHE) Mental Health Report (2007) estimates that there are over 5 million people who are Deaf in the United States who are in need of mental health treatment every year. Of these 5 million individuals, only about 2% receive appropriate treatment for their mental illness.

In the past, seeking mental health assistance has been too expensive for Deaf individuals, as they have been responsible for the cost of the mental health services as well as the services of the interpreter (Roe & Roe, 1991). As legislation continues to focus on individuals who are Deaf, more Deaf individuals are becoming aware of their right to equal access and accommodations to mental health counseling. As more Deaf individuals seek out professional mental health services, the need for individuals fluent in sign language and skilled in providing mental health services increases.

To respond to the increased demand for services, counselors and supervisors need to be highly skilled in providing services to the Deaf community. The increased demand for client-based services has been coupled with more Deaf individuals pursuing and excelling in higher education programs (Pollard, 1996). Many counselors, supervisors, and counselor educators are unaware and lacking in knowledge of Deaf culture, thus leading to possible misunderstandings and frustrations (Peters, 2007). One way of alleviating some of the misunderstandings and lack of cultural awareness is to hire a qualified interpreter to assist in the counseling and supervision process. This article will address counselor educators' and supervisors' legislative and ethical obligations, how to find a qualified interpreter, creating an accommodating classroom environment, and creating an accommodating supervision environment.

Legislation and Ethics

Legislation has influenced accessibility to services in the realm of education and supervision (U.S. Department of Justice, 2005). Because many universities receive federal funds, Section 504 directly impacts teaching and supervision practices as they relate to individuals with disabilities, including Deafness. Further, the Americans with Disabilities Act (ADA) mandate extends to non-federally funded agencies to provide "reasonable accommodations" and to provide accommodations beyond just access. Therefore, it is the legal obligation of the university to provide reasonable accommodations and equal access to information for those individuals who are Deaf, whether that is by means of an interpreter or some other accommodation such as note takers (Pollard, 1996; U.S. Department of Justice, 2005).

As supervisors recognize the legal requirements to providing services, ethical obligations arise and become another motivating factor to educate oneself about this unique supervisees' culture. According to the Association for Counselor Education and Supervision's (ACES) ethical guidelines for counseling supervisors (1993), supervisors are to promote the ethical and legal protection of clients' and supervisees' rights. In the matter of a Deaf counselor-in-training, Deaf individuals have the right to equal access and reasonable accommodations (U.S. Department of Justice, 2005). To be in accordance with these legal and ethical guidelines, it is the responsibility of the supervisor to protect the supervisee's rights by referring to another qualified professional who is fluent in sign language, acquire an interpreter to facilitate communication during the supervision process, or provide whatever accommodations appropriate for that Deaf supervisee that will assist in the communication process.

Counselor educators and supervisors are also obligated to adhere to the American Counseling Association's (ACA) *Code of Ethics* (2005). Section F of the ACA Code of Ethics attends to the supervision, training, and teaching facets. Within this section, there are various references to multicultural and diversity competence. In regards to student diversity, counselor educators are to strive to attain a diverse body of students.

This specific section attends to the goal of recruiting and retaining a diverse student body with diverse types of abilities to engage in training to become counselors, including Deaf counselors-in-training. Section F.11.c. goes on to outline the role of counseling supervisors as evaluators of services and the need for supervisors to be aware of potential limitations of the supervisee. Communication is a key component to evaluating the skills and potential limitations of supervisees. This again emphasizes the importance of using a sign language interpreter in order for the supervisor to ethically fulfill his/her supervisory role with a Deaf supervisee. After becoming aware that accommodations are needed, the question of what types of services need to be rendered comes to mind.

Deciding to Use an Interpreter

When making the decision of what types of services need to be rendered to provide an accommodating environment, asking the Deaf individual is typically the best starting point. In the case of all students with a disability, accommodations are typically requested through the educational institution's ADA offices or Disability

Resource Centers (DRC). Without a formal request and resulting accommodation letter, counselor educators are not legally mandated to provide services. The accommodation letter will state which accommodations are most appropriate and needed for the student with the disability.

For supervisors of Deaf supervisees, this accommodation letter may not be provided, especially if the supervision is occurring post degree. With or without the presence of an accommodation letter, it is recommended that the educator or supervisor ask the student or supervisee what the educator or supervisor may do to help facilitate communication. For the purpose of this article, the assumption will be that the Deaf individual prefers to use a sign language interpreter for communication purposes.

Often times, the best practice for working with a Deaf individual in an educational setting is by way of an interpreter (Humphrey & Alcorn, 1995). Interpreters relay the information simultaneously to allow for a more natural communication interaction to occur. Interpreters incorporate the speaker's tone and nonverbal communication into their interpretations to allow the Deaf consumer access to the message in its entirety (Humphrey & Alcorn, 1995; Roe & Roe, 1991).

Frequently, individuals with the ability to hear assume that all Deaf individuals can lip read and understand what is being said (Roe & Roe, 1991). Jeffers and Barley (1975) assert that speech reading is insufficient as it is estimated that only 40% of English speech sounds are visible on the mouth while the other 60% of English speech sounds are not visible on the mouth (as cited in Roe & Roe, 1991). If the supervisee is working hard to understand what is being said instead of the meaning, the supervisee is not receiving the full benefits of supervision.

Writing notes back and forth has also been posed as a method of communication when working with a Deaf student (Haley & Dowd, 1988). This method of communication lacks in effectiveness and efficiency. As many have found through e-mails and text messaging, written communication can often be misunderstood due to the lack of intonation, facial cues, body language, and nonverbal communication that add to the meaning. Because nonverbal communication is not transferred to our written words, misunderstandings often result. Consequently, ADA law also requires an interpreter to be employed if the communication is more extensive than just a few questions (U.S. Department of Justice, 2005).

Another benefit for supervisors engaging sign language interpreters is that the interpreters may also work as cultural mediators and may assist the supervisor in understanding some of the more subtle nuances that may emerge in the supervision process (Humphrey & Alcorn, 1995). The benefits and rationale for hiring an interpreter to assist in the supervision process are multifaceted, and they consist of time efficiency, respecting the native language of the supervisee, simultaneous communication, and cultural mediation.

Finding an Interpreter

When initiating services, finding a qualified interpreter may feel like a daunting task when one does not know where to begin the search. When working in an educational setting, the responsibility of finding a qualified interpreter falls on the shoulders of the ADA or DRC offices. Sometimes simply asking the Deaf individual if he/she has preferences or suggestions for interpreters will result in finding a qualified interpreter as well.

The benefit to asking the Deaf individual is that you convey a respect for his/her preferences. Caution should be used when going by word of mouth as there are no quality assurances with this method. The Deaf individual may prefer working with a specific interpreter, not because of their skills, but due to their open friendship. In the case of such a relationship, confidentiality may be readily breached. Word of mouth can be a great way to get in contact with someone who has a feel for the interpreting community in your area and that initial contact may be able to refer you on to other, more qualified interpreters.

For the purpose of supervision, it is important to find an

interpreter who is highly qualified. Just as we license individuals to counsel, there are governing agencies who certify individuals to advertise as qualified interpreters. The Registry of Interpreters for the Deaf (RID) and the National Association of the Deaf (NAD) have joined forces to create a national certification process to help ensure quality services (Registry of Interpreters for the Deaf [RID], 2005).

There are a variety of certification levels and some specialty certifications (RID, 2005). To date, there is not a national specialty certification for mental health interpreting. That is why it is vital to interview the potential interpreter regarding past experiences to ascertain if the interpreter is qualified for the job. By hiring a nationally certified interpreter, there is a minimum level of expertise one can expect (Seleskovitch, 1998). There is also the reassurance of having a reporting board to which a disciplinary counsel can be held if a certified interpreter's behaviors are considered unethical (RID, 2005).

The Internet can be a great resource when searching for a qualified interpreter. RID has established a web site to assist in finding nationally certified interpreters in a variety of geographic locations (www.rid.org). Included on the web site are various certifications the interpreter holds, contact information, and other relevant information. When hiring an interpreter for a mental health supervision assignment, it is important to ask what specialties the interpreter may possess as well as previous experiences of assignments similar to that of the current supervision assignment.

Another Internet resource is to simply use an Internet search engine and type the term "sign language interpreter agencies." If you are in a metropolitan area, there are typically a variety of agencies available. Rural areas may have an agency that serves your area as well. If you are not able to locate a qualified interpreter through this avenue, contacting your local university's ADA or DRC office is another potential starting point for your search.

Classroom Recommendations

Within an academic setting, an interpreter will be assigned to your class. Assuming that the Deaf student has provided his/her accommodation letter to you stating the need for a sign language interpreter, the first order of business to address is that of logistics. As a part of the certification process, interpreters are tested on how well one understands interpreting logistics such as how to position oneself for optimal communication and minimal distraction (Frishberg, 1990).

Early discussion of how to optimally use and place the interpreter will help to reduce later struggles of the counselor trainee not being able to see the interpreter and clearly receive the message being interpreted. Interpreters will typically place themselves behind and to the side of the speaking individual in order to ensure that the Deaf consumer can see both the speaker and the interpreter (Humphrey & Alcorn, 1995). In regards of interpreting logistics, the interpreter is typically the expert and will take the lead in placing himself/herself in the most appropriate situation. If at any time there is discomfort with where the interpreter is positioned, a private and open discussion with the interpreter and Deaf student is appropriate.

When utilizing the services of a sign language interpreter, there are some general guidelines to consider that may assist the interpreter in delivering the optimal interpretation of the counselor educator's lecture. Providing the interpreter with the lecture material greatly assists the interpreter when he/she is preparing for class. If the counselor educator is uncomfortable with the idea of the student potentially receiving the lecture notes through the interpreter, a simple discussion between the counselor educator and interpreter will often remedy this concern. The counselor educator may simply ask the interpreter to give his/her copy of the lecture notes back at the end of lecture. By receiving the copy of the lecture notes, the interpreter has access to specialized jargon the counselor educator may be using or can gain a clearer understanding of the counselor educator's focus for that lecture thus allowing the interpreter to provide a clearer interpretation for the Deaf student. This may be especially helpful if the interpreter is unfamiliar with this area of specialty.

Another way the counselor educator may assist in the interpreting process is by classroom management. By articulating the importance of speaking one at a time and raising one's hand to add to classroom discussion, the educator allows the interpreter time to identify for the Deaf individual who is speaking as well as allowing the student to have access to all comments. If more than one person is speaking, the interpreter must make a decision as to which comment to interpret first and the interpreter may have to drop the second comment due to the lack of time or inability of the interpreter to retain the other comment while interpreting the first comment.

Attending to the interpreter's mental and physical challenge of providing interpreting services in higher education is another recommendation for educators. If the class meeting time exceeds that of an hour, a ten minute break would be appropriate to allow the interpreter time to rest his/her hands and recharge mentally. A final recommendation for the counselor educator is to be aware of the content of the lecture and how often professional jargon is used. The counselor educator may want to discuss with the interpreter before class what specialized terms will be used to assist the interpreter in formulating an accurate interpretation. By attending to the needs of the interpreter, the counselor educator is working to ensure the Deaf student's equal access to the material.

Supervision Recommendations

Within supervision, an important step after acquiring an interpreter is to delineate roles (Bruin & Brugmans, 2006; Frishberg, 1990; Roe & Roe, 1991). This allows time for the supervisor and interpreter to create a working alliance that will enhance the supervisee's experience of supervision. After clearly discussing and agreeing on established roles, the supervision process is ready to begin.

Many of the classroom recommendations made previously

can also be useful within the context of supervision. The logistics of the supervision/interpreting environment is another point of discussion recommended to occur within the first supervision session. By discussing the logistics openly, both the interpreter and Deaf supervisee receive the message that the supervisor respects each of them and is willing to do his/her part to ensure a successful and beneficial supervision experience.

The supervisor may also want to allot time for a pre and post session review for the interpreter and supervisor. Bruin and Brugmans (2006) state that by conducting a pre and post session, those involved in the interpreting situation are able to communicate openly about the goals for the next session and how well the communication and interventions worked. Roe and Roe (1991) caution that a pre and post session may be detrimental to the relationship if the Deaf individual is not included in these sessions. When the Deaf individual is not included in these sessions, concerns about what the interpreter and supervisor are discussing may become a relationship and trust issue.

Conclusion

For counselor educators, supervisors, and practitioners, there are legislative and ethical requirements to consider when providing services for Deaf individuals. It is important to know how to access various accommodations for Deaf students and supervisees. By becoming more aware of logistical concerns as they pertain to Deafness, the educator/supervisor demonstrates a dedication to multicultural sensitivity and advocates for the Deaf student/supervisee by working to meet his/her needs. This article provided a discussion of the legal and ethical requirements as they pertain to serving Deaf students and supervisees. The process of locating and hiring a qualified interpreter as well as recommendations for educators and supervisors was provided.

References

American Counseling Association. (2005). *ACA code of ethics.* Retrieved February 21, 2007, from http://www.counseling.org/ Resources/CodeOfEthics/TP/Home/CT2.aspx

Association for Counselor Educators and Supervisors. (1993). *ACES code of ethics.* Retrieved February 21, 2007, from http://www.acesonline.com

Bruin, E., & Brugmans, P. (2006). The psychotherapist and the sign language interpreter. *Journal of Deaf Studies and Deaf Education, 11*, 360-368.

Frishberg, N. (1990). *Interpreting: An introduction* (2nd ed.). Silver Spring, MD: RID Publications.

Haley, T. J., & Dowd, E. T. (1988). Responses of Deaf adolescents to differences in counselor method of communication and disability status. *Journal of Counseling Psychology, 35*, 258-262.

Humphrey, J. H., & Alcorn, B. J. (1995). *So you want to be an interpreter: An introduction to sign language interpreting* (2nd ed.). Amarillo, TX: H&H Publishers.

Peters, S. (2007). Cultural awareness: Enhancing counselor understanding, sensitivity, and effectiveness with clients who are Deaf. *Journal of Multicultural Counseling and Development, 35*, 182-190.

Pollard, R. Q. (1996). Professional psychology and Deaf people: The emergence of a discipline. *American Psychologist, 51*, 389-396.

Registry of Interpreters for the Deaf. (2005, July). Retrieved February 21, 2007, from http://rid.org

Roe, D. L., & Roe C. E. (1991). The third party: Using interpreters for the Deaf in counseling situations. *Journal of Mental Health Counseling, 13*, 91-105.

Seleskovitch, D. (1998). *Interpreting for international conferences* (3rd ed.). Washington, DC: Pen and Booth.

U.S. Department of Justice. (2005). *A guide to disability rights laws.* Retrieved February 21, 2007, from http://www.ada.gov/cguide. htm#anchor65610

Western Interstate Commission for Higher Education (WICHE). (2007). InFocus: Deaf and hard of hearing populations in the west. *WICHE Mental Health Report, 1*, 1-6.

Article 17

Service Learning in Counselor Education Programs: Combating Truancy

Paper based on a program presented at the 2009 American Counseling Association Annual Conference and Exposition, March 19-23, Charlotte, North Carolina.

Gerra Perkins and Kristy Brumfield

Introduction

Service learning is a very important initiative in today's higher education arena (Baggerly, 2006; Burnett, Long, & Horne, 2005; Goodman & West-Olatunji, 2007; Kaye, 2004; Murray, Lampinen, & Kelley-Soderholm, 2006). Service learning is not volunteerism, community service, or community-based learning (Burnett et al., 2005; Kaye, 2004). Service learning, according to the Institute for Global Education and Service Learning (2008), is "made up of activities that connect serving the community with the learning already being done in a school, program or organization. Service learning provides a hands-on application of knowledge and skills to real life community needs." Service learning combines service objectives with learning objectives with the intent that the activities change both the recipient and the service provider. This is accomplished by combining service tasks with structured opportunities that link the task to self-reflection, self-discovery, and the acquisition and comprehension of values, skills, and knowledge content. Service learning is unique in that it benefits the students, university, and community (Burnett, Hamel, & Long, 2004; Burnett et al., 2005). Students involved in a service learning curriculum have opportunities to develop collaborative and empowering relationships with the community (Goodman & West-Olatunji, 2007; Kaye, 2004). Students reap the benefits of their involvement in service learning in areas such as curriculum enrichment, professional skill development, and personal growth (Burnett et al., 2005; Murray et al., 2006). Universities benefit from service learning because of the community outreach, improvement of college curriculum, the response to community and employer needs, and because it supports the college philosophy and mission. Lastly, communities benefit from service learning through improved service-delivery and by developing future citizenship support.

Service learning provides valuable learning experiences for students in counseling programs via engaged activities (Goodman & West-Olatunji, 2007) while increasing essential multicultural competence (Burnett et al., 2004) and aiding in the development of clinical skills (Arman & Scherer, 2002; Murray et al., 2006). Counseling trainees' service learning typically occurs during practicum and internship classes (Baggerly, 2006; Burnett et al., 2005). These field experiences are frequently more aptly defined as community-based learning and students would benefit from service learning throughout the curriculum (Burnett et al., 2004). In addition to increasing candidates' readiness for clinical interaction with clients (Burnett et al., 2005), utilizing these and other experiential methods enhances the learning process and offers practical application of classroom knowledge (Murray et al., 2006). Baggerly (2006) distinguishes between service learning assignments and similar tasks. Counseling students providing a guidance curriculum at a school servicing low-income students and reflecting on the experience could be called service learning, while simply interviewing students from such a school would not since such an assignment does not clearly benefit the students being interviewed. Both experiences could augment multicultural competence and other learning objectives, but the second lacks the reciprocity present in service learning (Kaye, 2004).

There are many ways service learning can be integrated into counseling programs. Service learning can be included in specific courses or may be implemented via supplemental activities throughout the curriculum (Burnett et al., 2005). Effective service learning requires preparation by involved counselor educators. Objectives and assignments for the course must be tied to service learning goals, and assessment should be ongoing. The counselor educator, as a facilitator of the learning experience, should provide opportunities for student reflection (Murray et al., 2006), connect theory and practice, and apply knowledge gained from the experiences. Counselor educators can maintain awareness of the growing field of service learning through the numerous continuing education opportunities currently available or by reviewing relevant literature. Finally, counselor educators must also maintain connections with service-learning coordinators at their respective institutions in order to maximize resources and utilization of service learning.

The process of implementing a service learning component or activity involves four separate and distinct stages: (1) Preparation, (2) Action, (3) Reflection, and (4) Demonstration. These stages will be further discussed through the lens of an extensive service learning project, *Combating Truancy*.

Preparation

The preparation stage lays the foundation for the stages that follow and includes steps such as identifying a real community and identifying potential partnerships. "Investigation, discussion, and analysis lead to plans for action" (Kaye, 2004, p. 10). Several key "events" occurred in this phase for the Combating Truancy project. First, the grant stipulated that the proposed project must in some way assist in hurricane recovery. For this reason, the project director, along with students, identified the New Orleans Recovery School District (RSD) as a potential partner. The issue of truancy was identified by the Counseling Coordinator of the RSD as one of the biggest problems with the schools, thus, the focus of the project became apparent. The next step was to examine ways the project could be incorporated into existing coursework, meeting both the needs of the District and the educational requirements of the counseling curriculum and instructors. In keeping with the roles and duties of a professional school counselor, the following assignments were proposed in order to provide a prevention and remediation component for the District: (1) parent workshops, (2) parent brochures, (3) guidance curriculum units, and (4) small group plans. Also, the rotation of the curriculum was examined to identify the courses in which the project could be incorporated.

The project was designed to follow the rotation of the counseling curriculum and involve students throughout the program. It was integrated into four courses: (1) School Counseling, (2) Multicultural Counseling, (3) Group Counseling in Schools, and (4) School Counseling Practicum.

With the need, the project, and coursework identified, it then became necessary to begin to prepare students to work on the identified learning products. For example, students researched the impact of Hurricanes Katrina and Rita on the educational system. In researching the current state of affairs, students read several articles and visited web sites related to recovery efforts in the various parishes in Louisiana. Additionally, students were encouraged to post research articles and web sites that they had found. Students then responded to several discussion board questions such as, *"What was the impact of Hurricanes Katrina and Rita on the educational system?"* Using this information and other information researched over the next three weeks, students then moved into the action phase.

Action

Students worked in groups to create the learning products for each of the identified courses.

Parent Information Brochure. Students enrolled in the Multicultural Counseling Course on-line participated in the service-learning project. Each group created an educational brochure for the

RSD that could either be distributed to parents or to members of the community. The brochure was to be a unique product that addressed the issue of truancy in the RSD. Each group chose its target population: (1) parents or (2) community members. If a group chose to target parents, they then chose a grade level on which to focus (i.e., elementary, middle, or high school). Three to five references/resources were cited in the brochures. If they selected community members, the students were then responsible for identifying agencies and/or specific groups of people who may benefit from the brochure.

Parent Workshop. Students enrolled in the beginning School Counseling on-line course created parent workshops that school counselors in the RSD could present to parents in their district. The students worked in groups of four and communicated with one another about the project via BlackBoard, e-mail, telephone, and fax.

The Parent Workshop the students designed were 30 minute presentations that school counselors could give to parents of a specific grade level (i.e., elementary, middle, or high school). The Workshop included: (1) an Introduction, (2) the Plan, and (3) Counselor "Talking Tips."

The Introduction consisted of the following elements: (1) an introduction stating what the workshop was about, (2) background information establishing the importance of the workshop, (3) a statement of purpose describing how the workshop was to be used, (4) the overall goals of the workshop, and (5) a comprehensive listing of materials needed for the workshop. The Plan was the actual workshop, organized through a PowerPoint presentation for parents. The workshop included learning objectives, an introduction to the workshop, activities that actively involved parents, and a conclusion detailing how the school counselor could assess parent learning and suggested ways to follow up with parents. The Counselor "Talking Tips" was a script that corresponded to each of the PowerPoint slides.

A total of seven workshops were created by students in the course (i.e., three elementary, two middle school, and two high school).

Truancy Curriculum Unit. Students enrolled in the beginning School Counseling on-line course also created truancy curriculum units that school counselors in the RSD could present in large-group classroom guidance lessons. The students worked in groups of three to five and again communicated with one another about the project via BlackBoard, e-mail, telephone, and fax.

Each curriculum unit included the following components: (1) an introduction stating what the unit was about, (2) background information establishing the importance of the unit, (3) a statement of purpose describing how the unit was to be used, (4) the overall goals of the unit, (5) a comprehensive listing of materials needed for the entire unit, and (6) a listing of additional references and resources. Each unit consisted of three to five guidance lessons on truancy that built on one another.

Each of the guidance lessons within the unit were required to state the American School Counseling Association (ASCA) standard(s) and competencies and contained learning objectives for the cognitive, affective, and psychomotor domains. Each lesson consisted of an introduction, developmental activities that actively involved classroom students and targeted multiple intelligences, a conclusion that required students to think about how the lesson applied to life outside of the classroom, and formal and informal assessments. Students were responsible for creating all materials that were mentioned in their lesson plans (e.g., samples of work, questionnaires, assessments and answers, etc.).

A total of seven curriculum units were created by students in the course (i.e., three elementary, two middle school, and two high school).

Small Group Plans. Two sets of five session integrated small group counseling plans were developed by students. One set was designed to be used with upper elementary students and the other set was designed for use with junior or senior high school students. Specific goals for each group session were given in the group plan, as well as all the activities that would take place in the group in that session. The sessions developed for the elementary students covered topics such as: reasons for truant behavior; consequences for missing school; getting ready for school in the morning; prioritizing reasons why "I" miss school; and overcoming the biggest personal obstacle to school attendance. The junior/senior high school group plans focused their sessions on: self-esteem; peer pressure (as a reason to miss school); relate attendance in school to graduation and occupations students are interested in; how truancy affects academic success – start visualizing their personal goals; and the role of family support in school attendance.

Reflection

After the learning products were created in each of the courses, students were asked to complete learning reflections. Reflection is an important component in the service learning process, because it "integrates learning and experience with personal growth and awareness" (Kaye, 2004, p. 11).

Students' learning reflections varied greatly. Although all reflections focused on what was learned in the process, several reflected how students were beginning to make connections to the real world and the profession. One student stated:

> On a personal note, the project was meaningful to me as a counselor. Although my school does not have a truancy problem as does New Orleans, it still has students and parents that don't feel school should be a top priority. Teachers of truant students spend countless hours trying to catch the student up to where the others are in class. Often the student becomes so far behind that it is impossible to complete all the assignments missed.

Another student found that not only did she learn information that was helpful in her day-to-day life, she was beginning to see some development in the remediation of the problem:

Working on the truancy project was eye opening. Not so much in the fact of how prevalent truancy has become, nor in how earning a high school diploma or GED impacts future earning potential. These things I have seen first hand. I was surprised at how many different factors contribute to truancy. For example, poor school climate, negative peer influences, child abuse and neglect, lack of family support for educational goals, poor academic performance, lack of self-esteem, and teen pregnancy are just a few.

Several themes were apparent in the students' reflections on their work: connection to future work, purpose, and empowerment. One theme in the reflections was the connection the projects had to the students' future work as professional school counselors. One of the students wrote that *having the opportunity to create these products allows me to feel comfortable, so when I do produce such products as a school counselor I will be competent in this area.* The project reflected a part of the real demands and expectations of what school counselors are expected to do, and the students appreciated the chance to have this learning experience. One of the students stated, *This was an exceptional learning tool and an experience towards becoming a well-equipped professional school counselor.*

Most students spoke of feeling purposeful and empowered in the products they created. In the words of a student, *the projects were more purposeful knowing that they were to be created for other school counselors in the New Orleans Recovery School District to use.* Students felt rewarded and empowered in their work. *Creating products that will actually be used by school counselors made me feel empowered and effective.* The students found and made meaning of the work they did. *Overall, I found myself not only learning about creating the lesson unit, but realizing that the purpose of the assignment is to make a difference in the life of a child.*

So, in participating in this service learning project, students were able to learn invaluable information not only about what was going on in New Orleans but also how to begin to address the issues they will face as future counselors.

Demonstration

Demonstration is the final stage of the service learning process and shows what the students have accomplished through their work. Kaye (2004) recommends that students show their expertise through public presentations (e.g., displays, performances, presentations) that demonstrate each of the previous stages (i.e., preparation, action, and reflection). In this particular project a group of students presented their learning products and met with the Counseling Coordinator of the Recovery District. The following are some excerpts from two of the reflections.

> As I was putting the materials together, I began to understand the amount of work that has gone into the service learning project. It wasn't until the group actually met with the Counseling Coordinator, however, that I really "got it." The work that students had done was truly going to make a difference. Everything that was done was so much more than a grade, it was material that would be passed on to counselors—counselors who are already struggling with truancy in their schools and who don't have the time to create the things that the students did.

> The Coordinator's gratitude and the look on her face as she flipped through the binder was the best "grade" anyone could ever get. I believe that this project is what service learning is all about—providing a service to a community in your own backyard and not only learning about the subject matter but learning what it feels like to know that you and your school community have potentially impacted lives.

The student reflections revealed that the gratitude of the Counseling Coordinator made a strong impact on them. Every one of the reflections mentioned this aspect and reflected on how her gratitude made them even more grateful that they had been a part of the project.

Conclusion

Service learning continues to grow in popularity and is an active and rewarding form of learning. Service learning has many positive effects and benefits for students, universities, and the communities they serve.

School counselors must be prepared to effectively deal with the difficult and unending problems they will face in today's schools. It is for these reasons that this model of service learning which integrates real community needs with coursework has been presented. This project focused on the issue of truancy. However the model is easily adaptable to other school issues, such as violence, test anxiety, and organizational skills. Despite its popularity and usage, much about service learning remains unknown. It is hoped this project can add to the growing body of knowledge and ideas about this movement within education, especially within counselor education programs.

References

Arman, J. F., & Scherer, D. (2002). Service learning in school counselor preparation: A qualitative analysis. *Journal of Humanistic Counseling, Education and Development, 41,* 69-86.

Baggerly, J. (2006). Service learning with children affected by poverty: Facilitating multicultural competence in counseling education students. *Journal of Multicultural Counseling and Development, 34,* 244-255.

Burnett, J. A., Hamel, D., & Long, L. L. (2004). Service learning in graduate counselor education: Developing multicultural counseling competency. *Journal of Multicultural Counseling and Development, 32*, 180-191.

Burnett, J. A., Long, L. L., & Horne, H. L. (2005). Service learning for counselors: Integrating education, training, and the community. *Journal of Humanistic counseling, Education, and Development, 44*, 158-167.

Goodman, R. D., & West-Olatunji, C. A. (2007). *Social justice and advocacy training for counselors: Using outreach to achieve praxis.* Retrieved October 10, 2008, from http://eric.ed.gov/ ERICDocs/data/ericdocs2sql/content_storage_01/0000019b/80 /2a/74/3c.pdf

Institute for Global Education & Service Learning. (2008). *Service learning professional development manual.* Levittown, PA: www.igesl.org.

Kaye, C. B. (2004). *The complete guide to service learning: Proven, practical ways to engage students in civic responsibility, academic curriculum, and social action.* Minneapolis, MN: Free Spirit.

Murray, C. E., Lampinen, A., & Kelley-Soderholm, E. L. (2006). Teaching family systems theory through service-learning. *Counselor Education and Supervision, 46*, 44-58.

Section IV

Effective Counseling Interventions

Article 18

Animal-Assisted Play Therapy: Canines As Co-Therapists

Paper based on a program presented at the 2009 American Counseling Association Annual Conference and Exposition, March 19-23, Charlotte, North Carolina.

Mary J. Thompson

Introduction

Research has shown that animals are significant in the overall development of children. Through animals, children learn about social interactions, boundaries, emotional reciprocity, and responsibility. Studies have shown that children who own pets have more empathy for others, higher self-esteem, and better social skills than other children (Jalongo, Astorino, & Bomboy, 2004). The child-animal bond is unlike any other relationship a child may have.

In reviewing the issue of children with emotional and behavioral problems, it has been determined that they also have a positive response to animals. In a study of neglected or abused children in foster care, it was found that the mere presence of a dog elicited laughter, lively conversation, and excitement among children who were generally withdrawn, hostile, and resistant (Gonski, 1985). Findings such as these form the foundation for incorporating animals, specifically canines, into play therapy.

Defining Play Therapy

To fully understand the importance of combining play therapy and animal-assisted therapy (AAT), it is important to first define both interventions more specifically. Virginia Axline introduced play therapy into the mainstream of psychotherapy during the 1940s. Since then, play therapy has been recognized as an effective approach for the psychotherapeutic treatment of children. Play therapy creates a safe atmosphere where children can express themselves, try new things, learn more about how the world works, learn about social rules and restrictions, and work through their problems. Play therapy is based on the fact that play is a child's natural medium of self expression and provides an effective way for the child to communicate with others (Axline, 1974). Play therapy allows trained play therapists to assess and understand children's play, use it in assisting the child in coping with difficult emotions, and find solutions to their problems (Kottman, 2001). For children, toys are their words and play is their conversation (Landreth, 2002). According to Piaget (1962), the symbolic function of play is critical because play represents children's attempts to organize their experiences; it may be one of the few times when they feel in control of their lives. Play gives concrete form and expression to the child's inner world. Of interest to the clinician is that emotionally significant experiences are given meaningful expression through play.

The two basic forms of the therapeutic play relationship are directed and nondirected. In the nondirected approach, children select their play materials from a group of items, set their own rules, and use the toys as they choose within safety and time limits (White & Allers, 1994). In directed approaches (often called structured play therapy), the therapist designs the activity, selects the play medium, and creates the rules. Therapists use structured play to focus attention, stimulate further activity, give approval, gain information, interpret, or set limits.

Defining Animal-Assisted Therapy

Animal-assisted therapy (AAT), the other intervention under investigation, involves the introduction of an animal into an individual's immediate surroundings with therapeutic intent. Current research suggests that it offers numerous benefits beyond those available through traditional therapies. AAT is not a style of therapy like cognitive-behavioral or rational-emotive therapy, as a therapist can incorporate the animal into whatever professional style of therapy the therapist already enacts.

The presence of the animal can facilitate a trust-building bond between the therapist and client. The animal relieves some tension and anxiety of therapy and interacting with the animal can be entertaining and fun. Through this interaction animals can help clients focus on difficult issues by aiding in the client's ability to get in touch with the associated feelings. Sharing these feelings with or about the animal can initiate the emotional sharing process with the therapist. For the client, the animal is seen as a friend and ally, thus presenting a safe atmosphere for sharing. The animal offers nurturance through a presentation of unconditional acceptance.

Chandler (2005) identified some of the major AAT therapy techniques. These can include (1) allowing clients to pet, touch, and hug an animal when the need or desire may arise, (2) using the animal to enhance the quality of the therapeutic relationship, (3) using the animal as a "co-therapist" to reflect, paraphrase, clarify, and summarize the behaviors and expressions of the therapy dog, the client, and the interactions between them, and (4) using the animals to provide access to emotions.

Integrating Play Therapy and Animal-Assisted Therapy With Canines

Canine-assisted play therapy (CAPT) is defined as the incorporation of a dog into a play therapy session to increase the amount of opportunities for tracking behavior and reflecting feelings.

The canine serves the role of co-therapist in the session by engaging the therapeutic powers of play. Therapists and canines engage with children through both directed and nondirected play therapy, with the goals of improving children's emotional health.

VanFleet (2008) highlights several key features of CAPT:

> (a) the therapist and animal are trained to do this type of work; (b) the interventions are systematic in nature, with forethought and evaluation of their usefulness in terms of therapeutic goals; (c) the primary modality of the interventions is play, including cross-species play; (d) the interventions are beneficial to the child developmentally and/or clinically; (e) the animal employed should benefit from the work as well; and (f) there is a focus on the various relationships of all those involved with each other—child, therapist, and animal. (p. 20)

Determining how to structure a CAPT session depends on a variety of factors. First, goals related to the use of the therapy dog should be set for each child. Second, how often the therapy dog is used needs to be determined. The presence of a therapy dog may not be necessary for every play session. There may be some children who respond well to the use of the dog in all sessions and other children who prefer the dog be used only on occasion. In nondirected play therapy it may be beneficial to include the dog in all sessions, as in this type of therapy it is important to maintain some consistency, predictability, and continuity in the play session. However, in directed therapy the dog may only be used in a few sessions in response to the child's treatment goals. Third, the dog's energy and stress levels must be considered as they may limit his use in sessions. If it is obvious the dog is disengaged, tired, or stressed, his use may no longer be therapeutic. Often it is important to allow the dog to leave the session when signs of stress become apparent. This can also be an important modeling opportunity for the child.

Nondirective Canine-Assisted Play Therapy

In nondirective play therapy the use of therapy dogs in play sessions tends to be fairly systematic in nature. The therapy dog attends every session throughout the day as all clients are screened for the appropriateness of the use of a therapy dog through a screening form. The therapy dog serves the role of "co-therapist" in sessions. The therapist introduces the therapy dog to the child at the initial play session. The therapist reads the child a book about play therapy and immediately engages the therapy dog by pretending as though the dog is also involved in the storytelling (in much the same way as using a puppet to talk to the child). The dog shows the child to the playroom after the purpose of play sessions is explained and after the child is introduced to the therapy dog. The child is given a tour of the playroom and is also shown an area known as the "Cozy Corner." This is an area dedicated to child-animal interaction. Here there are the dog's toys, a large pillow for the two of them to sit on, stories for the child to read to the dog, and a brush the child can use on the dog. A child is introduced to this in the same way he is introduced to all of the other toys in the fully stocked playroom.

While in the playroom, the therapy dog is an active part of the session. The therapist often makes reflective tracking statements to the therapy dog instead of directly to the child. This incorporation of another living being into the session allows the child to better accept the tracking of feelings and behaviors. For example, the therapist may say to the therapy dog, "Johnny is having a hard time deciding what he wants to play with next" or "Johnny seems frustrated with that thing today." Often the children respond to tracking from the dog more than from the therapist. We also use the value of fantasy in the pet play sessions. The therapist may pretend the therapy dog has a question to ask of the child or has a feeling or emotion to something the child may have said or done in the session. For example, the therapist may say to the child, "Razz wonders what happened to that doll" or "Razz is worried about how difficult school has been for you this week." This seems to be less threatening to the child and often allows for a response from the child.

Goals of Canine-Assisted Play Therapy

The following are some of the many goals of CAPT: (1) help establish rapport quickly, capitalizing on the natural interest that children have in animals; (2) improve social skills and confidence levels of children while also decreasing their aggressive and maladaptive behaviors; (3) enhance a child's self esteem and promote the expression of feelings; (4) foster healthy attachment relationships, not only with the dog, but also with people; (5) develop children's empathy, sharing, and care-giving capabilities; (6) help children share traumatic experiences in an emotionally safe way; (7) provide an opportunity to help children overcome a fear of dogs; (8) offer nurturance through a presentation of unconditional acceptance and interaction; and (9) improve cooperation and problem solving ability (VanFleet & Thompson, 2008).

Animals in psychotherapy can be used in a variety of ways to assist in meeting these goals, but few systematic approaches have been identified. Some clinicians use them merely as a presence to reduce anxiety where others use them more actively in role plays, metaphoric storytelling, or as co-therapists. Others see them as opportunities for children to exhibit control such as through obedience training or as diagnostic tools to solicit a child's social skills, aggressive tendencies, ability to emotionally self regulate, or ability to connect to another living thing.

Training and Certification of Therapy Dogs

Selecting a dog for therapy work is a difficult task. In an ideal situation, the therapy dog is chosen as a puppy based upon temperament testing and responsiveness to training. It is important to choose a breed that is suited for the work the dog is intended for and that will fit comfortably into the therapist's life. Just because a dog may be a marvelous pet does not mean it will be an effective canine therapist. Many factors and characteristics should be considered. Some of the preferred characteristics include: being well socialized (especially to children); having an interest in playing with humans; possessing the ability to calm itself easily; being able to handle loud noises, lots of activity, and quick movements by children; desiring human contact; having a high frustration tolerance; lacking aggressive tendencies; and getting along with other canines.

Beyond these characteristics, there are other considerations to be made when selecting a canine specifically for use in play therapy. Obviously, it is extremely important that the dog enjoys interacting with children and that he has a repertoire of tricks or activities he can do with them. It is also important to acclimate the dog to the play therapy environment, especially considering that there may be items in a playroom the dog typically is not exposed to. This can include toy guns, swords, or dress-up costumes that could initially alarm the dog. The dog should also enjoy physical contact with humans such as being petted or groomed. Finally, it is helpful for the dog to be "attentive to human affective expressions" and to be responsive to what the child needs at that particular time (VanFleet, 2008).

Once a therapy dog has been chosen the process of training him to fit into our world begins. Basic obedience training is the essential first step to help dogs integrate into the human world. Dog training should revolve around positive reinforcement, praise, fun, and showing the dog how to be successful. Positive training involves the use of rewards and praise for positive behaviors and firm but minimal corrections for undesirable behaviors. Forceful negative corrections can only overwhelm and confuse the dog. Therapy is not based on punitive or aversive measures and neither should the training of the therapy dog. Good dog training does not just happen; it is the product of enthusiastic instructors possessing a broad base of experience with dogs. Each dog is unique, has its own way of learning, and has its own problems and needs. You should always strive to bring out the best in every dog and work with a knowledgeable instructor.

Over the years, several certification programs have been developed within the animal-assisted therapy community. It is recommended that therapists who are considering the use of canines in their practices work toward one of these certifications before utilizing their dog in sessions. Therapy Dog International, Inc. (TDI) is the oldest and currently the largest therapy dog organization in the United States. It is a volunteer organization dedicated to regulating, testing, and registering therapy dogs and their volunteer handlers for the purpose of visiting nursing homes, hospitals, prisons, schools, and wherever else therapy dogs are needed. Dogs registered through TDI are rigorously evaluated and are graduates of basic obedience classes as well as other specialized forms of training. To maintain their therapy dog certification, the handler must renew their annual membership with TDI, which includes an annual veterinary visit, current vaccinations, and routine check-ups.

The Delta Foundation is another organization interested in therapy dog work. In the 1990s, Delta built on its scientific and educational base to provide the first comprehensive training in animal-assisted therapy to volunteers and health care professionals (Delta Society, 2006). They began their Pet Partners program in 1990, which trains and screens volunteers and their pets for visiting animal programs in hospitals, nursing homes, rehabilitation centers, schools, and other facilities.

Research on Canine-Assisted Play Therapy

Thompson, Mustaine, and Weaver (2008) completed the first known controlled study of the use of canines in nondirective play therapy. The purpose of this study was to present a model for combining animal-assisted therapy and play therapy as well as providing data on its effect on a child's response to play therapy. Methods combined quantitative and qualitative data collection to examine differences in children's behavior in the presence/absence of a certified therapy dog (ABAB design). Individual nondirective play sessions occurred weekly for 45 minutes across 16 weeks. Quantitative data collected with the Play Therapy Session Summary (PTSS) yielded an overall total behavior score based on the frequency of positive behaviors (participation in play, engagement in fantasy play, attention to task, response to tracking, positive affect, positive vocalizations, adherence to limits) and negative behaviors (play disruptions, distractibility, negative affect, resistance to tracking, negative vocalizations, breaking of limits, aggression) per session. Qualitative data were therapist-generated (MT) narratives. The study lasted for 6 months and captured 12 sessions with 5 participants and 16 sessions with 3 participants.

Results of the study showed that the presence of the therapy dog had a significant impact on a child's response to play therapy. In the presence of the dog, children in the study showed an improvement in mood and affect, an increased ability to engage in thematic play, and more readily established rapport. They also exhibited a decrease in aggressive behavior and play disruptions. Another interesting finding was when children with PTSD disclosed their abuse for the first time, it was always in the presence of the therapy dog. Seven of the eight children showed a clear differentiation between more positive and less negative behavior in the presence of the dog, suggesting that the therapy dog was associated with more organized behavior in anxious children.

VanFleet (2008) also recently wrote a book entitled, *Play Therapy With Kids & Canines: Benefits for Children's Developmental and Psychosocial Health*. This book was written for child and family play therapists who wish to incorporate their own dogs into their play therapy work. She addresses the human-animal bond, the methods and research for AAT and PT, and considerations for selecting, training, and using dogs in play therapy.

Conclusion

Animal-assisted play therapy has the potential to be a successful intervention for children if the proper steps are taken. It is important for therapists to have a solid foundation in play therapy before venturing to add the play therapy dog to the playroom. It is also important for the therapist to hand select their therapy dog for personality and temperament and to ensure the dog has the proper training and certification needed for the work. Dogs have been known to be wonderful teachers, friends, and companions and it appears now they also make wonderful therapists.

References

Axline, V. (1974). *Play therapy.* New York: Ballantine.
Chandler, C. K. (2005). *Animal assisted therapy in counseling.* New York: Routledge.
Delta Society. (2006). Retrieved August 8, 2006, from http://www.deltasociety.org.
Gonski, Y. A. (1985). The therapeutic utilization of canines in a child welfare setting. *Child and Adolescent Social Work Journal, 2,* 93-105.
Jalongo, M. R., Astorino, T., & Bomboy, N. (2004). Canine visitors: The influence of therapy dogs on young children's learning and well-being in classrooms and hospitals. *EarlyChildhood Education Journal,* 32(1).
Kottman, T. (2001). *Play therapy: Basics and beyond.* Alexandria, VA: American Counseling Association.
Landreth, G. L. (2002). *Play therapy: The art of the relationship* (2nd ed.). New York: Brunner-Routledge.
Piaget, J. (1962). *Play, dreams, and imitation in childhood.* New York: Norton.
Thompson, M., Mustaine, B., & Weaver, A. (2008). *Effects of a trained therapy dog in child centered play therapy on children with anxiety disorders.* Unpublished doctoral dissertation (Thompson), Argosy University, Sarasota, FL.
VanFleet, R. (2008). *Play therapy with kids & canines: Benefits for children's developmental and psychosocial health.* Sarasota, FL: Professional Resource Press.
VanFleet, R. & Thompson, M. (2008). *The power of cross-species play: Theory, research, and practice of canine-assisted play therapy.* Paper presented at the annual conference of the International Society for Anthrozoology, Toronto, Canada.

White, J., & Allers, C. T. (1994). Play therapy with abused children: A review of the literature. *Journal of Counseling & Development*, 72, 390-394.

Article 19

Counseling Management's Ethical Imperative: Responsible Quality Service

Paper based on a program presented at the 2009 American Counseling Association Conference and Exposition, March 19-23, Charlotte, North Carolina.

Richard F. Ponton

In the first decade of the millennium the cost to organizations and individuals of ethical violations has been measured in the loss of reputation and confidence, the loss of human life and health, the loss of environmental safety and ecology, and the loss of billions of dollars. The modern discourse on ethics seems to focus more on risk management and compliance than values and virtues. However, at its best, ethical discourse brings one's mind to the responsibilities of quality service, summarized by Bennis and Nanus (1985) as "doing the right thing" (p. 21). The purpose of this paper is to examine the role of counselor managers in the promotion of an ethic of responsible quality service and to provide practical strategies from management literature toward the fulfillment of that role.

Professional Identity and Ethics of Counselor Managers

Counseling as a profession, barely a century old, joins the ranks of the classical professions--medicine, law, and theology--and the myriad of modern professions that have emerged to address the needs of society. Welie (2004) defined a profession as:

> . . . a collective of expert service providers who have
> jointly and publicly committed to always give priority
> to the existential needs and interests of the public they
> serve above their own and who in turn are trusted by
> the public to do so. (p. 531)

Professional ethics can be seen as the implicit and explicit understanding of the relationship between the profession and society. Miller (1990) suggested that a model of understanding the relationship of a profession to society is the covenant. She suggested that a covenant model of the professional relationship with society and consequent obligations to society was useful in broadening the narrow *quid pro quo* agreement that is inherent in a contract model of professional responsibility. Miller (1990) pointed out that in the covenant model, each individual counselor "in assuming professional identity . . . promises to return the gift he or she has received in being trained for and granted professional status" (p. 121). It has been argued that the ethics of counseling are inextricably connected to the professional identity of counselors (Ponton & Duba, 2009). What counselors promise to do and the way they promise to do it emanates from who they are called by society to be. Counselors who are called to serve in the capacity of manager, at whatever level in an organization, continue their covenantal relationship with society as a counselor. They also enter into an additional covenantal relationship with society, the organization, and the people who comprise it. The successful transition from counselor to counselor-manager is measured by the degree to which the counseling habits of mind and covenants are merged with the habits of mind and covenants of management (Ponton & Cavaiola, 2008).

As counselors move to positions of leadership, their responsibility expands to include the provision of quality and ethical service not only by themselves but by the organization as a whole. While it is true that each counselor working in an organization is responsible for his or her own behavior, the manager is principally responsible for promoting the ethical behavior of the organization as a whole. The ACA code of ethics (ACA, 2005) clarifies the responsibility of counselor-managers in regard to the hiring competent counselors (C.2.c) and insuring their subordinates' maintenance of client privacy (B.3.a) and employee relations (Section D). However, by and large, the Code of Ethics is moot on the responsibilities of the counselor-manager to insure organizationally the same standards to which they are called personally.

Research suggests that managers play a significant role in the development of an organization's ethical culture and positive environment (Logsdon & Young, 2005). Whetstone (2005) pointed out that leaders control the most powerful means for embedding and reinforcing the culture of organizations by means of several mechanisms including reactions to critical incidents, allocation of resources, allocation of rewards and status, and the choice of issues to which they attend. It is in their day to day decision making, as well as the formal statements of mission, that managers announce, shape and reinforce the organizational goals and strategies, values, and behaviors that form the culture. Likewise, it is the culture of the organization, as it is formulated both formally and informally throughout its history, that calls forth the leader, determines the leader's fit to the organization, and thus the leader's effectiveness. It is the ability to shape the culture of an organization that calls counselor-managers to promote an ethic of responsible quality service. Such an ethic extends beyond the legalistic and minimalist view of compliance with the law and the standards of practice. Such compliance presents (to use a familiar phrase) the necessary but insufficient conditions of responsible quality service. Henderson (2009) suggested that managers promote the mission of their organization by establishing work environments that provide excellent, culturally responsive services to clients and she calls on counselor-managers to continuously update their management skills. As leaders of professional endeavors in the classroom or clinic, counselor-managers have much to learn from their counterparts in other industries in regard to quality assurance and organizational development.

Responsible Quality Service

Quality assurance and customer engagement have significant implications for counselor-managers and their organizations. Perhaps the most basic lesson counselor-managers learn from managers in other industries is the impact of quality on the bottom line. Counselors in private practice recognize how important it is to have people walk through the front door and how important it is to have them choose to return. Whether the enterprise is a small practice or a large multi-service agency, whether the counselor manager is an academic department chair or counseling center director, focus must be placed on the bottom line. Clients and students, directly or indirectly, support the organization. It is the responsibility of the manager to promote those practices and services that keep clients and students coming through the door.

Secondly, quality assurance assists counselor-managers in program improvement. As professionals, the covenant with society directs counselors toward excellence; therefore, managers of both treatment programs and educational programs have an implicit agreement with their constituencies to strive toward program improvement. Society expects better than "good enough surgery," more than "it'll get us by" dentistry, and attorneys whose ads read "we'll do in a pinch" would soon go out of business. The commitment to excellence stems in professions not from a competitive market but rather from the public trust. Consumers of professional counseling services, be they students or clients, in ways that are subtle and sometimes not so subtle, sacrifice their autonomy to be in a relationship in which there is a power differential. The truth is, counselors' customers are less likely and often less free to take their business elsewhere. This relationship suggests that our obligation for quality management exceeds that of other industries.

Perhaps the most compelling reason for counselor-managers to be concerned with quality management is its relation to the power of engagement. Customer and employee engagement research (Wagner & Harter, 2006; Fleming & Asplund, 2007) has demonstrated the relationship of a constellation of variables identifying customers who are emotionally satisfied and employees as committed to the organization. They have found that enterprises that have employees who are engaged and passionate about their work are more likely to have customers who are passionate and committed to the enterprise. It is reasonable to suggest that engagement at the organization level mimics the power of therapeutic alliance at the counselor level. Promoting both employee and customer engagement through a systematic quality management program is a strategy for improving client outcomes and enhancing organizational function.

The ethics of responsible quality service is shaped by the professional identity of the counselor. The effective counselor-manger can communicate this rich and complex understanding of the need to do the right thing that goes far beyond the risk-management mentality. From intake to discharge and from application to graduation the organization and all those working in it have a responsibility to the client and student to provide quality service. The receptionist and the C.E.O. and all the other employees have a commitment to serve in their unique roles toward the accomplishment of that mission. It is the role of the counselor-manager to maintain the focus of the work group on that mission and commitment. A simple five-step approach can assist the counseling-manager in maintaining the focus of responsible quality service.

A-Assess: The counselor manager can assess the organization's quality of service utilizing several formal or informal assessment tools. Gallup Institute provides tools that assess both customer engagement (Fleming & Asplund, 2007) and employee engagement (Wagner & Harter, 2006). Other formal instruments exist to provide similar information. However, such assessment may also be done on a less formal basis. Mayor Ed Koch of New York City, during his tenure would assess his administration by asking citizens on the street, "How'm I doin'?" A great way to find out how the organization is doing is to ask the stakeholders and the employees. Another informal method was introduced by Peters and Waterman

(1982) in their seminal work *In Search of Excellence*. They referred to it as "Management by wandering around." Essentially, they suggested that executives and managers get out of their office and talk to those who are doing the work, see the work being done, and learn. Counselor-managers wandering about their clinics may find that clients are put at ease by their receptionists, appointments are scheduled in a timely fashion, there are adequate parking places for staff and clients, and the temperature in the offices is comfortable — or maybe they will find room to go from good to great. Counselor-managers wandering about their counselor education programs may find support staff who are helpful to students, treating them as customers rather than interruptions. They may find faculty who are models of professional counseling, involved with their students and their professional colleagues in the academy and beyond. They may find phones that get answered, messages that get returned, and resources that are available. On the other hand, they may find room to go from good to great.

B-Build positive relationships. Positive relationships in the workplace have been seen as unique in their contribution to personal wellness and organizational success (Dutton & Raggins, 2007). Research in the area of organizational development has demonstrated the impact of positive relationships on collaboration (Powell, Kaput, & Smith-Doerr, 1996), organizational flexibility (Weick, Sutcliffe, & Obstfeld, 1999), safety and well-being (Wagner & Harter, 2006), and organizational success (Fleming & Asplund, 2007). If the counseling office or classroom becomes a silo of solitary endeavor, relationships beyond those walls are seen as non-essential interruptions to the work of dedicated, albeit disengaged, counselors or counselor-educators. It is the role of the counselor manager to shape the culture of the organization toward one that promotes positive relationships both within the organization and beyond it. The internal relationship building processes are shaped by the counselor-manager through attention to positive communication with and among staff and stakeholders. The counselor-manager provides the opportunity for relationships to develop through the allocation of space, time, and attention. It is the role of the counselor manager to insure that the organization develops positive relationships beyond its own walls. A successful organization is holistically integrated in the wider world of the community, the profession, and global concerns (Waddock, 2005). Longsdon and Young (2005) suggested that managers influence the organization's ability to interact positively with the world around it. The counselor-manager who attends to building such relationships actively promotes community awareness and connections in the work place, seeks out opportunities to involve the organization in community and professional activities, and promotes global social justice.

C-Clarify the mission. Counselor managers who are effective in promoting the ethics of responsible quality service recognize their role in formulating and announcing the mission of the organization. Champy (1995) suggested that managers have a primary role in articulating the mission of the organization as the "motivating explanations--why this business and its people must do what they're being called on to do" (p. 40). He refers to the manager's statement of the organization's mission as "…a master script…in which we all play out our different parts. It's the corporate meaning in which we find our personal meaning" (p. 58). The philosophical principle that once the *logos* is established, the *ethos* follows, applies to counseling work groups. Once the organization knows its meaning and organizing principles, the behaviors and customs follow. The counselor-manager's articulation and clarification of the organization's commitment to the ethic of responsible quality service provides meaning and direction to all levels of the organization. When clients are treated with respect and kindness by the reception staff, the manager articulates that to be in concert with the mission of quality service. When consideration is given to operating hours that meet the needs of clients, service delivery in languages spoken by the clients, and fee schedules that allow access to those who need service, the counselor-manager acknowledges the organization's fidelity to its mission.

D- Develop authentic leadership. Luthans and Avolio (2003)

defined authentic leadership as a process that draws on the positive qualities of both leaders and the organization, and also yields leaders in the organization who are self-aware, confident, hopeful, transparent, ethical, and future-oriented. The counselor-manager who is committed to quality recognizes that leadership does not reside in titles but rather in persons. Finding and promoting strengths in individuals within the organization expands the leadership network and promotes engagement. The counselor-manager committed to responsible quality management will implement a systemic approach to leadership development that is woven into staff assignments, performance evaluations, and succession planning.

E- Explore new horizons. Cooperrider and Sekerka (2003) summarized the need for positive exploration as foundational to organizational change, "Human systems grow in the direction of what they persistently ask questions about" (p. 234). Lewin's theory (1951) recognized the inevitability of change in the environment and the consequential need for organizations to change. The effective counselor-manager is aware of the impact of conditions on the organization and its need to adapt to those changes. Additionally counselor-managers are aware of the need to manage change in the organization in an effective manner that considers both the impact of the proposed change on the employee and the impact of the employee on the proposed change. The counselor-manager who scans the horizon for change may find that the primary language of the organization's constituency has changed, there is a need to provide childcare to keep talented workers, or there is no longer a need for a particular program that has "always" been provided by the agency. Awareness of such environmental change introduces the challenges of change and the opportunity for growth for both the organization and its employees.

Conclusion

The management of responsible quality service builds on the foundation of the Code of Ethics (ACA, 2005), and goes beyond those standards to recognize that counselors who manage counseling work groups in the community or the academy are responsible for the competence, effectiveness, viability, and well-being of the organization they serve. Browning (2007) pointed out that the skills of the counselor, while valuable in management, may not be sufficient to insure success. The covenantal promise of competence impels counselor-mangers to equip themselves with knowledge and skills of management and organizational development to insure that clients and students are well served by the work groups they manage.

References

American Counseling Association. (2005). *ACA Code of ethics.* Alexandria, VA: Author.

Bennis, W., & Nanus, B. (1985). *Leaders: The strategies for taking charge.* New York: Harper & Row.

Browing, F. (2007). *From counselor to CEO: Opportunities, challenges, and rewards.* Retrieved August 15, 2008, from http://counselingoutfitters.com/vistas/vistas07/Browning.htm

Champy, J. (1995). *Reengineering management.* New York: Harper Collins.

Cooperrider, D. L., & Sekerka, L. E. (2003). Toward a theory of positive organizational change. In K. S. Cameron, J. E. Dutton, & R. E. Quinn (Eds.), *Positive organizational scholarship: Foundations of a new discipline* (pp. 225-240). San Francisco: Berrett-Koehler Publishers.

Dutton, J. E., & Raggins, B. R. (2007). *Exploring positive relationships at work: Building a theoretical and research foundation.* New York: Erlbaum.

Fleming, J. H., & Asplund, J. (2007). *Human sigma: Managing the employee-customer encounter.* New York: Gallup Press.

Henderson, P. (2009). *The new handbook of administrative supervision in counseling.* New York: Routledge.

Lewin, K. (1951). *Field theory in social science.* New York: Harper & Row.

Longsdon, J. M., & Young, J. E. (2005). Executive influence on ethical culture: Self-transcendence, differentiation, and integration. In R. A. Giacalone, C. Jurkiewicz, C. Dunn (Eds.), *Positive psychology in business ethics and corporate responsibility* (pp. 103-122). Greenwich, CT: Information Age Publishing.

Luthans, F., & Avolio, B. (2003). Authentic leadership development. In K. S. Cameron, J E. Dutton, & R. E. Quinn (Eds.), *Positive organizational scholarship: Foundations of a new discipline* (pp. 241-258). San Francisco: Berrett-Koehler Publishers.

Miller, P. (1990). Covenant model for professional relationships: An alternative to the contract model. *Social Work, 35,* 121-125.

Peters, T. J. & Waterman, R. H. (1982). In search of excellence: *Lessons from America's best run companies.* New York: Warner Books.

Ponton, R. F., & Cavaiola, A. A. (2008). Positive leadership in counseling workgroups. In G. R. Walz, J. C. Bleuer, & R. K. Yep (Eds.), *Compelling counseling interventions. Celebrating VISTAS' fifth anniversary* (pp. 283-292). Ann Arbor, MI: Counseling Outfitters.

Ponton, R. F., & Duba, J. D. (2009). The code of ethics: Articulating counseling's professional covenant. *Journal of Counseling & Development, 87,* 117-121.

Powell, W. W., Kaput, K. R., & Smith-Doerr, L. (1996). Interactional collaboration and the locus of innovation: Networks of learning in biotechnology. *Administrative Science Quarterly, 41,* 116-145.

Waddock, S. (2005). Positive psychology of leading corporate citizenship. In R. A. Giacalone, C. Jurkiewicz, & C. Dunn (Eds.), *Positive psychology in business ethics and corporate responsibility* (pp. 23-45). Greenwich, CT: Information Age Publishing.

Wagner, R., & Harter, J. K. (2006). 12: *The elements of great managing.* New York: Gallup Press.

Weick, K. E., Sutcliffe, K. M., & Obstfeld, D. (1999). Organizing for high reliability: Processes of collective mindfulness. *Research in organizational behavior; 21* (81-123). Stamford, CT: JAI Press.

Welie, J. V. (2004). Is dentistry a profession? Part 1. Professionalism defined. *Journal of the Canadian Dental Association, 70,* 529-532.

Whetstone, J. T. (2005). A framework for organizational virtue: the interrelationship of mission, culture, and leadership. *Business Ethics: A European Review, 14,* 367-378.

Article 20

Developing Guidelines for Campus Suicide Prevention Anti-Stigma Posters: A Focus Group Approach

Paper based on a program presented at the 2009 American Counseling Association Annual Conference and Exposition, March 19-23, Charlotte, North Carolina.

Darren A. Wozny and Adetura Taylor

Introduction

One of the primary aims of our campus suicide prevention program is early identification of distressed at-risk students followed by appropriate referral to campus counseling services. Poor help-seeking attitudes and behaviors, on the part of the referring party (faculty, staff, and students) or the distressed student, can result in either referrals not being made or distressed students not following through on a counseling referral. One component of poor help-seeking behavior is a perceived stigma against those who receive mental health counseling (Suicide Prevention Resource Center [SPRC], 2004). SPRC (2004) indicated that one of the primary factors associated with the increased demand for campus counseling services for students with serious psychological issues was decreased stigma associated with mental illness and help-seeking on college campuses. However, this is not to say that mental health stigma is no longer an issue on college campuses, as there are still many college students with serious psychological issues that fail to seek counseling services (American College Health Association, 2001). Thus, an effective campus suicide prevention program must be able to early-identify at-risk college students and encourage those students to seek help from others (including friends, family, and campus counseling services). The anti-stigma project aims to increase early-identification of at-risk students and increase conducive help-seeking attitudes and behaviors among the campus community (faculty, staff, and students). The anti-stigma guidelines will be utilized to develop anti-stigma slogans and artwork for the campus.

Statement of the Problem

Going to college and staying in college is a protective factor for suicide risk. The Big Ten Suicide Study (Silverman et al., 1997) identified reported suicides among Big Ten University campuses over a 10 year period and reported a college suicide rate of 7.5 per 100,000 students. However, the general population suicide rate when matched for age, gender, and race was 15.0 per 100,000 (SPRC, 2004). Yet, suicide and related mental health issues are still a significant problem on college campuses. The American College Health Association (2001) national survey of 16,000 students across 28 college campuses reported that 9.5% of college students had suicidal ideation, 1.5% had made a suicide attempt, 50% reported feeling very sad, 33% reported feeling hopeless, and 22% felt depressed to the point of impaired functioning.

Although suicide and related mental health issues are a problem for the general college student population, there are college subpopulations that are at increased risk for suicide, particularly males, older students (25 years and older), and graduate students (both male and female; Silverman et al., 1997). Nontraditional college students (students 25 years and older) have some unique stressors that include commuting to college (less able to participate in extra-curricular college activities), loss of status if they have quit work to attend college (Silverman, 2004), work/family/school balance for those students that attend college while continuing to work and raise families, and academic-related challenges of returning to school after a prolonged absence (SPRC, 2004). Another college student subpopulation that overlaps with older nontraditional students are commuter students, who tend to have weak ties to their college whereby they only appear on campus to attend classes, lack "school spirit," and are difficult to engage in school-based programming (SPRC, 2004).

Despite the fact that suicide and related mental health issues are commonplace on all types of college campuses, including commuter campuses, many students fail to seek counseling services. The American College Health Association's study (2001) found a discrepancy between students who report that depression impaired their functioning (22%) and students who have been diagnosed with depression (6.2% of males and 12.4% of females). This highlights that many students with serious mental health issues are not seeking treatment. One of the primary reasons for not seeking counseling services is the stigma associated with counseling. This results in non-conducive help seeking attitudes and behaviors whereby, regardless of severity of mental health issues experienced, some students do not attend counseling even if referred.

The question then becomes how to increase help-seeking attitudes and behaviors on college campuses so that distressed students can receive counseling treatment when needed.

> While there is no evidence base supporting the efficacy of social marketing approaches at present, many suicide prevention practitioners believe that campus social marketing campaigns can stimulate cultural changes that destigmatize mental health problems, remove barriers to accessing appropriate care, and encourage help-seeking. (SPRC, 2004, p. 24)

Research Gaps

In addition to the lack of established efficacy in mental health anti-stigma programming, there is also a dearth of research associated with how to promote mental health or prevent suicides on commuter campuses (SPRC, 2004).

Research Question

What are the key guidelines for the development of effective anti-stigma posters for implementation on a commuter campus?

Anti-Stigma Project

Campus Setting

Our campus is a small regional campus (712 students) of a major public state university (16,206 students). It is located 100 miles from the main campus which houses most university services, including the college counseling center. Our campus is a commuter campus as many students commute to campus from surrounding counties. The regional campus student population (712 students) has the following characteristics related to academic class (71% undergraduate; 29% graduate); gender (76% female; 24% male); race (68% White American; 29% African American; 2.5% American-Indian); and age (71 % nontraditional students; 29% traditional students; 63% older students aged 25-49 years).

Campus Suicide Prevention Program Grant Activities

The SAMHSA federal grant guidelines stipulated that campus suicide prevention grant activities should be limited to the five primary project activities that include development of the following: mental health network; campus crisis response plan; integration of the National Suicide Prevention Lifeline in the campus crisis response plan; informational materials for students and their families; suicide prevention gatekeeper/awareness training workshops, early identification of students-at risk, and promotion of help-seeking behaviors among distressed students. The primary grant project activity of promoting help-seeking behaviors is principally concerned with reduction of stigma associated with students seeking help for mental health issues.

Method

Participants

Seven counselor education graduate students took part in a 90 minute focus group regarding the development of anti-stigma poster guidelines. The participants' demographic characteristics included: gender (85.7% female); age (average age 38.4 years, range 27-57 years); education (100% graduate students); employment status (85.7% work full-time; 14.3% work part-time); marital status (71.4% married; 14.3% divorced; 14.3% single); number of children (average 1.43 children per participant).

Procedures

Focus group participants were shown three student-developed suicide prevention anti-stigma posters as well as a four-part professionally developed anti-stigma poster series (*Don't Erase Your Future*, n.d.) that have different anti-stigma messages and are visually different in design.

Focus Group Questions.
All focus group participants were asked the following questions:

1. What is your *initial reaction* to the posters?
2. What do you think is the *purpose or intent* of these posters?
3. How well do you think that these posters *achieve their purpose*?
4. In terms of *visual design of the posters, what seems to work* and *what changes would you recommend* for future posters?
5. In terms of the *content or message of the posters, what seems to work* and *what changes would you recommend for future posters*?

Task. All focus group participants were instructed to write anti-stigma slogans (maximum one sentence/slogan) for our campus aimed at raising awareness of campus mental health issues and encouraging help-seeking behaviors among campus students. Each of the anti-stigma slogans was critiqued by the focus group to maximize their potential effectiveness. For each developed anti-stigma slogan, focus group participants were asked, "What, if any, *changes would you recommend* with this developed anti-stigma message?" All suggested changes were debated among the focus-group participants until a group consensus was reached on each slogan.

Data Analysis Methods

Researchers read the focus group transcript to become familiar with content. The first researcher wrote in the margin the basic meaning of each participant's statement (in black ink). The second researcher read the transcript and the first researcher's basic meaning statement in the margin. If the second researcher concurred with the basic meaning statement of the first researcher, the meaning statement was left unchanged in the margin. If the second researcher disagreed with the basic meaning statement of the first researcher, the second researcher wrote a second meaning statement beside the first meaning statement (in blue ink). The member check process involved returning the focus group transcript and their respective meaning statements to the participants to have them provide feedback on the meaning of their original statement. The participants agreed with the first or second researcher's meaning statements (with a check mark in red ink) or wrote a third meaning statement beside the existing meaning statements (in red ink). Participant meaning statements were then organized and sorted into categories to answer the research question (developing guidelines for anti-stigma posters).

Results

The analysis of the focus group transcript was sorted into three primary categories. Each of the three primary categories of mental health anti-stigma guidelines had subcategories of more specific guidelines.

Category 1: Visually Engaging Aspects of Mental Health Anti-Stigma Posters

Sub-category 1: Use of color is visually engaging. "My initial reaction is that it's colorful."

Sub-category 2: Use of pictures on poster is visually engaging. "My initial reaction was to see if there is anyone I know."

Sub-category 3: Creative artwork on posters is visually engaging. "Because like aside from what is actually said content wise, just art alone could actually engage us even if we don't particularly like the message."

Sub-category 4: Must use appropriate font size and attractive font. "When you read the bottom (of the poster) it makes sense. If I was just walking by I would not have stopped to read it. If it (font) was bigger it (poster) would have caught my eye."

Sub-category 5: Use of non-message space on poster is more visually engaging (brief messages result in larger non-message space). "With the 'I have a dream' (poster), my initial reaction was that it was a good theme but why did they erase the dream off (chalkboard in poster)."

Sub-category 6: Use of visual contrast through color is visually engaging. "The poster with all the people on it (student anti-stigma poster), if it had one single person maybe be black and white instead of color, that was obviously unhappy, I think would probably catch the attention in a way that the message was trying to bring out."

Sub-category 7: Pictures that show human diversity are visually engaging. "My initial reaction is that there are a lot of people (student anti-stigma poster), different people from different walks of life, background and age."

Category 2: Engaging Aspects of Mental Health Anti-Stigma Poster Messages (Slogans)

Sub-category 1: Message has to be age-appropriate (use of common issues). "I was thinking maybe this (*Don't Erase Your Future* poster) would be geared toward an elementary child because of the blackboard and the cursive writing."

Sub-category 2: Message can be culturally targeted. "But the Martin Luther King one and the one with Rosa Parks (*Don't Erase Your Future* posters) those are the ones we as African Americans hear often. The 'I have a dream' one kind of catches my eye to read it…and you just know those words. They caught my attention more than the others. I didn't read the other (posters)."

Sub-category 3: Messages need to be clear and unambiguous. "Talking can help."

Sub-category 4: Message needs to arouse curiosity. "Okay, why did they start writing (on chalkboard on the *Don't Erase Your Future* poster series) and then erase it off?"

Sub-category 5: Message needs to be in positive terms. "Talking is helpful."

Sub-category 6: Messages that use "play on words" of existing slogans are engaging. "Yeah, she was the one who took an existing slogan ('great taste, less filling'), and then did a play on words with it ('great taste, less feeling'), right? And that part of it was good."

Category 3: Aspects of Anti-Stigma Poster Messages (Slogans) That Fail to Engage

Sub-category 1: Too much information on poster. "My initial reaction was that there is a lot of stuff to read at one time."

Sub-category 2: Some parts of poster message not emphasized on poster. "All of the stressful things (mental health issues on poster) stand out to me, but you kind of miss the 'seek counseling for everyday dilemmas part' until I looked at it a second time."

Sub-category 3: Poster message is unclear or ambiguous. "My first reaction to it was that it didn't seem like a poster at all about hurting people because the people had happy expressions on their faces. But the poster doesn't tell me anything. I don't even know what it was about."

Sub-category 4: Poster message may arouse curiosity but still fail to engage. "I wondered why they left it off (*Don't Erase Your Future* poster series). It wouldn't have been something I would have stopped to read if I was just walking by in the hallway."

Sub-category 5: Some choice of language in the poster message fails to engage readers. "I'm not really sure that it does decrease stigma because I get what they are saying (*Don't Erase Your Future* series). You know, saying that if those people (historical figures represented in the poster series) committed suicide they wouldn't have done the great things they did, but it really doesn't relate to the average person being depressed or whatever."

Through a group critique process, the focus group participants developed 10 mental health anti-stigma slogans (messages) that would be appropriate for our commuter campus.

1. You are not alone. There is a way out of sadness.
2. Depression makes you feel small, seek help before you disappear.
3. Are you going down for the last time? There is help to be had!
4. Don't let the pressure of life get you down – talk to others!
5. Chill out! Exercise more. Take charge of your life! Run, play and have fun!
6. Just do it! Talk about your daily dilemmas.
7. Everyone struggles at times in life. It is okay to talk about it.
8. What time is it? Time to talk! Talk about what? Talk about you!
9. Is stress taking over your life? Talk to someone.
10. Is it time…to seek advice for those concerns troubling you?

Discussion and Future Directions

How are the *research results to be utilized* in the campus suicide prevention project? The focus group participants developed mental health anti-stigma slogans (see results section above) based on their guideline discussions on what makes an effective anti-stigma message (see results section – categories 2 and 3). The mental health anti-stigma slogans (messages) and the visual-based guidelines (see results section – category 1) were given to a creative arts teacher education class to paint the canvases for the mental health anti-stigma paintings. The campus mental health anti-stigma painting series (15 paintings; some slogans utilized twice with different artwork) will be part of a permanent campus art collection and will include card boxes under each painting with campus counseling services contact information and emergency phone number wallet cards.

The next step after the campus mental health anti-stigma artwork series is displayed on campus is to evaluate the effectiveness of the project. Why is it important to evaluate this anti-stigma project? Evaluating our anti-stigma project will begin to address the research gaps of establishing efficacy in anti-stigma social marketing programming, as well as how to promote mental health or prevent suicides on commuter campuses (SPRC, 2004).

The future evaluation plans for the campus mental health anti-stigma project include evaluation of campus students' help-seeking attitudes as well as their help-seeking behaviors. To evaluate the campus students' help-seeking attitudes, the Attitudes toward Seeking Professional Psychological Help Scale (ATSPPHS) will be included in the evaluation process so that the campus students' attitudes can then be compared prior to anti-stigma project implementation (pretest) and at one-year post-implementation (posttest) for returning students. To evaluate campus help-seeking behaviors, all campus faculty/staff and student peer helpers will report monthly: (a) number of distressed students that they encountered overall; (b) number of distressed students that they attempted to engage; (c) number of distressed students that they successfully engaged without need for referral; and (d) number of distressed students that they referred for campus counseling services. Our contracted campus counseling service provider will track the following information: (a) number of referrals (quarterly); (b) referral source (self; campus source – faculty, staff, student peer helper; other student, family, or other); (c) follow-through on referral for counseling (first session attendance). Campus students who attend counseling will be asked as part of the intake process which, if any, of the campus suicide prevention project activities, including anti-stigma project, influenced their decision to attend counseling. Students will have the opportunity to check all the activities that apply.

Why should counselors be interested if mental health anti-stigma projects work? Evaluating an anti-stigma project to establish if it decreases mental health stigma and increases help-seeking attitudes and behaviors should be of major interest to all practicing counselors because it begins to address a broader issue of how to encourage individuals with mental health issues to seek help when necessary. Underutilization of counseling services by individuals in need is a continuing problem to the field of counseling. Many helpful guidelines associated with developing a commuter campus mental health anti-stigma artwork campaign were learned through our focus group approach. This focus group approach allowed our commuter campus to develop an effective, targeted, and visually engaging mental health anti-stigma artwork campaign that will be an integral part of our campus suicide prevention program for years to come.

References

American College Health Association (2001). *National College Health Assessment: Aggregate report, spring 2000.* Baltimore: Author.

Don't Erase Your Future. (n.d.). Don't Erase Your Future: Mental Health Anti-Stigma Campaign. Retrieved January 20, 2008, from http://www.donteraseyourfuture.org

Silverman (2004, March). College suicide prevention: Background and blueprint for action. College Mental Health (Special Issue). *Student Health Spectrum*, 13-20.

Silverman, M., Meyer, P., Sloan, F., Raffel, M., & Pratt, D. (1997). The Big Ten student suicide study. *Suicide and Life Threatening Behavior, 27*, 285-303.

Suicide Prevention Resource Center. (2004). *Promoting mental health and preventing suicide in college and university settings.* Newton, MA: Education Development Center, Inc.

Funding for this conference presentation was made possible (in part) by grant no. 1H79SM057854-01 from SAMHSA. The views expressed in written conference materials or publications and by the speakers and moderators do not necessarily reflect the views, opinions, or official policies of the Department of Health and Human Services and SAMHSA.

Article 21

Deviant Sexuality in Children and Adolescents: A Protocol for the Concurrent Treatment of Sexual Victimization and Sex Offending Behaviors

Paper based on a program presented at the 2009 American Counseling Association Annual Conference and Exposition, March 19-23, Charlotte, North Carolina.

David D. Hof, Julie A. Dinsmore, Catherine M. Hock, Michael A. Bishop, and Thomas R. Scofield

Increased attention has recently been given in mental health literature to better understanding the impact of personal victimization on child and adolescent sex offending behaviors (Burton, 2003, 2008; Hunter & Figueredo, 2000; Kulesz & Wyse, 2007; Veneziano, Veneziano, & LeGrand, 2000). During the 1990s, the number of sex offenders processed through court systems increased by 50%, highlighting the need to identify effective interventions for this growing client population (Snyder & Sickmund, 1995). Studies have found that between 40 and 80% of sex offenders have been sexually abused themselves (Hunter, Goodwin, & Becker, 1994; Ryan & Lane, 1997). Research supports the idea that youth who are victimized or see others victimized may go on to repeat this behavior (Burton, 1999, 2008; Burton & Meezan, 2004), which would suggest that treatment of offending behaviors should concurrently address sexual victimization and engage the client in trauma resolution. Specific attention to victimization issues can enhance clients' goal attainment in their sexual offending treatment in several ways. It not only helps them gain a better understanding of the root cause of their anger and their need for power, control, and revenge, but it can also help clients conceptualize and implement more appropriate replacement behaviors. However, currently there are no universally accepted treatment protocols that address concurrent treatment of offending behaviors and victimization issues (Burton, 2008; Ryan & Lane, 1997).

This article provides an overview of a suggested treatment protocol for use with children and adolescents who display offending behaviors and also have a history of sexual abuse. It treats victimization issues and sexual offending behaviors simultaneously, integrating evidence-based treatment methods of both issues for the most effective treatment (see Table 1 for detailed protocol). The protocol goals are considered beneficial for the treatment of a child or adolescent who is considered to be sexually reactive. Sexually reactive children have been exposed to inappropriate sexual activities and engage in a variety of age-inappropriate sexual behaviors as a result of their own exposure to sexual experiences. They begin to engage in sexual behaviors or relationships that may include excessive sexual play, inappropriate sexual comments or gestures, mutual sexual activity with other children, or sexual molestation and abuse of other children. These children may not understand the harmfulness of their behaviors (Cavanaugh Johnson, 1999). Conversely, sex offenders would be individuals who understand the unlawfulness and harmfulness of their sex offending behaviors and yet choose to offend repeatedly (Ryan & Lane, 1997). Based on years of experience using this protocol, the authors recommend that the goals, as well as the steps to implement them, be addressed in the order given. Although the intention is to provide a universally accepted protocol for concurrent treatment of this population's issues, the protocol can be customized to meet individual clients' needs.

Summary of Treatment Protocol

Goals 1-3 of the protocol focus on building rapport and creating a safe environment for clients. This can be challenging for individuals with offending behaviors, as therapy is often court ordered. Similar to other therapeutic relationships, trust is essential to the change process (Ivey & Ivey, 2003), and working with individuals with offending behaviors is no different. Because participation is not voluntary, clients may feel isolated and incapable of making change. It is essential for the therapist to join with clients, helping clients not feel alone. Court-ordered clients cannot choose whether or not they attend therapy, so giving power to clients in how they would like to participate can be a key factor in helping to increase client motivation.

Goals 4-5 are designed to help clients openly share their stories of offending behaviors and personal victimization as well as their entire sexual histories, both healthy and unhealthy behaviors. Initially, therapists should have clients share their offending behaviors in detail, both verbally and in writing. At times, clients may only self-disclose offending behaviors they have been caught doing or legally charged with. By coming back to the written history throughout the course of treatment, the therapist is able to facilitate further self-disclosure by clients and uncover additional offending behaviors the client has not disclosed as well as unrecognized victimization experiences. When writing and discussing the client's victimization history it is often helpful to talk not only about sexual abuse, but also physical and emotional abuse. Clients may need assistance differentiating between offending behaviors, victimization, healthy sexual behaviors, and unhealthy sexual behaviors.

In implementing Goals 6-8, therapists use clients' histories to help them explore how their offending behaviors are illegal and unhealthy and to take ownership for ways in which they abused other human beings. It is equally important for clients to identify unhealthy and illegal behaviors that were done to them, which can help them make sense of how they developed unhealthy patterns of sexual behavior.

Goal 9 involves exploration and understanding of clients' fantasies and how they played a role in their choice to offend. Clients may be reluctant to share their darkest fantasies; however, it is essential for clients to learn how to recognize and replace, rather than reinforce, unhealthy fantasies.

Goal 10 requires clients to write their thoughts, feelings, and behaviors before, during, and after their offense. In this way, clients begin to understand what thoughts and feelings trigger their offending behaviors and to see moments during the offending cycle when they may be able to intercede. In this goal area, it is important to help the client understand that many people do not offend for enjoyment of a sexual act, but to meet their needs for power, control, revenge, and/or expression of anger. A better understanding of the impact of being victimized may help the client understand the feelings triggering the offending behaviors.

Goals 11-15 focus on teaching clients a model of healthy human sexuality, a process necessary to help them create and nurture healthy relationships and have better understanding as to how their current perspectives on gender roles, sexual orientation, intimacy, relationships, and reproduction were impacted by their victimization.

After clients have a better understanding of healthy relationships, Goal 16 asks them to reexamine their current relationships and determine which are healthy and how their offending behavior has damaged those relationships. It may also be helpful to identify multigenerational abuse and victimization patterns within the family system. This awareness is often helpful in clients' taking responsibility for how they have impacted others' lives.

Goals 17-18 expand the focus on clients taking responsibility for their actions by asking clients to identify by name the individuals they victimized, how they impacted their victims, and how their victims might respond to them. This process begins to build empathy and an increased awareness of their long-term impact. It may be beneficial for clients to write a letter of clarification to the survivor of their offense to aid in taking full responsibility and to aid in the treatment of the survivor.

Goals 19-22 incorporate education about the sex offender assault cycle and lapse contracts to help clients understand what they have control of in their lives and what they do not, especially within the context of their own victimization. Clients should begin by mapping the steps in the assault cycle so they can see their patterns of sexual offending and visualize getting out of their cycle before offending. A lapse contract helps clients identify realistic and useful replacement behaviors at each step in their cycle. In helping clients develop their lapse contracts, it is important to help them understand how their victimization has impacted their decision making process.

As clients gain a better understanding of healthy relationships and their decision-making processes in relationship to their assault cycles, it is time to create and maintain healthy relationships. Goals 23-24 facilitate the building of clients' support systems. Their support systems should start with individuals who are least likely to trigger their assault cycles, should be in writing, and should be carried on clients' bodies so that they have access to these names at all times.

Goals 25-26 encompass the development of a relapse prevention plan (RPP; Laws, Hudson & Ward, 2000) for offending behaviors that includes cues, risk factors, replacement behaviors, and primary support persons who can keep clients accountable. In addition to the RPP that is specific to offending behaviors, a separate process of identifying risk factors that increase likelihood of being re-victimized and replacement for these behaviors is equally as important.

Aftercare, addressed in Goals 27-28, provides a safety net if client's struggle to maintain healthy behavior and follow through with their treatment. The termination process should include reviewing the aftercare plan with clients' primary support systems. A referral to an aftercare group should be required if such a group is available.

Discussion

The counseling profession is attempting to respond to the needs of the growing number of clients experiencing the impact of sexual victimization and displaying sexual offending behaviors. This suggested treatment protocol provides a holistic approach to these issues while allowing for the flexibility to respond to individual client needs. It is hoped this protocol provides direction for those seeking a uniform and integrated approach to concurrent treatment of offending behaviors and victimization for sexually reactive children and adolescents that can be implemented in both inpatient and outpatient settings.

References

Burton, D. L. (1999). An examination of social cognitive theory with differences among sexually aggressive, physical aggressive and nonaggressive children in state care. *Violence and Victims, 14*, 161-178.

Burton, D. L. (2003). Male adolescents: Sexual victimization and subsequent sexual abuse. *Child and Adolescent Social Work Journal, 29*(4), 277-296.

Burton, D. L. (2008). An exploratory evaluation of the contribution of personality and childhood sexual victimization to the development of sexually abusive behavior. *Sexual Abuse: A Journal of Research and Treatment, 20*(1), 102-115.

Burton, D. L., & Meezan, W. (2004). Revisiting recent research on social learning theory as an etiological proposition for sexually abusive male adolescents. *Journal of Evidence-Based Social Work, 1*(1), 41-48.

Cavanaugh Johnson, T. (1999). *Understanding your child's sexual behavior.* Oakland, CA: New Harbinger Publications.

Hunter, J., & Figueredo, J. (2000). The influence of personality and history of sexual victimization in the prediction of juvenile perpetrated child molestation. *Behavior Modification 24*, 241-263.

Hunter, J., Goodwin, D. W., & Becker, J. V. (1994). The relationship between phallometrically measured deviant sexual arousal and clinical characteristics in juvenile sexual offenders. *Behavior Research and Therapy, 32*, 533-538.

Ivey, A.E. & Ivey, M.B. (2003). *Intentional interviewing & counseling* (5th ed.). Pacific Grove, CA: Brooks/Cole.

Kulesz, K. M., & Wyse, W. J. (2007). Sexually abused children: Symptomatology and incidence of problematic sexual behaviors. *Journal of Evidence-Bases Social Work, 4*(1/2), 27-45.

Laws, R. D., Hudson, S. M., & Ward, T. (Eds.). (2000). *Remaking relapse prevention with sex offenders: A sourcebook.* Thousand Oaks, CA: Sage Publications.

Ryan, G., & Lane, S. (Eds.). (1997). *Juvenile sexual offending: Causes, consequences, and correction.* San Francisco: Jossey-Bass.

Snyder, H., & Sickmund, M. (1995). *Juvenile offenders and victims: A national report.* Washington, DC: U.S. Department of Justice, Office of Juvenile Justice and Delinquency Prevention.

Veneziano C., Veneziano, L., & LeGrand, S. (2000). The relationship between adolescent sex offender behaviors and victim characteristics with prior victimization. *Journal of Interpersonal Violence, 15*, 363-374.

Table 1: Protocol for Concurrent Treatment of Sexual Victimization and Sexual Offending Behaviors
(Offending Behavior Goal = O; Victimization Goal = V)

Goal 1: Develop Rapport (O & V)
- Get to know each other
- Understand purpose and process of therapy

Goal 2: Making it Safe (O & V)
- Discuss fears and expectations
- Review confidentiality

Goal 3: Develop Trust (O & V)
- Define trust and distrust, and why it is important to be able to trust others
- Understand how sexual abuse has affected ability to trust self and others
- Develop an atmosphere that encourages disclosure

Goal 4: Disclose and discuss healthy and unhealthy sexuality history including offending behaviors (O)
- Write and present sexual history in therapy
- Write and share weekly sexuality journal

Goal 5: Share victimization story in a safe and supportive environment (V)
- Identify fears around disclosing
- Increase understanding of reason for maintaining the secret, addressing feelings of responsibility, blame, and helplessness
- Validate disclosure of abuse and discuss other people's denial and minimization at previous disclosures

Goal 6: Understand how client was sexually, physically, and emotionally abused and the impact of this abuse (V)
- Write abuse history to include story previously shared
- Explore how client survived abuse
- Begin to understand how to nurture self in healthy ways
- Name the abuser

Goal 7: Understand the difference between sexually reactive behavior and sex offending behavior (O & V)
- Review written histories
- Identify ways both types of behavior have contributed to client development
- Identify illegal behaviors

Goal 8: Gain awareness of what client is feeling and why (O & V)
- Identify and name feelings
- Translate feelings expressed through behaviors into words
- Identify appropriate and inappropriate expression of feelings and encourage appropriate expression

Goal 9: Explore healthy and unhealthy fantasies and how these fantasies impacted offending behaviors (O)
- Chart fantasies in writing and present in therapy
- Review fantasies related to sexual offense
- Replace with healthy sexual fantasy

Goal 10: Understand thoughts, feelings and behaviors specific to sexual offenses (O)
- Write and present thoughts, feelings, and behaviors, before, during, and after offense
- Identify why client acted out sexually

Goal 11: Teach healthy intimacy, relationships, sex, reproduction, and touch (O & V)
- Gain a comprehensive understanding of healthy human sexuality
- Begin to implement into client's life

Goal 12: Learn about and begin to develop healthy human relationships (O & V)
- Understand sexual identity
- Understand and begin to accept sexual orientation

Goal 13: Increase client's awareness of how victimization impacted identity development (V)
- Identify qualities client likes and dislikes about self
- Examine positive/negative memories and how they influence self-image and the power client has over internalizing those messages
- Identify characteristics client would like to associate with self, the motivation behind their desire, and if healthy, steps to adopt these characteristics

Goal 14: Identify etiology of client feelings about the person who abused him/her (V)
- Understand and normalize what client currently feels about abuser
- Help client understand etiology of feelings
- Help client let go of feelings getting in the way of promoting recovery

Goal 15: Understand client's beliefs specific to gender roles and the impact of these beliefs (O & V)
- Write and discuss beliefs related to gender roles

Goal 16: Understand how relationships have changed between client, family, and friends (O & V)
- Examine client's relationship with family before and after abuse
- Examine client's relationship with friends before and after abuse
- Identify how client would like to change these relationships

Goal 17: Increase client capacity for empathy and ability to validate, support, and understand others (V)
- Become more open to the emotional responses of others
- Continue to normalize victimization

Goal 18: Name individuals client has abused and understand immediate and long-term impact on their lives (O)
- List each individual the client victimized
- Write and discuss how victim(s) may have felt then and now
- Write clarification letter(s) to each victim

Goal 19: Understand assault cycle and how it applies to client's offending behaviors (O)
- Write and present in therapy client's assault cycle: (a) deviant fantasy, (b) reinforcement of fantasy, (c) objectification, (d) victim selection, (e) decision to offend, (f) planning, (g) grooming, (h) offense, (i) rationalization, (j) shame, and (k) back to normal

Goal 20: Understand how victimization affected client in the past and present: emotionally, physically, sexually, and psychologically (V)
- Write and examine in therapy how specific abuse impacted client in the past and present: emotionally, physically, sexually, and psychologically
- Determine changes client would like to make emotionally, physically, sexually, and psychologically

Goal 21: Understand elements of client's life over which they have control and how to exercise change (O & V)
- Identify what client has control of and want they want to change
- Create plan of change

Goal 22: Understand assault cycle and know how to get out of it before offending (O)
  • Write and present lapse contract in therapy
Goal 23: Creating healthy relationships (O & V)
  • Understand client's personal space and boundaries issues
  • Create a plan to assert boundaries in client's life
Goal 24: Identify and create support system (O & V)
  • Identify individuals client can talk to about abuse and offense
  • Identify individuals who may not know about client's abuse and offense yet can be supportive
  • Formally contact individuals and ask them to be part of support system
  • Create a list of names and numbers that can be carried on client
Goal 25: Develop and implement relapse prevention plan (O)
  • Create relapse prevention plan
  • Share plan with support system
Goal 26: Identify risk behavior for victimization and create plan for replacement behaviors (V)
  • Identify risk behavior that may get in the way of recovery and overall mental health
  • Create replacement for risk behaviors
  • Plan how to implement replacement behaviors into everyday life
Goal 27: Develop and implement aftercare plan (O & V)
  • Create and present aftercare plan in therapy
Goal 28: Provide closure and reinforce aftercare plan
  • Review aftercare plan with support system
  • Refer to aftercare group
  • Terminate

Article 22

En-Trancing People Who Are a Pain and the Bullies in Your Clients' Brains

Based on two programs presented at the 2009 American Counseling Association Annual Conference and Exposition, March 19 -23, Charlotte, North Carolina.

Kate Cohen-Posey

Like the mythical, two-faced god Janus, the first program, "Using Hypnotic Language in Everyday Life," poises people to deal with difficult characters by using hypnotic syntax to promote desirable conduct. The second workshop, "Semi-Hypnotic Self-Talk for Briefer, Deeper Therapy," looks inward to identify thought demons and makes use of thinking processes to mindfully observe and ask questions that derail subvocal monologues. In both presentations, overbearing people or undermining thoughts are en-tranced, but hypnotic trance never occurs. This use of evocative language ventures into uncharted territory in the social and psychic realms and offers fertile soil to cultivate compelling counseling interventions. The rest of this paper will make those clear.

I. Teaching Clients to Deal With Difficult People

Often it is difficult to focus on intra-psychic issues because clients bring their "war stories" of problems they are having with spouses, children, in-laws, and co-workers to sessions. In a troubled relationship or a dysfunctional family, the parties that seem to need help the most frequently refuse to come for treatment. While this may leave counselors feeling helpless, an important reframe is needed. Murray Bowen (1978), the originator of Family Systems Therapy, believed that the most productive work could be done with the healthiest member of the family and that is frequently the person most likely to seek treatment.

Bowen had the foresight to realize that anytime a person takes a stand that goes against the prevailing beliefs of a system, threats, attacks, name calling, and other types of *emotional reactivity* <u>must</u> occur. He recommended that people maintain contact with the system while under attack with casual responses and he gave some fine examples of such rejoinders. But he did little to define or expand them into an arsenal of responses that allow people to stay connected to adversaries while under fire with empowering grace.

Sources for Empowering, Casual Responses

The part of this paper that deals with difficult people codifies a set of skills inspired by two main sources: (1) Taoism shows the way of using opposing forces to find harmony and balance. Along with Buddhism and Zen, it inspired the martial art of *aikido* which absorbs an adversary's energy. (2) Hypnosis and hypnotic language is the practical source that shows how to evoke desired responses in people or disrupt habitual patterns of behavior.

People frequently use hypnosis in their everyday language with undesirable outcomes. Saying, "Don't ever *lie to me again*," is an order that provokes resistance with an (*italicized*) <u>embedded suggestion</u> to be deceitful. The alternative, "You can *always... tell me the truth*," is a statement of fact or a <u>truism</u> with an embedded suggestion that encourages honesty. Orders provoke instinctive, *fight/flight* reactions. A truism is a *flow* response. Once learned, it is surprisingly easy to execute. The overall strategy is to eliminate resistance with hypnotic or verbal aikido responses. There are four main tactics to this strategy. The fine nuances of each one will be <u>underlined</u>, illustrated, and defined in the following sections.

Four Types of Casual Responses

Acting-As-If

Acting-as-if is the verbal art that confirms the best in people by treating a harsh comment as if it were harmless. We have come a long way from Art Linkletter's *House Party* where kids said the darndest things. We now live in a Jerry Springer world where even our friends can say the darndest things that are anything but cute. Suppose a frenemy said to you, *"It's amazing that you were picked to speak at the ACA conference. Just be careful not to bore people."* This remark is rife with not-so-hidden rudeness. Several acting-as-if responses would remove the veiled barbs.

1. *Why thank you for your heartfelt confidence in me.* Saying <u>thank you</u> is the easiest way to handle any cruel comment. The reply is unexpected and responds to insolence with etiquette, throwing people off their game. Suggesting that the person has heartfelt confidence is called "<u>speaking things as you want them.</u>" It undermines the insinuation that you might be boring and <u>takes it as a compliment.</u>
2. *You're such a good friend for giving me that reminder, but I've already got "don't bore people" on my packing list.* This casual response starts by <u>complimenting</u> the instigator, which is always disarming. The compliment is then negated with the <u>hypnotic word</u> *but* that discounts whatever comes before it. Putting *don't bore people* on a fictional packing list is the tactic of <u>agreeing</u> with an opponent in fact or theory, which eliminates resistance.
3. *Actually, I have been known to bore people to death. It's one of my special powers that I reserve for certain occasions.* This reply can best be thought of as <u>dramatizing</u> the worst-case scenario to embrace an insult. In this case a "<u>golden nugget</u>" of truth or greatness is also found by being able to turn on special powers at a whim.

Asking Questions

Asking questions, or the Art of Inquiry, is the most natural of the verbal arts. On some level, it does not make sense for people to make random, rude remarks. If stress did not get in the way, curiosity would be roused. All questions have the effect of taking the spotlight off victims, forcing instigators to look at themselves and start a focused inward search. This basic tenet of hypnosis is illustrated in the following inquiries.

1. *Actually, I'm curious. Why are you amazed that I was picked to speak at the conference?* This simple, <u>open-ended question</u> exposes the assumption about qualifications and puts the frenemy on the spot. In such situations people will often deny presumptions or admit them more meekly and leave avenues open for other casual comments.
2. *I wonder why you're amazed that I'm speaking at the conference.* This <u>hidden question</u> is posed in the form of a statement with the words *I wonder*. It does not require a response, plants ideas to ponder, and implies that there is nothing surprising about being chosen.
3. *Are you trying to keep me on my toes or build my confidence?* This question creates a <u>false choice</u> between two acceptable alternatives rather than trying to fathom the reason for rudeness. In a sense, it speaks things as the person wants them by assuming that the frenemy is looking out for her best interest.

A false choice puts people in a <u>bind</u> —*heads I win, tails you lose.* A <u>double bind</u> creates a forced choice that assumes success: *Do you know how this paper will help you think of new counseling interventions?* Regardless of how the question is answered, there is a covert agreement that the paper will be of assistance.

Active Listening

Active listening is familiar to counselors from the work of Carl Rogers (1951) when he introduced his single-point (nondirective) method. In the interest of making casual comments while under fire, it will be looked at from the Taoist perspective of the Mirror Mind that reflects but does not absorb verbal attacks (Lao Tzu, 1972). Thus, the Art of Understanding is not only a meditation on another person's experience, but it offers protection from personalizing insults by seeing through to underlying issues:

1. *You're suggesting my news is unexpected and you want to caution me.* Instead of rephrasing with the usual, "I hear you saying...," a hypnotic video talk is used to narrate verbal process with words like "You're wondering, pointing out, recommending, remembering, hinting, and so on.
2. *It makes sense that you're warning me not to be boring since that is the biggest worry of many people with a fear of public speaking.* The listener validates the speaker's emotional logic whether or not it is reasonable.
3. *You're* surprised *that I was picked and* apprehensive *about how I'll perform.* This is deep listening that requires empathy or seeing into (*em*—Latin) the feelings (*pathos*—Greek) of others.

Hypnosis and Humor

All of the above comments contain elements of hypnosis that bypass resistance and evoke involuntary responses. The third *as-if* response uses humor because an absurd or unexpected connection is made between the cliché of boring people to death and its literal meaning. The examples of a truism, embedded suggestion, bind, and double bind above are outright hypnotic verbiage. More complex evocative language follows.

1. *Keep thinking of all the ways I might mess-up (while presenting), because over-confidence killed the cat.* Advanced hypnotic ploys encourage undesirable behavior in order to place it under the speaker's control. This is called utilization and is more commonly known as reverse psychology. An incorrect cliché subliminally focuses on curiosity, rather than confidence.

2. *While we bite into this scrumptious desert, lets both see if we can* dare *to... remember giving a talk without the bother of worrying.* A serial suggestion starts with an easy, currently occurring behavior and links it to a more difficult task. Dare is a hypnotic word because it draws attention to and challenges the listener to endorse a difficult concept.

3. *When you remember to ... forget about worrying me, you can take another bite of this delicious dessert.* An implied directive is the opposite of a serial suggestion. A command (*forget about worrying me*) is tied to an easy, almost involuntary behavior to signal readiness to comply. Using paired opposites (*remember to forget*) sneaks in a suggestion by focusing on one end of the polarity.

The four tactics, Acting-As-If, Asking Questions, Active Listening, and Humor and Hypnosis, can be remembered by the acronym AAAH. It suggests an expression that breathes enlightenment into any tense moment. Responding to difficult people with casual comments offers a shortcut to self esteem and empowerment. However, when people are overwhelmed with a cacophony of inner voices, they may not be able to execute these maneuvers.

II. Teaching Clients to Deal With Distressing Thoughts

Madelyn came to counseling under the onus of dealing with a hypercritical mother who had recently chastised her for not helping with a family barbecue. Simply attempting to role-play the words, "You sound upset with me," had triggered a flood of tears and such thoughts as—*The entire welfare of the family depends on me; I cannot trust my own judgment; My mom knows what is best for me*; and so on (Cohen-Posey, 2008b).

Even the frenemy's remark in Part I is suspect. Few people have friends of any sort who would express amazement that they were speaking at a conference and caution them not to be boring. Those ideas are more likely to have been generated by an inner critic that rambles in a non-stop fashion:

I can't believe they picked me to speak... I'll probably bore everyone... Maybe I won't make any sense... What if I won't be able to answer people's questions... They might think my ideas are too far out... and on and on.

It would seem that cognitive therapy would be the treatment of choice to confront these automatic thoughts. However, this approach uses the person of the therapist to challenge disturbing ideas and restructure them. Semi-hypnotic self-talk begins in a similar fashion by identifying faulty thinking, but three intermediary steps are taken to distance people from their beliefs before addressing them.

Distancing People From Disturbing Thoughts

1. *Speaking in the second person.* Non-stop (subvocal) monologues like the ones above are voiced in the first person. We mistake our thoughts for ourselves. The first step to creating distance is to rephrase disturbing thoughts in the second person. *I'll bore everyone* becomes *You'll bore everyone.* Thoughts turn into objects to be faced.
2. *Naming thoughts.* Turning thoughts into objects poses the questions: What or who are these mental elements that are being faced? They are easily recognized by such names as Inner Critic, People Pleaser, or Terrorist that cries, "What if this..., What if that..."
3. *Representing thoughts.* Once thoughts have been isolated and have an identity, they can be further objectified with images and everyday items. Edvard Munch's famous painting, *The Scream*, is a perfect portrait for an Inner Terrorist that predicts catastrophes. A Halloween witch can symbolize an Inner Critic and a cute stuffed puppy dog can stand for a People Pleaser. When all else fails, an emoticon such as /8-[can portray a pushy inner voice saying, *"You haven't done enough."*

Once these steps have been taken, a person has begun to dis-identify from disturbing thoughts. Roberto Assagioli, the founder of Psychosynthesis (1965/2000) said people are ruled by the things with which they identify (their thoughts). They can control inner voices from which they dis-identify.

Identifying with Resourceful Thought Processes

When the bond between beliefs and Being is broken, one's true identity can be revealed. *I think, therefore I am*, becomes, *I have thoughts and I AM the observer of those thoughts.* This is the *I AM* that is the witness of distressing thoughts. It is an inner resource that can mindfully observe beliefs and make inquiries for the sake of curiosity, not to force change. Therapists begin to help clients discover this inner resource with three steps.

1. *Asking questions* to recognize resourceful thought processes. Have you ever heard a still small voice that kept you going in the midst of a crisis? When have you been surprised by your courage, calm, or creativity? Tell me about that. What has helped you get through your worst moments?
2. *Representing thinking processes* that are observant, intuitive, reasonable, flexible, and compassionate with illustrations or figures. Images can easily be found and printed with a Google image search: *The Hands of God and Man* (Michelangelo), the Scales of Justice, a soaring eagle, a flowering rose, or the yin/yang symbol. The curious, unflappable Winnie the Pooh wonderfully embodies Being that just IS (Hoff, 1982). Angels or a compass can symbolize guiding spirits.
3. *Naming Thinking Processes.* Clients can readily find words to label these thinking processes—Knower, Reason, Intuition, Witness, Observer, or Presence. When all else fails, the words *True Self* or *Self* can be used to distinguish the originator of compassionate observations and inquiries from thoughts that criticize, warn, and pressure.

Hypnotic Observations and Inquiries

The stage is now set to coach clients to make observations and inquiries that en-trance disturbing thoughts. A negative thought has been re-worded in the second person: *You'll bore everyone.* Perhaps it comes from a fretful, piglet part. The counselor can ask this person's "Knower" to go inside and silently say to the fretful part, *You're making a prediction that gives Kate a tight stomach.* This is the same as the <u>narrating verbal processes</u> tactic under active listening in Part I. The consequence of the maladaptive thought is also pointed out. This hypnotic video-talk feeds back exactly what is happening in order to establish credibility and rapport, and to narrow a person's focus of attention. A constricted focus of attention is one definition of trance (O'Hanlon, 1992). The client reports back anything she hears from within.

To further the dialogue, the Knower can ask the fretful part questions: *What is the chance of everyone being bored? Where do you think that worry comes from? Would anything bad happen if you stopped giving Kate warnings? Are you trying to help?* Questions continue a focused inward search. At some point clients will report that they do not hear anything, which is usually experienced as relief from constant mind chatter. It is important that questions and observations suggested by counselors be repeated silently by clients. Subvocal verbiage energizes the frontal lobes of the cortex that become dominant during meditation (Cohen-Posey, 2008a). The following is an example of a dialogue that unfolded with a young, overweight girl that we'll call Chyanne. Responses for the Self were suggested by her counselor:

Shy Part: *People are always looking at you in the lunch room.*
Self: What's bad about people looking at Chyanne?
Part: *They're judging her.*
Self: What are their judgments?
Part: *They think she is stupid and a waste of space.*

Self: That's pretty harsh. Do you look to see if they're scowling as they judge? …. You got pretty quiet. Are you OK? Are you going to keep your eyes down or look around and see if people are watching Chyanne?
Part: *Someone has to protect her.*
Self: Are you protecting her or scaring her?
Chyanne: It's quiet for now. That feels better.

Counselor: How do you feel towards that shy part?
Chyanne: I'm tired of her. I start doing better and then she pops up. I wish she'd get over herself.
Counselor: So a controlling part inside is trying to order her to grow up….

The work continues: the object is not to rid Chyanne of her shyness, but to help her recognize the notions that trigger it and to separate those maladaptive beliefs from calming, empowering thought processes. A sure sign of detachment from distressing ideas occurs when they can be looked at with compassion, goodwill, and even humor. Chyanne's counselor will continue to feed her Self observations and inquiries that yield other moments of quiet clarity.

It is apparent that dialogue with disturbing thoughts is different from the casual comments that can quash quarrels in social arenas. The inner bullies of the psychic realm can become tyrants who require a special diplomacy. This is possible once illuminating powers of observation and inquiry are revived.

References

Assagioli, R. (2000/1965). *Psychosynthesis: A collection of basic writings*. Amherst, MA: Synthesis Center.
Bowen, M. (1978). *Family therapy in clinical practice*. Northvale, NJ: Jason Aronson.
Cohen-Posey, K. (2008a). *Empowering dialogues within: A workbook for helping professionals and their clients*. New York: John Wiley & Sons.

Cohen-Posey, K. (2008b). *Making hostile words harmless: A guide to the power of positive speaking for helping professionals and their clients.* New York: John Wiley & Sons.

Hoff, B. (1982). *The Tao of Pooh.* New York: Penguin Books.

Lao Tzu. (1972). *Tao Te Ching* (Vintage Books ed.). New York: Random House.

Linkletter, A. (1945-1970). *House Party.* CBS Corporation.

O'Hanlon, W., & Martin, M. (1992). *Solution-oriented hypnosis: An Erickson approach.* New York: W. W. Norton.

Rogers, C. (1951). *Client-centered therapy: Its current practice, implications, and theory.* Boston: Houghton Mifflin.

Section V

Research and Evaluation

Article 23

Advocating for Minority Clients with Program Evaluation: Five Strategies for Counselors

Paper based on a program presented at the 2007 Association for Counselor Education and
Supervision Conference, October 11-14, Columbus, Ohio.

Randall L. Astramovich and Wendy J. Hoskins

Over the past twenty years, evaluating the outcomes of counseling services has taken a central role in professional counseling practice (Leibert, 2006; Studer, Oberman, & Womack, 2006). Increasingly, counselors working in education and human services settings are expected to demonstrate effectiveness and efficiency in the services they provide to clients. Accountability has therefore become a routine expectation in virtually every counseling specialty. In order to meet accountability demands, counselors have been encouraged to utilize program evaluation methods for systematically planning, implementing, and evaluating outcomes of counseling services (Astramovich, Hoskins, & Coker, 2008). Concurrent with the increased emphasis on evaluating the outcomes of counseling services, multiculturalism, advocacy, and social justice have become major forces in counseling (D'Andrea & Heckman, 2008; Kiselica & Robinson, 2001). Today's professional counselors are expected to have the knowledge and skills to advocate on a client's behalf (Council for Accreditation of Counseling and Related Educational Programs [CACREP], 2008; Lewis, Arnold, House, & Toporek, 2003) and to help clients develop the ability to self-advocate

(Astramovich & Harris, 2007). Major professional counseling organizations including the American Counseling Association (ACA), American School Counselor Association (ASCA), and the American Mental Health Counselors Association (AMHCA) have all endorsed the need for counselors to develop skills to advocate for minority and underserved client populations. In recent years, the specialty of professional school counseling has been particularly active in promoting advocacy among its practitioners (Bemak & Chung, 2005; Hipilito-Delgado & Lee, 2007; Ratts, DeKruyf, Chen-Hayes, 2007; Trusty & Brown, 2005).

Although advocacy has become a major initiative among professional counselors, few concrete advocacy techniques have been developed for counselors to implement (Astramovich & Hoskins, 2008). Some pioneering work in professional school counseling has highlighted the potential of advocacy-based interventions (e.g., Bemak, Chung, & Sirosky-Sabado, 2005). Yet much of the literature on advocacy in counseling is more philosophical or theoretical in nature and may not be easily translated into counseling practice. Counselors who may aspire to advocacy work in counseling need more explicit examples of interventions. Specifically, counseling program evaluation can be an effective and action-oriented advocacy tool for counselors who may be working with minority and underserved client populations.

Overview of Counseling Program Evaluation

Considered a planned and systematic process, counseling program evaluation refers to the ongoing use of evaluation principles to monitor and assess the impact and effectiveness of counseling programs and services (Astramovich et al., 2008; Loesch, 2001). Program evaluation has been identified as an emerging best practice for counselors (Astramovich & Coker, 2007) and it has been featured in frameworks for counseling practice, including the ASCA *National Model* (2005). Counseling program evaluations can help counselors answer multiple questions about their programs and services including how well clients are being helped, what services are most beneficial and effective to various client groups, and what gaps exist in current counseling services. Additionally, from an accountability perspective, program evaluation data can be effective in helping counselors demonstrate the effectiveness and outcomes of their programs to stakeholders (ASCA, 2005; Myrick, 2003; Studer et al., 2006).

Process of Counseling Program Evaluation

Counseling program evaluation can be conceptualized as occurring in two major cycles, one emphasizing the micro-level, or actual counseling services, and the other emphasizing the macro-level, or context of the counseling program. In a school setting, for example, the micro-level of program evaluation examines the specific services and interventions developed and implemented by the school counselor. On the macro-level, program evaluation looks at the impact of school counseling services upon the larger school environment and community. Accountability to stakeholders helps bridge the counseling program with the broader context of the school environment and the community. Ultimately, information gathered from each program evaluation cycle is then used to enhance the counseling services provided to students and their families.

According to Astramovich and Coker (2007), counseling program evaluation involves eight major steps including: 1) needs assessment; 2) identifying service objectives; 3) program planning; 4) program implementation and monitoring; 5) assessing program outcomes; 6) providing accountability to stakeholders; 7) gathering feedback from stakeholders; and, 8) strategic planning. Information gathered during each step in the counseling program evaluation process is used to inform practice and to help with decision making in later steps. For example, needs assessments can help identify specific counseling services that are desired by client populations. Information gathered from needs assessments can then help counselors make decisions about service objectives and specific counseling programs to offer clients. In turn, such program offerings help counselors identify variables for measuring outcomes of services provided to clients. Counseling program evaluation therefore involves a cyclical process of developing, monitoring and refining counseling services with the goal of improving client outcomes.

Advocacy Strategies Using Counseling Program Evaluation

With its focus on systematically collecting and evaluating outcomes information, counseling program evaluation can be strategically used by counselors to advocate for minority client populations and for improved counseling services. Data collected from program evaluations can be used as an effective means to advocate with stakeholders for the resources and support needed to provide services to minority clients. Five advocacy strategies drawn from counseling program evaluation procedures are discussed below. Each strategy is based on a major step in the counseling program evaluation process.

Advocacy Strategy 1: Identifying Unique Needs of Minority Populations

Conducting needs assessments specifically with minority or underserved clients can help pinpoint the unique concerns of these populations. A primary means of advocating for minority clients involves an accurate understanding of the socio-political and cultural factors that influence their development (Lewis et al., 2003). Needs assessments can help counselors become more knowledgeable about the various issues faced by minorities and help counselors develop services that are targeted to address these issues. For example, a community mental health counselor working in an urban community agency may be interested in identifying the primary concerns of lesbian, gay, bisexual, transgender, and questioning (LGBTQ) clients seeking counseling services with the agency. Using a brief needs assessment questionnaire, the counselor may find that relationship issues are the most frequently cited concern of this population. In order to address these needs more specifically, the counselor could then advocate that the community agency implement a relationship counseling group for its LGBTQ clients.

Advocacy Strategy 2: Addressing Barriers to Accessing Counseling Services

A primary way counselors can advocate for minority and underserved client populations is to identify and address barriers to accessing counseling services. Minority clients may face many challenges to seeking counseling help including limited financial resources, travel difficulties, and the stigma associated with seeking help for mental health issues (Overton & Medina, 2008). Other barriers to accessing counseling services may be culturally based (e.g., not seeking help outside the family unit) or related to broader socio-political oppressive practices faced by minorities (Astramovich & Harris, 2007). Counselors need to be culturally knowledgeable and sensitive when addressing barriers to access, yet they must also be proactive in addressing issues which may not have been championed by other professionals (Bemak & Chung, 2008). For example, an urban school counselor recognizes that for an after-school parenting skills program to be successful, transportation and child care issues will need to be addressed. The counselor surveys parents interested in the program to determine ways the school can help them make arrangements to participate. The school counselor then reports the data to the school administration to garner resources for creating on-site child-care options and creating a car pooling network.

Advocacy Strategy 3: Developing Targeted Counseling Services

Counseling services offered to majority populations may be inappropriate or ineffective in addressing the concerns of minority clients. Counselors can advocate for minority and underserved client groups by developing interventions that target the specific needs of these populations. In order to be effective advocates, counselors must be active in creating opportunities for clients through their counseling services (Ratts et al., 2007). For instance, a career counselor at a predominately Caucasian state university might expand the career counseling center and develop a mentoring program geared at encouraging minority students to pursue careers in education. Because the field of education is in need of more minority educators, the career counselor's mentoring program could create pathways into education careers for minority students.

Advocacy Strategy 4: Using Descriptive and Outcomes Data

A central component of counseling program evaluation involves the collection and analysis of data about the success of counseling services and interventions. From an advocacy perspective, descriptive and outcomes data can be a powerful tool for highlighting the needs of minority clients and in demonstrating the success of services provided to minority populations (ASCA, 2005; Gysbers, 2004). Descriptive data can be used to identify gaps in services or specific challenges faced by minority clients. In a school setting, a counselor might use descriptive data to show administrators the disproportionate number of minority students who are enrolled in advanced placement classes and to then advocate for developing opportunities and support for minority students to take advanced placement coursework. Outcome data about the program's eventual success could then be presented at a school board meeting in order to advocate for a district-wide implementation of the program.

Advocacy Strategy 5: Garnering Stakeholder Support & Resources for Counseling Services

A common goal of counseling program evaluation and advocacy efforts is to generate stakeholder support for specific counseling services and interventions. Information gathered at each stage of the counseling program evaluation process can be strategically used to help promote stakeholder support and generate resources for programs. As discussed by Astramovich and Coker (2007), accountability to stakeholders should be a proactive, rather than reactive, process. Counselors can actively advocate for minority clients by developing accountability reports and making presentations to stakeholder groups which highlight successes and continued needs for the sustainability of counseling services. For example, a community counseling agency which has been funded by a grant to develop and implement an aftercare program for people in recovery from substance abuse, might use outcomes data to help demonstrate the initial effectiveness of the program. Based on the promising results, counselors at the agency could then seek additional grant funding to expand the program and offer targeted services for minority clients needing additional aftercare services.

Recommendations and Conclusion

Counseling program evaluation has great potential for use as an advocacy tool by professional counselors. Generally, counselors express an interest in conducting program evaluations; however they frequently report having very limited training or experience in evaluation methods (Astramovich, Coker, & Hoskins, 2005). Likewise, counselors generally aspire to adopt advocacy and social justice philosophies in their practice, yet may fail to do so because of concerns about creating too much conflict within their work setting (Bemak & Chung, 2008) or because it is difficult for them to identify specific advocacy interventions they might utilize (Astramovich & Hoskins, 2008).

In order to address these concerns, counselor educators should help counselors develop strong evaluation and advocacy skills during their graduate level training in order to help new professionals meet the continued calls to be advocates for minority clients. Furthermore, major professional counseling organizations should develop conferences and workshops that help practicing counselors put program evaluation and advocacy theory into practice. One approach to helping counselors actualize advocacy and social justice philosophy involves the active use of program evaluation methods in their counseling practice. Finally, professional counselors should seek opportunities for furthering their knowledge and skills in counseling program evaluation and advocacy by attending and presenting at professional conferences and by seeking mentors and supervisors who may help guide their development of these skills.

In conclusion, counseling program evaluation and advocacy have separately been major initiatives within professional counseling. Each offers important foundations from which counselors in the twenty-first century aspire to practice. Ultimately, by joining the philosophies of advocacy and social justice with the practical steps of program evaluation, counselors can address barriers to access and actively promote the provision of effective counseling services to minority and underserved client populations.

References

American School Counselor Association. (2005). *The ASCA national model: A framework for school counseling programs* (2nd ed.). Alexandria, VA: Author.

Astramovich, R. L., & Coker, J. K. (2007). Program evaluation: The Accountability Bridge model for counselors. *Journal of Counseling & Development, 85*, 162-172.

Astramovich, R. L., Coker, J. K., & Hoskins, W. J. (2005). Training school counselors in program evaluation. *Professional School Counseling, 9*, 49-54.

Astramovich, R. L., & Harris, K. R. (2007). Promoting self-advocacy among minority students in school counseling. *Journal of Counseling & Development, 85*, 269-276.

Astramovich, R. L., & Hoskins, W. J. (2008, October). Advocacy evaluation: Using program evaluation to advocate for minority client populations. Paper presented at the meeting of the Rocky Mountain Association for Counselor Education and Supervision, Breckenridge, CO.

Astramovich, R. L., Hoskins, W. J., & Coker, J. K. (2008). *The Accountability Bridge: A model for evaluating school counseling programs.* Dubuque, IA: Kendall-Hunt.

Bemak, F., & Chung, R. C. Y. (2005). Advocacy as a critical role for urban school counselors: Working toward equity and social justice. *Professional School Counseling, 8*, 196-202.

Bemak, F., Chung, R. C. Y., & Sirosky-Sabado, L. A. (2005). Empowerment Groups for Academic Success (EGAS): An innovative approach to prevent high school failure for at-risk urban African American girls. *Professional School Counseling, 8,* 377–389.

Bemak, F., & Chung, R. C. Y. (2008). New professional roles and advocacy strategies for school counselors: A multicultural/ social justice perspective to move beyond the nice counselor syndrome. *Journal of Counseling & Development, 86,* 372-382.

Council for Accreditation of Counseling and Related Educational Programs. (2008). *CACREP 2009 standards.* Retrieved October 1, 2008, from: http://www.cacrep.org/2009standards.html

D'Andrea, M., & Heckman, E. F. (2008). Contributing to the ongoing evolution of the multicultural counseling movement: An introduction to the special issue. *Journal of Counseling & Development, 86,* 259-260.

Gysbers, N. C. (2004). Comprehensive guidance and counseling programs: The evolution of accountability. *Professional School Counseling, 8,* 1-15.

Hipilito-Delgado, C. P., & Lee, C. C. (2007). Empowerment theory for the professional school counselor: A manifesto for what really matters. *Professional School Counseling, 10,* 327-332.

Kiselica, M. S., & Robinson, M. (2001). Bringing advocacy counseling to life: The history, issues, and human dramas of social justice work in counseling. *Journal of Counseling and Development, 79,* 387-397.

Leibert, T. W. (2006). Making change visible: The possibilities in assessing mental health counseling outcomes. *Journal of Counseling & Development, 84,* 108-113.

Lewis, J., Arnold, M. S., House, R., & Toporek, R. (2003). Advocacy competencies. Retrieved October 1, 2008, from http://www.counseling.org/Publications

Loesch, L. C. (2001). Counseling program evaluation: Inside and outside the box. In D.C. Locke, J. E. Myers, & E. L. Herr (Eds.), *The handbook of counseling* (pp. 513-525). Thousand Oaks, CA: Sage.

Myrick, R. D. (2003). Accountability: Counselors count. *Professional School Counseling, 6*, 174-179.

Overton, S. L., & Medina, S. L. (2008). The stigma of mental illness. *Journal of Counseling & Development, 86*, 143-151.

Ratts, M. J., DeKruyf, L., & Chen-Hayes, S. F. (2007). The ACA advocacy competencies: A social justice advocacy framework for professional school counselors. *Professional School Counseling, 11*, 90-97.

Studer, J. R., Oberman, A. H., & Womack, R. H. (2006). Producing evidence to show counseling effectiveness in the schools. *Professional School Counseling, 9*, 385-391.

Trusty, J., & Brown, D. (2005). Advocacy competencies for professional school counselors. *Professional School Counseling, 8*, 259-265.

Article 24

Psychological First Aid: An Evidence Informed Approach for Acute Disaster Behavioral Health Response

Paper based on a program presented at the 2009 American Counseling Association Annual Conference and Exposition, March 19-23, Charlotte, North Carolina.

Julie A. Uhernik and Marlene A. Husson

Counselors are increasingly called to respond to acute emergency and disaster situations. Immediate counseling interventions in a disaster scenario are by necessity short, population based, and supportive of the natural resiliency of affected individuals and communities. Among a number of response modalities, Psychological First Aid (PFA) is emerging as the preferred response and is now recommended in Federal guidelines as specified in the 2008 National Response Framework (U.S. Department of Homeland Security, 2008). This paper will discuss the origin of PFA, identify eight core concepts of PFA, review current research and evidence-informed practice in Disaster Behavioral Health Response, and direct the counselor towards further training and utilization of components of PFA.

Psychological First Aid is an evidence-informed model utilized in disaster response to assist those impacted in the hours and early days following emergency, disaster, and terrorism. *The Medical Reserve Corp Psychological First Aid Field Operations Training Manual* (National Center for Child Traumatic Stress Network, 2006) stresses that PFA is designed to reduce the initial distress caused by traumatic events, and to foster short- and long-term adaptive functioning and coping. According to the manual, the principles and techniques of PFA meet four basic standards, including: (a) PFA is consistent with research evidence on risk and resilience following trauma; (b) PFA is applicable and practical in field settings; (c) PFA is appropriate to developmental level across the lifespan; and (d) PFA is culturally informed and adaptable. At the most basic level, counselors who utilize the concepts of PFA will assist, through these early contacts, in helping alleviate survivor's painful emotions and promote hope and healing.

A growing number of counselors are becoming involved in disaster response. Counselors are finding that the principles and recommended actions of PFA provide tools and guidance for response efforts. Many counselors are involved in disaster response efforts through organizations such as the American Red Cross, Salvation Army, and other groups. Some counselors are joining community mental health agency teams as they organize to provide community disaster response. A number of counselors and other licensed mental health professionals have joined Medical Reserve Corps (MRC) teams. The Medical Reserve Corps program is fairly new, created in 2002 by the Office of the Surgeon General, United States Public Health Service (2008). There are presently over 400 individual MRC units with over 73,000 members with teams of responders from disciplines including medical, nursing, public health, and mental health professionals. The Medical Reserve Corps has worked in partnership with the National Center for Child Traumatic Stress Network (NCTSN) and National Center for PTSD to develop a Psychological First Aid Field Operations Guide, adapted from the original PFA manual (National Center for Child Traumatic Stress Network, 2006). Their efforts have provided advisory information, research review and given recommendations based upon current research findings. Counselors, whether MRC members or otherwise, need to familiarize themselves with the theory and application of PFA. Many counselors and other mental health professionals have not been trained or updated in disaster mental health and may have a difficult time shifting from conventional clinical practice models to the requirements of disaster behavioral health response. New counselors completing Council for Accreditation of Counseling and Related Educational Programs (CACREP) accredited educational programs will learn the basics of PFA and emerge as practicing counselors with this knowledge. The new CACREP 2009 Standards include clear language and guidance on incorporation of PFA components into the curriculum of accredited higher education programs in counseling. The 2009 Standards include specific PFA references. An example would be under *Helping Relationships, sec g*, programs are to include "crisis intervention, and suicide prevention models, including the use of psychological first aid strategies" (CACREP, 2008). Current counselors will require training in PFA and a paradigm shift to understand that basic PFA concepts and applications are different than "psychotherapy" as many currently practice.

History

In the late 1970s and 80s, disaster responders typically utilized components of a Critical Incident Stress Management (CISM) model developed originally for military use. This model was expanded on, and subsequently credited to paramedic and EMS Coordinator Jeffrey T. Mitchell, for use by fellow EMS responders. The Mitchell model, as it came to be known, was later widely adopted by police and fire responders for emergency response use. The model included a component called Critical Incident Stress Debriefing (CISD). By the mid 1990s, research protocols began to investigate the efficacy of CISD procedures. The research did not support the efficacy of CISD in reducing symptoms of post-traumatic stress disorder and other trauma related symptoms following disaster (Van Emmerik, Kamphuis, Hulsbosch, & Emmelkamp, 2002). Debriefing models that included a cathartic ventilation of feelings and emotion in particular were shown to potentially cause harm and re-traumatization of survivors and first responders. In general, the research showed that CISD participants initially indicated satisfaction with the immediate experience of debriefing within the CISM system. However, further outcome and follow-up studies indicated that this form of early intervention had the potential to actually increase the signs and symptoms of Post Traumatic Stress Disorder as well as Major Depression (Raphael, Meldrum, & McFarlane, 1995; Rose, Bisson, Churchill, & Wessely, 2008; Van Emmerik et al., 2002).

In response to growing concerns, experts at the Center for the Study of Traumatic Stress met to compile new guidelines for behavioral health response that would help to standardize and clarify effective response efforts. At the same time, new studies on the concept of individual and community resiliency determined that the majority of people post disaster do not go on to develop PTSD and other trauma-related mental health sequelae (Reissman, Klomp, Kent, & Pfefferbaum, 2004). Specific components of natural resiliency and supportive functions were identified and developed into the concepts of Psychological First Aid we have today.

PFA Components

Psychological First Aid (PFA) is a structured intervention that has been developed over the past few years to replace the various forms of "psychological debriefings." Reference to the development of PFA can be found in the *Field Operations Guide for Psychological First Aid* published by the National Center for Child Traumatic Stress Network and National Center for PTSD (2006).

Psychological First Aid includes a set of eight interventions that can be used to support survivors after a disaster or traumatizing event. These eight core actions and focus goals include:

1. *Contact and Engagement.* The goal is to respond to survivors and to engage in a non-intrusive and supportive manner.
2. *Safety and Comfort.* The goal is to help meet immediate safety needs and to provide emotional comfort.
3. *Stabilization.* The goal is to reduce stress caused by a traumatic event.

4. *Information Gathering.* The goal is to assess the immediate needs of the survivors.
5. *Practical Assistance.* The goal is to create an environment where the survivor can begin to problem solve.
6. *Connection with Social Supports.* The goal is to assist survivors to connect or re-connect with primary support systems.
7. *Coping Information.* The goal is to offer verbal and written information on coping skills and the concept of resilience in the face of disaster.
8. *Linkage with Collaborative Services.* The goal is to inform survivors of services that are available to them.

Current Research

As outcome data on previous disaster response methods began to surface, a closer scrutiny of efficacy and effectiveness of existing methodology began. This resulted in the need for re-consideration of current response focus and the development of evidence driven theory and approach. The National Center for Child Traumatic Stress Network and National Center for PTSD formed a collaborative team to begin a systematic review of existing data on various components of disaster behavioral health response. When research pointed to efficacy of various individual components (i.e., the importance of contact and engagement, or of fostering social support systems), the team was able to formulate new recommendations that collectively formed eight basic actions of what has become known as Psychological First Aid. This collaboration led to the development of the PFA Field Operations Guide (2006). The beauty of PFA is that it can be used in any location where trauma survivors may be found; it is ideal for immediate response and for the practical administration in field settings. PFA supports the concept of resiliency, in individuals and in communities, which encourages self-efficacy and decreases victimization and dependency. While there is a continuing need for evaluation and research of the application of

PFA principles, the development of Random Controlled Trials (RCTs) in a spontaneous disaster environment poses numerous ethical and research obstacles. Nevertheless, research efforts continue to provide further support on the overall efficacy of PFA. According to Ruzek (2007), "There is a great need for both program evaluation and RCTs that will evaluate the effectiveness of Psychological First Aid principles in a number of contexts" (p. 5). The basic premise of PFA is to support individual and community resiliency, to reduce acute distress following disaster, and encourage short and long term adaptive functioning. Napoli (2007), outlines the characteristics of resiliency to include "inquisitiveness, optimal optimism, active coping and problem-solving, effectiveness despite being fearful, emotional self-regulation, bonding for a common mission, positive self-concept, internal control, desire to improve oneself, altruism, social support, the ability to turn traumatic helplessness into learned helpfulness, humor and meaning" (p. 2). PFA promotes these concepts of resilience among disaster survivors. For disaster responders, the principles of PFA honor the adage of Primum non nocere or 'First Do No Harm' as an appropriate initial guide for the application of PFA.

Applications of PFA

The concept of Psychological First Aid has evolved to make PFA applicable for working with specific subgroups of individuals who may have special needs during a disaster. Some of these subgroups include children and adolescents, first responders, groups of disaster survivors, the military and their families and those who may require additional assistance beyond PFA.

There is a recognized need for use of appropriate disaster responses with children and adolescents, based upon the increasing recognition of PTSD in children (Pfefferbaum, 1997). The core concepts of PFA are applicable for working directly with vulnerable populations of children and adolescents in disasters. PFA assists families by providing safety and comfort, by supporting a calm environment of adults who are better able to care for and aid their children, and assisting in connecting with social supports and community resources. Further, the extent to which counselors can provide assistance and support to parents can make a critical difference in post-disaster functioning for many families. While there is an ongoing need for research in this area, the PFA manual draws on the available research to provide responders with specific and effective tools which focus on this population.

First Responders are an often overlooked population that may benefit from the application of PFA principals. According to Phillips and Kane (2006), PFA is considered "best practice" for intervention with First Responders in the aftermath of a disaster. First Responders have unique needs for support following a disaster. For example, First Responders operate under a "Mission First" perspective placing the group goals and focus ahead of the individual. First Responders knowingly enter into traumatic situations in order to assist others in need. The basic principles of PFA can be applied as appropriate support for First Responders. For example, the PFA action of 'connection with social supports' could be extended to the First Responder by the encouragement of buddy care and peer support following the trauma of disaster response. The PFA action of 'safety and comfort' can include providing information on and encouragement of self-care behaviors for First Responders.

Psychological First Aid basic tenets have now been incorporated into a training course designed to reach out to military families. As the use of PFA has been shown to be effective in promoting resilience and increasing healthy coping in the face of disaster, a training course entitled "Coping with Deployment / Psychological First Aid for Military Families" (2008) has been developed collaboratively by the American Red Cross and Armed Forces Department. This new course will enable military family members to provide emotional support for themselves and outreach to other military families.

Another area of PFA application includes a focus on developing "Secondary Psychological Assistance" as follow-up to identified higher-risk subgroups who might benefit from more specialized and subsequent therapeutic support. According to Ruzek (2007), Secondary Psychological Assistance will provide "additional interventions focused on psychoeducation, developing and practicing coping skills and a greater focus upon promoting calmness, connectedness, self and collective efficacy and hope" (p. 9).

Research into the utilization of theoretic approaches such as CBT after the immediate phase of the disaster is being explored (Ruzek, 2006). Adapting PFA theory to a small group format is being considered. According to Everly, Phillips, Kane and Feldman (2006), "clinically, it may be argued that in situations where groups of individuals were exposed to the same amplitude and chronicity of traumatic exposure, there may be strong rationale for implementing PFA practices in that natural homogeneous cohort" (p. 2).

Finally, the concepts behind PFA are being extended to apply to international disaster relief efforts, bringing to bear PFA tenets of support and resiliency of the individual and communities throughout the world (Van Ommeran, Saxena, & Saraceno, 2005).

Recommendations for the Counselor

As Psychological First Aid has become the recommended evidence-driven disaster response, and as the call for counselor expertise in disaster response continues to grow, counselors should familiarize themselves with Psychological First Aid. The counselor should understand how disaster behavioral health response fits into the larger disaster response system by review of the National Incident Management System (NIMS) and the operational management and structure of the Incident Command System (ICS). Basic level ICS courses are available online through http://training.fema.gov/IS/crslist.asp. In addition, disaster field response trainings that include PFA can be taken through agencies or groups such as the American Red Cross and local or state public health departments. Counselors in all settings will need to become familiar with PFA, whether they are new to counseling or are veteran counselors. Recognition of the unique approach of PFA and incorporating PFA tenets may initially challenge the counselor with a paradigm shift, but ultimately bolster the assistance role of the counselor to reach out to populations in their time of greatest need.

References

American Red Cross. (2008). *Coping with deployments--PFA for military families. Training guide and manual.* Washington, DC: Author.

Council for Accreditation of Counseling and Related Educational Programs. (2008). *2009 CACREP standards.* Retrieved Oct 1, 2008, from www.cacrep.org/2009standards. html

Everly, G. S., Phillips, S. B., Kane, D., & Feldman, D. (2006). Introduction to and overview of group psychological first aid. *Brief Treatment and Crisis Intervention, 6*(2), 130-136. Retrieved October 2008 from http://brief-treatment.oxford journals.org

Napoli, J. C. (2007) *Resiliency, resilience, resilient: A paradigm shift?* Retrieved September 18, 2008, from www.resiliency.us

National Center for Child Traumatic Stress Network and National Center for PTSD, U.S. Department of Veterans Affairs. (2006). *Psychological first aid: field operations guide* (2nd ed.). Retrieved October 28, 2007 from http://www.ncptsd.va. gov/ncmain/index.jsp

Office of the U.S. Surgeon General. (2008). Office of the Civilian Volunteer, Medical Reserve Corps. Retrieved from http://www.medicalreservecorps.gov/About

Pfefferbaum, B. (1997). Posttraumatic stress disorder in children: A review of the past 10 years. *Journal of the Academy of Child and Adolescent Psychiatry, 36*, 1503-1511.

Phillips, S. B., & Kane, D. (2006). *Guidelines for working with first responders (firefighters, police, emergency medical service and military) in the aftermath of disaster.* New York: American Group Psychotherapy Association. Retrieved from http://www. agpa.org/events/index.html

Raphael, B., Meldrum, L., & McFarlane, A.C. (1995). Does debriefing after psychological trauma work? *British Medical Journal, 310,* 1479-1480.

Reissman, D. B., Klomp, R. W., Kent, A. T., & Pfefferbaum, B. (2004). Exploring psychological resilience in the face of terrorism. *Psychiatric Annals, 34*(8), 626-632.

Rose, S., Bisson, J., Churchill, R, Wessely, S. (2008). Psychological debriefing for preventing post traumatic stress disorder (PTSD). *Cochrane Database of Systematic Reviews* 2002, Issue 2.

Ruzek, J. I. (2006). Bringing cognitive-behavioral psychology to bear on early intervention with trauma survivors. In V. M. Follette & J. I. Ruzek (Eds.), *Cognitive-behavioral therapies for trauma,* 2nd ed. (pp.433-462). New York: Guilford Press.

Ruzek, J. I. (2007). Psychological first aid. *Journal of Mental Health Counseling 29*(1), 17-33.

U.S. Department of Homeland Security. (2008) National Response Framework. Retrieved October 2008, from www.fema.gov/emergency/nrf/

Van Emmerik, A. A. P., Kamphuis, J. H., Hulsbosch, A. M., Emmelkamp, P. M. G. (2002). Single session debriefing after psychological trauma: a meta-analysis. *The Lancet 360,* 766-771.

Van Ommeran, M., Saxena, S., & Saraceno, B. (2005). Mental and social health during and after acute emergencies: Emerging consensus. *Bulletin of the World Health Organization 83*(1) Retrieved September 18, 2008, from http://www.who.int/en/

Article 25

Reconnecting Science to Practice: An Innovative Model for Supporting a Counseling Research Identity

Paper based on a program presented at the 2007 Association for Counselor Education and Supervision Conference, October 11-14, Columbus, Ohio.

James M. Devlin, Robert L. Smith, Stephen Southern, and Richard Ricard

Within the converging identities of the 21st century counselor and counselor educator lays the focus of a research identity. Traditionally and contemporarily the counseling field has placed great emphasis on empiricism as a vehicle of academic training, which illustrates the underlying reciprocal role that practice and research share (Murdock, 2006). Complimenting this paradigm, the Council for Accreditation of Counseling and Related Education Programs (CACREP, 2001) encourages counselors to develop an understanding of research methods, program evaluations, and statistical analyses. However, as the role of the counselor educator and counselor has changed in response to the fluid nature of the field, so does the change occur in establishing and redefining a research identity.

Reformulating a research identity arrives at a time in the counseling profession when the incongruence between counseling and research has gained salient attention (e.g., Bishop & Bieschke, 1998; Borders & Bloss, 1994; Lundervold & Belwood, 2000; O'Brien, 1995; Okech, Astramovich, Johnson, Hoskins, & Rubel, 2006; Reisetter et al., 2004). The factors contributing to the divergence between counseling and research have been suggested to stem from the humanistic identity inherent in counseling (Reisetter et al., 2004). Moreover, current research practices and methodologies may represent an impractical area of research informed practice (Lundervold & Belwood, 2004; Murdock, 2006). These discrepancies may lead to the further estrangement of practitioners from traditional methods of epistemology and thus reinforce the boundaries between both disciplines (Murdock, 2006; Reisetter et al., 2004).

However, in the face of these identity challenges, the field of counseling has attempted to answer these schismatic concerns. As the field of postmodernism expands within the profession, certain research methodologies offer an insight into capturing a constructivist epistemology. The increase of qualitative research designs provides counselors with the opportunity to utilize a vast amount of research methods, which may reconnect practice and research (Hanson, Creswell, Clark, Petska, & Creswell, 2005; Reisetter et al., 2004). Concurrently, mixed-method paradigms, which combine the strategies of both quantitative and qualitative methods, offer a new avenue of research adherence (Hanson et al., 2005). However, it should be noted that one method or the combination of methods should not be conceptualized as providing the best solution for the chosen research method, but rather the research question should guide the selection of the research design (Hanson et al., 2005).

Furthermore, researchers have attempted to identify the various factors associated with counselor research productivity and the interaction of these variables to increase research productivity. Findings suggest that the interplay amongst research-related variables has been illustrated through a suggested person and environment fit (e.g., Brown, Lent, Ryan, & McPartland, 1996; Gelso, 2006; Gelso, Mallinckrodt, & Judge, 1996; Kahn & Scott, 1997; Mallinckrodt & Gelso, 2002). The influence of these person and environmental variables either directly or indirectly predicts subsequent research productivity (i.e., publications, presentations, etc.). The conceptualization of how these variables interact may be best understood through a reciprocal path analysis.

The use of a path analysis model illustrates the causal paths of predictive variables (i.e., independent variables) and their effect on research productivity (i.e., dependent variable). In addition, the path analysis provides the opportunity to view how the predictive variables are indirectly influenced by their effect on research productivity. Specifically, the research training environment offers itself as one of the major variables associated with research productivity. Gelso (2006) proposed that the graduate training environment is the most suitable atmosphere in which to shape and guide the research attitudes of students. Moreover, Gelso suggested that early exposure and integration of students into research is critical for training and subsequent productivity.

The purpose of the present paper is to describe an innovative research organization which specifically addresses the role of counseling and research. The organization, known as the Counselor Education Research Consortium (CERC), represents a counseling society that is dedicated to creating a positive and reinforcing environment intended to foster the research identity of counselors. The creation of CERC brings faculty and counseling students together in a collaborative effort to increase research productivity and research self-efficacy in counseling students, as well as support research agendas of counseling faculty. Consequently, the article's authors expound the mission and structure, intended benefits, and implications of CERC. It is the hope of this article that through the creation of such a society, the reconnection of research and practice can be obtained, supported, and maintained.

Mission and Structure of CERC

CERC's mission is to promote the scholarly productivity of research as well as increase individuals' research self-efficacy. CERC has been established in the Counselor Education Program at Texas A&M University-Corpus Christi. The development of CERC was driven primarily by the positive variables (e.g., research productivity, connectedness, etc.) associated with the creation of a research training environment (Gelso, 2006). Moreover, one of the longstanding visions of CERC is the facilitation of the professional development and support of a research counseling identity. These long term goals are intended to be accomplished through the collaborative efforts of faculty and counseling students, which in turn may create a positive cascade of events that support the practitioner as well as the investigator identity of counselors.

CERC's structure is grounded within a developmental trajectory which identifies individuals in their current research-related abilities and acts to encourage these individuals to participate in research focus groups. Although the developmental progression of research skills is inherent within the structure of CERC, so is the sense of equality. Equality creates and fosters an environment of collaboration and positive reinforcement. These concepts provide individuals within the group the opportunity to be active within the organization as well as develop their research abilities. Furthermore, the essential elements of CERC's foundation are the creation of a non-threatening and reinforcing environment.

CERC's operation provides individuals with the opportunity to develop research focus groups within the main organization. These focus groups operate in order to identify potential research interests and avenues of exploration. Agreed upon group facilitators work to establish a research agenda in order to provide a tentative timeline for the completion of the various components of the agreed upon research. Group members additionally develop a provisional agreement between members regarding areas of delegated work and authorship concerns. It is essential for the smaller focus groups of CERC to establish these informal bylaws in order to promote and maintain ethical research considerations.

Upon completion of these agenda items, the focus groups meet with the entirety of CERC and present the areas of interest. The executive committee of the group consists of elected representatives (e.g., faculty advisors, president, etc.). These representatives facilitate the functional meetings of CERC to open discussions regarding focus groups' research and provide a collaborative environment for feedback and additional considerations.

CERC's executive board primarily functions in order to foster the creation of focus groups as well as support the research endeavors of these entities. Furthermore, the executive board functions within a mediating role in order to resolve possible communication and interpersonal problems. Members of CERC have the opportunity to be actively involved in the structural components of the organization (i.e., elections, voting, etc.) as well as offer feedback to the executive board. As with any organization, the development and function of the elected officials provides structure and governance for the collective; however, in the essence of counseling, these structures are open for change and improvement.

Another component of CERC which offers itself to its innovative properties is the area of technology. CERC operates on the World Wide Web and is accessible for registration to individuals who are interested in research collaboration. The web site operates as a registration based foundation that allows individuals the opportunity to obtain usernames and passwords, as well as identify areas of research interest. Upon completion of registration, individuals have the opportunity to search the web site database according to research interests, locations, and universities. The ability to search according to research interests provides a connection between individuals from virtually any location to others who share similar interests. The result of such an association offers the ability to develop international, national, and regional projects and data sharing.

Intended Benefits of CERC

CERC offers a vast amount of systemic benefits that operate in order to enhance the research training environment and productivity of counseling departments. Furthermore, the benefits of CERC are not limited to those areas related to research but rather have far reaching effects. The creation of a positive and structured environment that brings students and faculty together provides a greater sense of connectedness. Additionally, the opportunity to develop mentoring relationships may be obtained among faculty, advanced students, and novice students. Mentoring opportunities may be formed within the research organization; however, the effects of such relationships may be carried over to other areas of counselor preparation as well as faculty and pre-tenured faculty relationships.

CERC provides the opportunity for students to overcome a previous fear of research as well as to increase enthusiasm for research. The modeling of supportive behaviors as a function of faculty, and possibly advanced students, provides a necessary form of support for beginning student involvement. The participation of novice counseling students may prove critical to the adoption of research-relevant attitudes as they continue with their career. These attitudes are invaluable for individuals who are only seeking terminal masters' degrees and enter the field as practitioners. Furthermore, CERC provides individuals with the opportunity to have others involved in their thesis and dissertation endeavors. The support offered to complete these projects decreases completion time and strengthens positive attitudes toward these academic hallmarks.

As befits the essence of counseling, CERC also provides members with opportunities to enhance communication and group process skills. Moreover, individuals have the opportunity to become involved in projects they find personally relevant, thus supporting introspective abilities. Individuals can surround themselves with others who support their research identities, thus fostering professional development and networking.

Through involvement in the various components of the research process, CERC members may be exposed to regional and national conferences. The ability to participate within these environments provides increased networking opportunities. Furthermore, based on the agreed upon mission of the focus group, the intended project may result in manuscript submission. These opportunities provide individuals with valuable professional experiences. The intended benefits of CERC's development are far reaching and may be specifically tailored to meet the needs of various departments and universities. CERC's inherent malleability offers individuals the opportunity to shape and guide the organization's impact relevant to their department's mission and vision.

Future Research and Implications

The future research and implications of CERC provide opportunities to identify the longitudinal influence of a structured research-based organization on research productivity. The identification of such influences creates a more thorough understanding of the processes which may foster and support a counseling research identity. CERC's organizational format and the standardized assessments created in order to study related research variables offer additional empirical support for previous research findings. Furthermore, the portability of the CERC organization may make it possible for other counseling departments and institutions to adopt the CERC model for their students and subsequent research may be gathered regarding their reported outcomes.

The collaboration between universities through the development of CERC acts as a catalyst in the counseling profession to adopt the CERC model. The adoption of such a model potentially leads to the recognition of a counseling research identity as being parallel to that of a practitioner identity. The promotion of research through the vehicle of the CERC model leads to the enhancement of counseling and counselor education departments' research productivity. The ramifications of such productivity have beneficial effects for the reconnection of science and practice. The provision of best practices for clients has been traditionally and contemporarily informed by practice, thus suggesting that increased research within the counseling field would greatly contribute to clients' well-being.

It is within the scope of CERC to create a positive environment for students and faculty wishing to pursue similar research interests. The pursuit of such interests grounded within the framework of CERC offers numerous benefits for the professional and personal development of its members. The increased sense of connectedness within counseling departments, as well as between students and faculty, provides a setting to enhance the overall effectiveness in the preparation of counselors. CERC is an organization that strives to support a counseling research identity as well as a sense of community. Mutually, these goals have far reaching implications for the counseling profession and all colleges and universities who wish to join this innovative organization.

References

Bishop, R., & Bieschke, K. (1998). Applying social cognitive theory to interest in research among counseling psychology doctoral students: A path analysis. *Journal of Counseling Psychology, 45*, 182-188.

Borders, D., & Bloss, K. (1994). Helping students apply the scientist-practitioner model: A teaching approach. *Counselor Education & Supervision, 34*, 172-178.

Brown, S., Lent, R., Ryan, N., & McPartland, E. (1996). Self-efficacy as an intervening mechanism between research training environments and scholarly productivity: A theoretical and methodological extension. *The Counseling Psychologist, 24*, 535-544.

Council for Accreditation of Counseling and Related Educational Programs. (2001). The 2001 CACREP standards. Retrieved January 26, 2007, from http://www.counseling.org/2001 standards.html

Gelso, C. (2006). On the making of a scientist-practitioner: A theory of research training in professional psychology. *Training and Education in Professional Psychology, S(1)*, 3-16.

Gelso, C., Mallinckrodt, B., & Judge, A. (1996). Research training environment, attitudes toward research and research self-efficacy: The revised research training environment scale. *The Counseling Psychologist, 24*, 304-322.

Hanson, W., Creswell, J., Clark, V., Petska, K., & Creswell, J. D. (2005). Mixed methods research designs in counseling psychology. *Journal of Counseling Psychology, 52*, 224-235.

Kahn, J., & Scott, N. (1997). Predictors of research productivity and science-related career goals among counseling psychology doctoral students. *The Counseling Psychologist, 25(1)*, 38-67.

Lundervold, D., & Belwood, M. (2000). The best kept secret in counseling: Single-case (n=1) experimental designs. *Journal of Counseling & Development, 78*, 92-102.

Mallinckrodt, B., & Gelso, C. (2002). Impact of research training environment and Holland personality type: A 15-year follow-up of research productivity. *Journal of Counseling Psychology, 49(1)*, 60-70.

Murdock, N. (2006). On science-practice integration in everyday life: A plea for theory. *The Counseling Psychologist, 34*, 548-569.

O'Brien, K. (1995). Enhancing research training for counseling students: Interuniversity collaborative research teams. *Counselor Education & Supervision, 34*, 187-199.

Okech, J., Astramovich, R., Johnson, M., Hoskins, W., & Rubel, D. (2006). Doctoral research training of counselor education faculty. *Counselor Education & Supervision, 46*, 131-145.

Reisetter, M., Korcuska, J., Yexley, M., Bonds, D., Nikets, H., & McHenry, W. (2004). Counselor educators and qualitative research: Affirming a research identity. *Counselor Education & Supervision, 44*(1), 2-16.

Article 26

The Role of Evidence-Based Therapy Programs in the Determination of Treatment Effectiveness

Paper based on a program presented at the 2009 American Counseling Association Annual Conference and Exposition, March 19-23, Charlotte, North Carolina.

Paul L. West and Judith Warchal

The call for greater accountability in counseling has resulted in attempts to include outcomes research as a component of clinical treatment. "Evidence-Based Practice" has become an accepted term used to describe the integration of research and practice. First used by a Canadian medical group to describe "evidence-based medicine" (Evidence-Based Medicine Working Group, 1992), a widely accepted definition for use in the human services was developed by Gibbs (2003) who stated: "evidence based practitioners adopt a process of lifelong learning that involves continually posing specific questions of direct practical importance to clients, searching objectively and efficiently for the current best evidence relative to each question, and taking appropriate action guided by evidence" (p. 60). This definition has been used by the American Psychological Association to develop a list of empirically validated treatments that "have been referenced by a number of local, state, and federal funding agencies, which are beginning to restrict reimbursement to these treatments" (Levant, 2005). The consequences associated with the rush to adopt empirically supported treatments without careful consideration for the clinical utility of the treatment, the professional expertise of the counselor, and the unique characteristics of the clients, are serious and will impact the future of the profession. Although practitioners may be well-meaning, not all interventions are effective and some may be harmful (Rubin & Babbie, 2005).

Greater emphasis on accountability in the human services has encouraged counselors to consider methods to support their clinical decisions with research initiatives. The American Counseling Association (ACA) *Code of Ethics* (2005) stops short of requiring professional counselors to actively engage in formal outcomes research activities to support their clinical services, but specific codes are present that promote greater accountability. Sections A.1.c and C.2.d specifically call for professional counselors to pay attention to the issue of counseling effectiveness; section C.2.a requires counselors to practice within the boundaries of their competence; and section C.2.f requires counselors to "acquire and maintain a reasonable level of awareness of current scientific and professional information in their fields of activity." These codes lay the foundation for the evolution of evidence-based counseling practices among professionals with appropriate training and experience.

The transition from laboratory to practice is not without controversy. The difference between treatment efficacy and clinical effectiveness with actual clients who present with a broad range of co-occurring disorders is yet to be established. Borckardt et al. (2008) suggest that a case-based timed-series research approach has many benefits over the use of group research initiatives, the predominant feature of randomized clinical trials (RCTs). Messer (2004) questions whether RCTs and experimental, single-case studies yield more useful information than philosophical outlook, theory, other research sources, and practical experience on which most practitioners rely. Sharpley (2007) cites numerous studies that suggest the use of RCTs to guide the development of preferred counseling approaches is inappropriate and leads to inaccurate results when applied to practice.

Controversy over effectiveness measures in the human services has led to the emergence and promotion of evidence-based practices that attempt to merge research with practice and demonstrate some level of accountability to the public. However, are counselors to provide services that are strictly objective and data based or purely subjective and experience based (Messer, 2004)?

Rubin (2007) defines evidence-based practitioners as "those who use scientific evidence to guide their own practice and who conduct or participate in evaluations of their own practice or programs" (p. 290). However, in practice the use of the term "scientific evidence" seems to cover a broad range of research approaches, some of which represent more rigorous application of research methodologies than others.

The Continuum of Evidence-Based Practices

It is tenable to assume that all counseling is evidence-based. Some counselors may pursue a course of treatment based on intuition anchored by their experiences with clients with similar characteristics while others may choose a treatment approach based on research found in the literature that recommends certain clinical approaches with clients with certain disorders. Still others may choose to make clinical decisions based on formal, site-based outcomes research activities. This range in the rationale supporting clinical decision making forms a continuum based on research rigor.

At one end of the scale, counselors depend largely on intuition which is often influenced by their training and experience. This includes the "clinical impressions" often cited in discharge summaries providing an evaluation of a client's progress. Such impressions are often supported by references to in-session observations, client self-reports, and feedback from clients regarding the benefits of therapy.

Further along this continuum are counselors who depend on their training and experience and incorporate programs of study that have been developed to increase a client's knowledge base or awareness level of a particular clinical problem. Gains in knowledge or awareness are subsequently considered evidence of counseling effectiveness.

Other counselors depend on their training and experience and incorporate outcomes research using global indicators reported in professional journals regarding specific client populations (Stewart & Chambless, 2007). Some of these indicators include psychological, medical, or social characteristics that appear in the literature relative to certain client populations. Examples of this approach include a review of services provided to inmates with co-occurring disorders (Chandler, Peters, Field, & Juliano-Bult, 2004) or the use of a family-based, behaviorally oriented, multimodal, multisystemic approach for children with attention deficit disorder with hyperactivity (ADHD; Edwards, 2002).

Toward the scientific end of this continuum, counselors' professional training and experience may lead them to expand their reliance on research and incorporate "best practice" treatment approaches supported by literature references. Often these references to "best practices" represent the collective opinion of professionals regarding a treatment strategy for a particular client population with a particular problem and may include some global data regarding client progress. An example of this would be the use of Dialectic Behavioral Therapy as a predominant approach for clients with borderline personality disorder (Linehan, 1993) or the use of Cognitive Behavioral Therapy for individuals experiencing phobic or anxiety disorders (Rubin & Babbie, 2005).

At the scientific end of the scale, counselors use their professional training and experience and engage in formal research activities. These activities include an assessment of client progress, adaptation of treatment to account for the individual characteristics of the client, review of initial assessment information at the end of therapy to identify changes in qualitative indicators, and incorporation of pre- and post-treatment quantitative test data to confirm the changes that have been identified.

Challenges to Evidence-Based Research Approaches

Messer (2004) provides a comprehensive discussion of evidence supported therapies (ESTs) and Randomized Clinical Trials (RCTs) and describes limitations relevant to both approaches. This discussion leads to the conclusion that practitioners need to follow a model of evidence-based psychotherapy practice, such as the disciplined inquiry or local clinical scientist model, that encompasses a theoretical formulation, empirically supported treatments, empirically supported therapy relationships, clinicians' accumulated practical experience, and their clinical judgment about the case at hand (p. 580). Client characteristics, specifically personality, cultural, socioeconomic, developmental, stressors, and personal preferences, need to be considered because treatments are most likely to be effective when tailored to fit the individual needs of the client (Norcross, 2002).

The continuum of evidence-based practices presented above appears to follow Messer's (2004) recommendations. Questions emerge, however, regarding the rigor of the research methodology used to support evidence-based counseling approaches and the application of these approaches in a counseling setting.

Intuition and Clinical Impressions

Intuition and clinical impressions are often anchored in a therapist's training and experience. Such impressions may be offered by paraprofessionals who possess little or no formal counseling training or by licensed professionals with graduate or advanced graduate degrees including exposure to research strategies and techniques.

Intuition and clinical impressions introduce the potential for bias, especially when the clinician is also the researcher. A counselor's devotion to a particular treatment theory may influence objectivity and create situations where clinicians simply seek to confirm their clinical hypotheses, possibly ignoring indicators that do not fit their treatment schema.

Programmed Studies

Clinicians who use programs of study to help define clinical effectiveness must assume there is a connection between knowledge gain and behavior change. The connection between these two variables has never been established.

Global Indicators

Global indicators supported by research often provide a checklist of psychological, medical, or social characteristics generally determined through clinical studies or gleaned from state or national databases. While global indicators might signify common characteristics among a particular client population, the connection between changes in the levels of these indicators and treatment effectiveness, represented by behavior change, has not always been established.

Best Practices

The concept of "best practices" has been promoted to direct the treatment activities of counselors toward interventions that groups of professionals consider to be most appropriate for particular client populations or for clients with particular clinical issues. Following a medical model, best practices research aims to identify specific techniques or treatments that are "best" for particular categories of client problems. Thus, the mechanisms of change in counseling, according to the "best practices" point of view, are specific techniques, not features common to all counseling orientations (Hansen, 2006).

Two fundamental issues challenge the efficacy of best practices. The first focuses on the nature of the evidence supporting the use of best practices and the second raises concerns about the application of best practices.

In a comprehensive review of decades of outcomes research, Wampold (2001) found that specific ingredients or techniques in the counseling approach played an insignificant role in overall client progress. Messer (2004) appears to confirm this position in a meta-analysis that found a very substantial association between the researchers' preferred therapy model and the therapy that was more successful. It emerged despite the fact that differences in efficacy between the therapies were rather small and clinically insignificant to begin with (p. 581).

Coupled with the challenge of the research supporting "best practices" are questions regarding the application of best practices in a clinical setting. To what degree do theoretical applications compare among counselors with different levels of formal education? Is it reasonable to assume that a paraprofessional with no graduate education would be able to apply the principles of Cognitive Behavioral Therapy at the same professional level as a licensed professional therapist with an advanced graduate degree?

Instrument Selection

Professional counselors have access to a broad range of instruments that can be used for data collection during the counseling experience. Some of these instruments are designed for diagnostic purposes only (e.g., MMPI-2). Others, such as interest inventories and opinion surveys, are designed to open avenues for discussion.

Not all instruments have the psychometric properties appropriate for use in research designs that require parametric data for analysis. Therefore, counselors who generate quantitative data utilizing test data need to pay attention to scales of measurement of data being collected and use the corresponding test of significance.

Understanding Evidence-Based Therapy

There may be some discussion regarding the placement of the various evidence-based approaches along the research continuum presented above. The research continuum provides the opportunity for counselors to select from many evidence-based practices, some that offer more rigorous approaches to research than others, but all documented, to some degree, in the literature.

The merits of evidence-based therapy hinge on two critical

issues that may not be easily recognized or understood by the general public. First, the rigor of the "evidence" associated with evidence-based therapy represents a broad range of possibilities ranging from personal opinion to formal repeated measures designs using valid and reliable instruments. Currently, there is no method for the public to distinguish between the various research approaches implied by the term "evidence-based therapy." It is reasonable to assume the use of the term "evidence-based practice" might encourage potential clients to select a particular counseling program. It is unreasonable to assume, however, that potential clients would take the time or have the expertise to evaluate the research used to support claims that a particular counseling practice was evidence-based.

Second, research to support clinical initiative might be generated by professional practitioners, those with advanced specialized graduate degrees (Gladding, 2009), or paraprofessional practitioners, those practicing without the benefit of a formal graduate education. Graduate education exposes individuals to research methodologies and proper statistical procedures, necessary components for conducting formal outcomes research. Without restricting the use of the term "evidence-based practice" to research generated by qualified professionals, the general public has no way to readily determine if the evidence has merit.

It might be time for professional counselors to consider establishing a classification system to provide the public with a quick reference to evidence-based practices conducted by qualified researchers and based on rigorous research approaches. Such a system could include a two-tier system. The first tier could represent the researcher's qualifications and second tier could represent a ranking of rigor of the research approach. A multidisciplinary, non-profit organization could be developed to establish and monitor the research classification system and provide the public with accurate information regarding outcomes research activities.

Conclusions

The demand for greater economic efficiency in the delivery of counseling services is likely to continue into the foreseeable future (Norcross, Hedges, & Prochaska, 2002). The integration of research and counseling services is gaining the attention of state legislatures and third-party payers in an attempt to determine "what is appropriate to do in practice, what is to be reimbursed, and what the rates of reimbursement will be" (Kasdin, 2008, p. 156).

It is tenable to assume that counseling entities will explore integrating "evidence-based therapy" into day-to-day practices. A major concern should be whether all of these research approaches satisfy the definition of "evidence-based practices" or offer sufficient evidence that reflects effective therapy. Further, a major concern should focus on the integrity and rigor of the evidence being generated.

It is unreasonable to assume that the public will become familiar enough with formal research concepts to be able to explore the differences in research used as support for evidence-based practices. Without rigorous research being conducted by qualified researchers, the question is whether some "evidence-based therapy" is actually supported by qualified research or simply a marketing ploy to attract new clients.

As the role of outcomes research in the human services continues to be debated, other questions emerge regarding the responsibility of professional counselors to verify the effectiveness of the clinical services they provide. To what extent are professional counselors ethically bound to produce valid, empirical evidence to support their clinical services? What role should clinical impressions and client satisfaction surveys play in the overall evaluation of the effectiveness of clinical services? How should valid and reliable test instruments be utilized in measuring treatment effectiveness? To what extent can current qualitative and quantitative research principles and practices contribute to a measure of client behavior change noting common limitations regarding subject sampling and research designs that do not necessarily have control groups for comparison? As these questions continue to be debated, individuals seeking counseling are faced with a major challenge in trying to identify effective treatment sources.

References

American Counseling Association. (2005). *Code of ethics.* Alexandria, VA: Author.

Borckardt, J. J., Nash, M. R., Murphy, M. D., Moore, M., Shaw, D., & O'Neil, P. (2008). Clinical practice as natural laboratory for psychotherapy research: A guide to case-based time-series analysis. *American Psychologist, 62,* 77-95.

Chandler, R. K., Peters, R. H., Field, G., & Juliano-Bult, J. (2004). Challenges in implementing evidence-based treatment practices for co-occurring disorders in the criminal justice system. *Behavioral Sciences and the Law, 22,* 431-448.

Edwards, J. H. (2002). Evidence-based treatment for child ADHD: "Real-world" practice implications. *Journal of Mental Health Counseling, 24,* 126-139.

Evidence-Based Medicine Working Group. (1992). Evidence-based medicine. A new approach to teaching the practice of medicine. *Journal of the American Medical Association, 268,* 2420-2425.

Gibbs, L. E. (2003). *Evidence-based practice for the helping professions: A practical guide with integrated multimedia.* Pacific Grove, CA: Brooks/Cole-Thompson Learning.

Gladding, S. T. (2009). *Counseling: A comprehensive profession* (6th ed.). Upper Saddle River, NJ: Prentice Hall.

Hansen, J. T. (2006). Is the best practices movement consistent with the values of the counseling profession? A critical analysis of best practices ideology. *Counseling and Values, 50,* 154 – 160.

Kasdin, A. E. (2008). Evidence-based treatment and practice: New opportunities to bridge clinical research and practice, enhance the knowledge base, and improve patient care. *American Psychologist, 63,* 146-159.

Levant, R. F. (2005, February). Evidence-based practice in psychology. *Monitor on Psychology, 36* (2), 5.

Linehan M. M. (1993). *Cognitive-behavioral treatment of borderline personality disorder.* New York: Guilford Press.

Messer, S. B. (2004). Evidence-based practice: Beyond empirically supported treatments. *Professional Psychology: Research and Practice, 35*, 580-588.

Norcross, J. C. (Ed.). (2002). *Psychotherapy relationships that work: Therapist contributions and responsiveness to patient needs.* New York: Oxford University Press.

Norcross, J. C., Hedges, M., & Prochaska, J. O. (2002). The face of 2010: A delphi poll on the future of psychotherapy. *Professional Psychology, Research and Practice, 33*, 316 – 322.

Rubin, A. (2007). *Statistics for evidence-based practice and evaluation.* Belmont, CA: Thompson/Brooks-Cole.

Rubin, A., & Babbie, E. (2005). *Research methods for social work.* Belmont, CA: Thompson/Brooks-Cole.

Sharpley, C. F. (2007). So why aren't counselors reporting n=1 research designs? *Journal of Counseling and Development, 85*, 349-356.

Stewart, R. E., & Chambless, D. L. (2007). Does psychotherapy research inform treatment decisions in private practice? *Journal of Clinical Psychology*, 63, 267-281.

Wampold, B. (2001). *The great psychotherapy debate: Models, methods, and findings.* Mahwah, NJ: Erlbaum.

Section VI

Technology and Counseling

Article 27

The Collaborative Counselling Website:
Using Video e-Learning via Blackboard Vista
to Enrich Counselor Training

Paper based on a program presented at the 2007 Association for Counselor Education and
Supervision Conference, October 11-14, Columbus, Ohio.

Cristelle T. Audet and David A. Paré

Introduction

With the increased availability of technology on campuses, incorporating technology as a tool in counselor education is becoming commonplace for students and professors alike (Baggerly, 2002; Baltimore, 2002; Granello, 2000). Examples of technological applications include the posting of courses online, distance education, online supervision, and even online counseling. The review of video-recordings is probably the most common technological application in counselor education; however, it is typically a one-off event incorporated in a classroom lecture. This article discusses some useful extensions of that fundamental practice.

The Collaborative Counselling Website was inspired by the pedagogical possibilities suggested by housing video resources at a location accessible 24/7 by graduate students. As the project has unfolded, however, we have come to see that this technology offers expanded possibilities. In particular, two agendas of importance to us are effectively served by the project.

The first agenda pertains to the elevation of what anthropologist Clifford Geertz (1983) has called "local knowledge." We believe in the parallels between counseling practice on the one hand, and counselor education on the other. The collaborative approaches to counseling that inspired this web site (cf. Anderson, 1997; Anderson & Gehart, 2007; White, 2007) construe counseling conversations as sites for uncovering and celebrating client knowledges. We see the same empowering possibilities in counselor education: rather than merely "transmitting" (Sfard, 1998) so-called expert knowledge, we are interested in tapping into students' existing skills and resources, and showcasing them as a way to circulate accounts of their competence. Indications are that unilateral, top-down transmission of information fails to engage practitioners as active partners in their own learning (Lee & Garvin, 2003; Waddell, 2001). The web site described here offers an alternative that centers students in knowledge production.

A second agenda well served by this initiative pertains to knowledge exchange. Barwick et al. (2005) concluded that "potential users of research knowledge are unconnected to those who do the research, and consequently a huge gap ensues between research knowledge and practice behaviors" (p. 25). *The Collaborative Counselling Website* is a prime vehicle for promoting knowledge exchange (in both directions) between the university and the surrounding counseling community. Indeed, this function is gaining ground as we accumulate additional resources worthy of sharing with diverse stakeholders.

To introduce this pedagogical innovation, we begin with a brief review of the use of video in counselor education. A discussion ensues on how *The Collaborative Counselling Website* was built, structured, and utilized, followed by lessons we learned along the way.

Using Videos in Counselor Education and Increasing Student Accessibility to Videos

There have been mixed reviews on instruction methods using different forms of media and technology, with some indication that technological applications do not necessarily enhance performance (Hayes, Taub, Robinson, & Sivo, 2003). However, there is growing consensus that incorporating diverse technological resources in the learning process motivates and engages students. We believe this engagement is critical to the creation of a vital and creative counseling program. Our own interest in integrating technology into counselor training has centered on (a) expanding access to learning resources, (b) creating a forum for highlighting and sharing student "expertise," and (c) initiating knowledge exchange activities with the surrounding counseling community.

Video-recordings of counseling sessions or role-plays have long been central pedagogical tools in counselor education, particularly for demonstrating specific counseling concepts, modeling counselor behaviors for future practice, and enhancing the learning process of counselors-in-training in general (Baum & Gray, 1992; Kaplan, Rothrock, & Culkin, 1999; Keats, 2008). We have found video demonstrations helpful for concretizing what might otherwise be abstract theoretical discussions; helping students visualize how an intervention might appear in practice; and providing students with a point of reference from which to plan their own interventions.

The benefits of counseling videos led us to seek ways to increase accessibility of videos beyond the classroom context. In early experiments making videos temporarily available through a campus listserv, we sought informal feedback from our students, asking them what it was like to have the opportunity for multiple viewings of videos outside of class. The advantages they cited included (a) ability to rewind/fast-forward for individualized viewing, (b) assistance in prepping for sessions, (c) opportunity to see full sessions which is time-consuming for classes, (d) point of

307

comparison between one's own style and that of videotaped counselor, (e) useful preparation for in-class role-play exercises, and (f) particularly effective learning vehicle when paired with a transcript. A frequent comment from students has been their astonishment at the subtle skills and conversational turns revealed upon close, repeated inspection. This feedback is the basis of our growing interest in the use of a web-based medium for showcasing the skills and knowledge of counselors-in-training.

How the Site Works

The Collaborative Counselling Website is hosted on Blackboard Vista (BBV), an educational platform used at many universities. Although traditionally used to post "courses" online, we modified its purpose to become a web environment, accessible by all of the counseling students in our program, for housing counseling videos and other resources. Because BBV is an "intranet" medium, access to the site is controlled by a password, and content can be displayed selectively for the different users. This allows us to delimit consent to particular viewer groups, and tailor the site specifically for each user.

Students create and edit videos of their counseling practice as part of various course requirements in the Counseling Program. Counseling sessions – actual and role-played – are recorded digitally using cameras installed in our facility. A committee of faculty members and graduate students engaged with the web site select whole videos, or portions of videos, as potential additions to the web site. In these cases we solicit students' permission; those interested (clients and counselors) in displaying their work sign a consent form. With the selective release feature, users who log on see only the materials released to them without any sense of sections being "censored." This chameleon-like quality is one of the platform's attractive features because it allows the site to be many things to many people.

To ensure compatibility of multiple video and playback formats, we convert edited video clips from the starting format into Flash format using a conversion software called Swish. We post video clips on the site using DreamWeaver software, which are then organized into meaningful categories for easy navigation. The site also includes a wide range of faculty-produced counseling role-plays on topics such as sharing the limits of confidentiality with clients, setting goals, and using metaphor. To orient the viewer, each video is accompanied by a brief description and a clickable frame of the clip to start playing the video. In some cases, a verbatim transcript is also included.

How the Site Was Built

While the uploading of videos to the Internet has become a commonplace event (e.g., YouTube), the development of a dedicated intranet web site has been the product of a prolonged process – approximately two years from its inception to its release for student consumption. Our hope is that we might shorten that process considerably for others by sharing our learnings here. The process included multiple steps: consultation, securing funds for the project, project planning and approval, programming and design of the web site, pilot testing, and debugging.

Consultation. We began with a consultation process with the University of Ottawa's Centre for e-Learning, a resource to assist professors in the development of innovative technology-based pedagogical tools. The consultation process enabled us to (a) determine the feasibility of the project, (b) establish key components of the project and a projected timeline for completing it, and (c) identify internal sources of funding we had not considered.

Funding. Web site development requires expertise not always freely available. It is also a time-consuming endeavor for professors, but can be shared with graduate assistants. We secured a $15,000 grant allotted by an internal funding program with the mandate of supporting the development of innovative use of technology as a pedagogical tool. We also secured two smaller internal grants of $4,000 each through the same program and our Faculty to hire a graduate student to act as a part-time web site resource manager for two years. We leveraged these grants by committing some of the funds we had received from a federal body, the Social Sciences and Humanities Research Council of Canada. The project associated with that grant had a broader mandate, part of which involved the development of a web site.

Project planning. A team from the Centre for e-Learning – comprised of web design and programming specialists – helped us develop a concrete plan to realize our vision of what the finished site would look like and how it would operate. The team engaged us in a prioritizing process to ensure the site be built within the constraints of available funding. Key elements we deemed necessary at this stage were (a) using an intranet system for restricted use by students to ensure confidentiality, (b) a video player function accessible to the widest range of users with differing access to technology and competency levels, and (c) establishing autonomy for site maintenance with minimal reliance on external assistance.

Programming and design. We met every few weeks with the team to consolidate our preferred web features, map out the terrain of the site, and provide content. Using our input for the desired "look and feel" of the site, the programmer generated a template from which subsequent web pages would be built. We then converted and uploaded many self-produced videos we had accumulated over the years.

Pilot-testing and debugging. Once completed, we invited two students to surf the web site. They shared their impressions aloud while navigating the site in the presence of the project manager. Some adjustments were made based on this process.

How the Site Is Used

The web site is a tool to enrich training and student learning processes by facilitating student exposure to, learning about, and acquisition of counseling skills and concepts through video technology. To date, there are different ways we have utilized the site and ways we plan to use it in the future as relevant resources are consolidated further. Here are some examples:

- "Priming" students with an introductory viewing of a technique to be discussed in class.
- Offering multiple viewings at their own pace prior to practicing the technique.
- Tailoring a video through editing, titles, accompanying text, etc. to achieve specific pedagogical objectives for in-class instruction or course assignments.
- Inviting students to post their work and soliciting feedback from classmates.
- Adding student videos demonstrating effective use of specific counseling skills for use by future cohorts.

We believe multiple viewings can foster more thoughtful and integrative discussion since pre-processing has occurred and different perspectives emerge with subsequent viewings.

Lessons Learned

We have learned valuable lessons along the way that parallel many experiences depicted in the literature regarding counselor educators using technology with counselors-in-training (Baggerly, 2002; Newman & Abney, 2005). These lessons can be grossly divided into those that are specific to technology and to site users.

Technology. The process of developing the web site involved a series of conversations not unlike cross-cultural counseling. We struggled to make ourselves understood, and to understand the technical experts, learning to slow things down and unpack meanings, one by one, to ensure that neither party ended up down a blind alley of misunderstanding. Anticipating the multiplicity of media technologies was the biggest challenge. For example, we had many discussions around which default player should be used on the site (e.g., Windows Media Player, QuickTime, Real Player, etc.). This hinged on the video file type, which hinged on recording capabilities and whether the video would be streaming video, which hinged on whether the server we would use had appropriate streaming capabilities. Several challenges of this nature taught us the complexity that multiple interacting systems can yield and the importance of anticipating compatibility issues early on. We suspect system compatibility will improve as technology progresses, which may reduce, but not completely eliminate, the learning curve involved.

Site users. Technological competence varies across counselor educators and students. We have learned the importance of (a) helping users navigate the process of simply accessing the site and videos and (b) encouraging users to develop, edit, and post videos of their own counseling work to share with their peers. We have learned that although there is a trend toward increased use of technology in education, competencies, confidence, and motivation vary widely from student-to-student, requiring different degrees of guidance. This necessitates mentorship of students in the technical skills needed to benefit from the site's pedagogical potential. To this end, we plan to offer students a tour of our recording facilities, direct them to library-based workshops on camera use, and generate user-friendly "how-to" documents to guide them in their recording and editing projects.

Supporting Ongoing Autonomy

One of our central goals for this project has been to attain autonomy around managing the web site without the need for ongoing technical consultation and the potential expense associated with it. This autonomy extends to the administration of access to the site by users, the ongoing creation and uploading of new resources, and the selective release of content to various groups.

A vital resource has been the *Web Management Guide* authored by the Centre for e-Learning project team. It details in a tutorial style all the features and functions needed for site maintenance. Further support from a hired assistant with technological savvy has facilitated the general maintenance of the site to date as well as helped address technical difficulties as they arise. This is an ongoing process: the resource manager has continued to generate new documents which we have integrated with the *Web Management Guide.*

Future Directions

While our focus has mostly been on the pedagogical benefits of *The Collaborative Counselling Website*, we are excited by the possibilities it offers for community-building. The web site enables us to connect our graduate students with counselors from the broader community beyond the academic setting. So far our energies have been focused on bringing knowledge and expertise from the community to our campus. We also look forward to initiatives that will promote knowledge exchange in the reverse direction: there are fertile possibilities for our graduate students to share their learnings with local practitioners who have limited means for accessing literature and related resources.

This lateral knowledge exchange is a refreshing alternative to the conventional top-down "expert" approach to training practitioners, and is empowering to the counselors whose work is featured. It also helps to knit together the local professional community, forging ties between our graduate program and local agencies. In this respect, *The Collaborative Counselling Website* has proven to be far more than a repository of pedagogical resources; rather, it acts as a powerful vehicle for community building. We are filled with anticipation for the many knowledge-sharing possibilities that await us.

References

Anderson, H. (1997). *Conversation, language, and possibilities: A postmodern approach to psychotherapy.* New York: BasicBooks.

Anderson, H., & Gehart, D. (2007). Collaborative therapy: Relationships and conversations that make a difference. New York: Routledge.

Baggerly, J. (2002). Practical technological applications to promote pedagogical principles and active learning in counselor education. *Journal of Technology in Counseling, 2*(2). Retrieved August 21, 2008, from http://jtc.colstate.edu/vol2_2/baggerly/baggerly.htm

Baltimore, M. L. (2002). Recent trends in advancing technology use in counselor education. *Journal of Technology in Counseling, 2*(2). Retrieved August 21, 2008, from http://jtc.colstate.edu/vol2_2/editor.htm

Barwick, M. A., Boydell, K. M., Stasiulis, E., Ferguson, H. B., Blase, K., & Fixsen, D. (2005). *Knowledge transfer and evidence-based practice in children's mental health.* Toronto, ON: Children's Mental Health Ontario.

Baum, B., & Gray, J. (1992). Expert modeling, self-observation using videotape, and acquisition of basic therapy skills. *Professional Psychology: Research and Practice, 23*(3), 220-225.

Geertz, C. (1983). *Local knowledge: Further essays in interpretive anthropology.* New York: Basic Books Inc.

Granello, P. F. (2000). Historical context: The relationship of computer technologies and counseling. In J. W. Bloom & G. R. Walz (Eds.), *Cybercounseling and cyberlearning: Strategies and resources for the millennium* (pp. 3-15). Alexandria, VA: American Counseling Association.

Hayes, B. G., Taub, G. E., Robinson, E. H., III, & Sivo, S. A. (2003). An empirical investigation of the efficacy of multimedia instruction in counseling skill development. *Counselor Education and Supervision, 42*(3), 177-188.

Kaplan, D., Rothrock, D., & Culkin, M. (1999). The infusion of counseling observations into a graduate counseling program. *Counselor Education and Supervision, 39*(1), 66-76.

Keats, P. A. (2008). Buying into the profession: Looking at the impact on students of expert videotape demonstrations in counsellor education. *British Journal of Guidance and Counselling, 36*(3), 219-235.

Lee, R. L., & Garvin, T. (2003). Moving from information transfer to information exchange in health and health care. *Social Science & Medicine, 56*, 449-464.

Newman, J. M., & Abney, P. C. (2005). The use of digital video editing software in microskills based on counselor education programs: A technology perspective. *Journal of Technology in Counseling, 4*(1). Retrieved August 21, 2008, from http://jtc.colstate.edu/Vol4_1/Newman/Newman.htm

Sfard, A. (1998). On two metaphors for learning and the dangers of choosing just one. *Educational Researcher, 27*(2), 4-13.

Waddell, C. (2001). So much research evidence, so little dissemination and uptake: Mixing the useful with the pleasing. *Evidence-Based Mental Health, 4*(1), 3-5.

White, M. (2007). *Maps of narrative practice.* New York: Norton.

Article 28

Requisite Computer Technologies and Infrastructures for Providing Live, Remote, Clinical Cybersupervision

Paper based on a program presented at the 2007 Association for Counselor Education and Supervision Conference, October 11-14, Columbus, Ohio.

Kenneth L. Miller, Salvatore A. Sanders, and Susan M. Miller

Introduction

The meteoric rise of computer technologies and infrastructures during the past three decades now makes it possible to deliver live, clinical supervision from virtually any place on Earth. This capability is, of course, no small accomplishment and stands as a crowning achievement in a long history of technology use to deliver clinical supervision. Since the 1950s, counselor educators have slowly but consistently adapted emerging technologies to enhance the quality of supervision. During that decade, telephones were used to provide supervisory feedback during live counseling sessions. Although intrusive, this technology has stood the test of time in supervision practice with only minor modifications to the hardware employed (e.g., cell phones, digital telephones with text/video messaging). Advances in audio technologies gave rise to the use of audiocassette recorders and "bug-in-the ear" devices for supervision. Other improvements in video technologies prompted the widespread use of video cameras and videocassette recorders to tape counseling sessions for post-session reviews as a component of clinical

317

supervision. However, it has been the upsurge in digital technologies that now enables clinical supervisors to not only view counseling sessions from remote locations in "real time," but also to provide "live" evaluative feedback both during and after counseling sessions.

Live, remote clinical supervision, a form of cybersupervision (Miller & Miller, 2008), is a constellation of processes by which counselor supervisors provide real-time evaluative feedback to supervisees who are delivering counseling services in another (i.e., remote) location. In these processes, a supervisor uses her computer and a broadband Internet connection to access a digital video camera, microphone, and computer monitor housed in a remote counseling room. With a full view of the supervisee and client(s) and access to verbal communications through her computer monitor and speakers, the supervisor observes the counseling session and provides evaluative feedback during or after the session, or both. Depending on location, type of supervision process desired, hardware and software configurations, and the speed, reliability, and security of the Internet connection, feedback can be delivered in several formats. Figure 1 depicts a common hardware configuration for delivery of cybersupervision from an observation room (e.g., located in a counseling clinic) to a supervisee who is providing counseling in one of the clinic's counseling rooms.

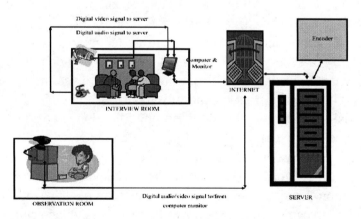

Figure 1. Common Hardware Configuration for Delivery of Live, Remote Cybersupervision to a Single Supervisee in a Training Clinic.

System Feasibility

Live, remote clinical supervision is technically feasible using current equipment and video protocols. The authors conducted a pilot project using notebook computers and Polycom® cameras and software over a broadband wireless network to simulate supervision of a mock counseling session. Although audio and video qualities are subjective factors, participants were able to communicate clearly with good video quality. Videoconferencing equipment has been successfully utilized for conducting live, remote, clinical supervision (Miller, Miller, & Evans, 2002). This equipment is similar to that used in telemedicine (Mora, Cone, Rodas, & Merrell, 2006) and distance education (Trauner & Yafchak, 2005) applications. A number of companies offer hardware, software, and services that can be adapted for the delivery of live, remote cybersupervision.

System Requirements and Costs

Technologies that support the delivery of cybersupervision have expanded at explosive rates and include high-speed computer chips, mass-storage devices, broadband Internet access, instant messaging programs, wireless technologies, and videoconference software. In order to implement a system that supports live, remote supervision, the supervisor (minimally) and both supervisor and supervisee (in order to maximize options) must have access to computers equipped with the hardware and software options identified previously. It is important to note that many notebook and desktop computers sold today in the United States are equipped to support most forms of live cybersupervision as part of an overall videoconferencing system. Specifications for each computer system must be selected to meet the hardware (e.g., type of video camera) and software (e.g., videoconferencing program) requirements of the videoconferencing system.

In addition to the computer requirements identified above, consideration must also be given to hardware/software requirements in the counseling room, counseling center, and at the university. The counseling room must be equipped with a digital camera accessible by a wireless signal, a digital microphone, and (in some methods described below) a stand-alone, flat-screen monitor that can be wall mounted. Figure 2 illustrates a common hardware configuration for live, remote cybersupervision of multiple sessions within a training clinic.

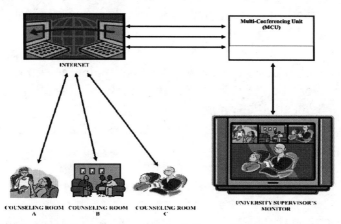

Figure 2. Common Hardware Configuration for Delivery of Live, Remote Cybersupervision to Multiple Supervisees in a Training Clinic.

Initial set-up costs vary considerably depending on existing equipment and infrastructure and desired capability. The actual costs of implementing a wireless videoconferencing system will also depend on the number of remote sites connected. The information that follows was obtained through discussion with technical personnel (J. Brandenstein, personal communication, October 2008; J. Paolucci, personal communication, September 2007) to identify key components and approximate costs of a videoconferencing system.

- Multi-conferencing Unit (MCU; Optional), $50,000-$100,000. More cost-effective options include foregoing the MCU and registering CODECS with videoconferencing services to provide conferencing to multiple sites at a cost of approximately $150/month/CODEC.
- Encoder-Decoder (CODEC), $10,000-$15,000. One per counseling session room to be monitored. Some onboard options

may decrease other costs. For example, some onboard CODEC options may facilitate multi-site calling.

- Digital cameras, $1,000. One per counseling session room. Less expensive portable cameras for each supervisor's computer will be necessary if not "built in."
- Personal Computers (notebook or desktop), $1,000. One per supervisor – optional for each counselor station depending on capabilities desired. Video displays ($500) are needed at each counselor station as a minimum.
- Headsets, $30. One per supervisor.
- Bandwidth (T1 example), $25/month/per 1MB.
- Video Encoder (PC System), $2500.
- Server Storage, $3,000-$10,000.

Components necessary for wireless Internet access may add to the cost of the system if such access is not already in place and a wireless connection is desired. The costs for wireless components are not provided because they are highly variable depending on the physical characteristics of the area and distances from the counseling site to the receiver.

The authors advise consulting with institutional technical experts and with representatives from common commercial vendors such as AT&T, Life Size, Polycom, RADVision, Tanberg, and Trinity Global L.L.C. These vendors are a small sample of companies that supply such equipment and services.

Supervision Options

Depending on technological capabilities and the supervisor's preference for providing live evaluative feedback during or after counseling sessions, a variety of live, remote supervision options are available. Bug-in-the-Eye (BITE) supervision is an adaptation of an approach described by Neukrug (1991) and more recently implemented by Miller et al. (2002). BITE supervision requires that the counseling room be equipped with a digital camera and microphone, as well as a computer monitor that is mounted either behind the client(s) or on a swiveling wall mount and positioned so that only the counselor can view the screen. As the supervisor remotely views the counseling session from her computer, she uses an instant messaging program to provide immediate feedback on the supervisee's performance. Appearing as either text or iconographic messages (see Figure 3) that are digitally transmitted by the supervisor onto the monitor in the counseling room, the supervisor looks for evidence that the supervisee has read the message, then uses a combination of keystrokes on her computer to withdraw the message in preparation for the next.

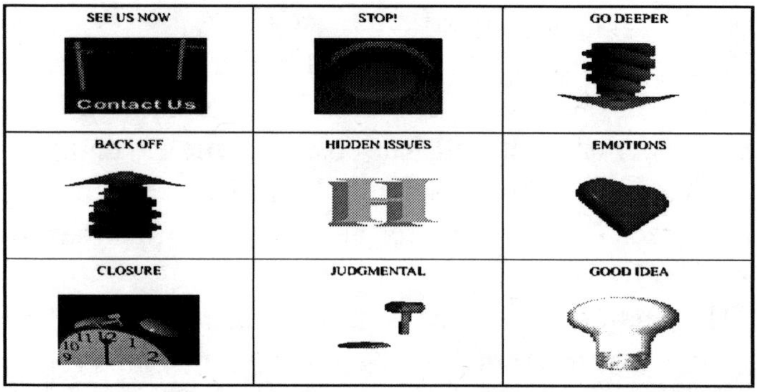

Figure 3. Examples of Iconographic Messages Used in BITE Supervision. Source: Miller, Miller, & Evans, 2002. Copyright 2002 by the American Counseling Association. Reprinted with permission. No further reproduction authorized without written permission of the American Counseling Association.

Audio-Track Overlay Protocol (ATOP; Evans, Miller, Miller, & Lucey, 2005) is a process that enables supervisors to provide comprehensive audio feedback in real time during counseling sessions for post-session review by supervisees. In this process, a supervisor remotely observes the counseling session from her computer (as described above) and uses a digital microphone to record substantive feedback regarding the supervisee's performance at specific points during the session. The supervisor's comments are synchronously recorded as a digital audio file with the digital video file of the session, which are saved to a server. Because the audio signals are recorded in real time as the session progresses, supervisees are able to play back the video digital file of the session and hear the supervisor's evaluative feedback at junctures that correspond to communications that occurred during the session.

Perhaps the most comprehensive option for delivering live, remote, clinical supervision is through post-session videoconferences. This method requires that both the supervisor's computer and the one located in the counseling room be equipped with digital video cameras, microphones and speakers, broadband Internet access, and videoconferencing software. In this approach, supervisors observe the live counseling session from a remote location as described previously and use any number of live supervision options previously noted. Following the session, the supervisor opens a live videoconference with the supervisee in order to provide evaluative feedback. During this process she may examine portions of the counseling session that are retrieved from the server and viewed on both computers, review supervisor feedback saved in ATOP files, or discuss a host of other supervision issues.

Benefits and Limitations

Several benefits can be realized from the use of live, remote, clinical supervision. These include time, cost, convenience, and efficacy advantages. Time is an important resource and remote supervision offers opportunities to conserve time by eliminating travel to counseling sites. Live, remote supervision is economical: saving mileage, tolls, parking fees, and other travel expenses. In situations where the supervisor visits multiple sites, savings are magnified. Live, remote, clinical supervision is convenient. Imagine the ease of supervising from the office; no driving, parking, packing a lunch, and so forth. Taken together, these advantages yield increased efficiency in the delivery of clinical supervision.

Live, remote supervision allows supervisees in remote locations and rural environments access to a greater pool of professional talent. Because qualified supervisors are in demand, they can provide more supervision services to larger numbers of supervisees. Live, remote supervision also permits counselor supervisors to observe sessions that are not practical to visit in person due to cost or travel limitations. Figure 4 illustrates a common hardware configuration for delivery of live, remote cybersupervision from an off-campus site (hotel) to an agency site.

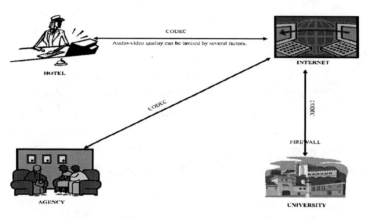

Figure 4. Common Hardware Configuration for Delivery of Cybersupervision From an Off-Campus Site to an Agency Site.

An advantage of digital audio and video communications, an element of live, remote cybersupervision, is the ease of archiving and retrieving digitally recorded counseling sessions for review in supervision sessions. Counseling sessions that are monitored via a videoconferencing system can be saved to a hard disk or other media storage system. Compared to analog systems (e.g., videotape), digital storage (i.e., files saved to a server) permits more precise retrieval of files and file segments, which can be indexed by date, time, or digital counter.

Despite the advantages of live, remote cybersupervision, supervisors must consider a host of potential technical, legal/ethical, and interpersonal limitations before adopting its use. These limitations include potential breaches of confidentiality through unauthorized access to live counseling or supervision sessions, constraints on the development of the supervisor-supervisee relationship, and lack of research on the use of theoretical models in online environments. Although authors address technical issues in the following paragraphs, other limitations are addressed in the professional literature (e.g., Kanz, 2001; Layne & Hohenshil, 2005; Mallen, Vogel, & Rochlen, 2005; Miller & Miller, 2008; Wegge, 2006).

A major technical concern results from insufficient bandwidth and varying traffic through available bandwidth. Insufficient bandwidth can result in problems such as pixelization and freezing of the video and audio transmission during live supervision sessions. Insuring sufficient bandwidth dedicated to the videoconference is the best way to avoid or minimize these problems. This problem may be more likely to occur in off-campus settings (e.g., hotel) and while using wireless mobile computing where the background traffic, location, and other unpredictable factors may cause fluctuations in the transport channel (Liu & Zarki, 2006).

Even with dedicated bandwidth and ideal configurations, live, remote digital communications are characterized by a slight but perceivable delay as audio and video signals are transmitted. In order to address this problem, practice (plus patience) on the parts of supervisor and supervisee are critical. If not addressed, videoconference participants may inadvertently "talk over" one another. Depending on the speed of the video transmission, video may blur at high rates of movement. Avoiding sudden movements of the head, limbs, or body can reduce this problem. Background noise can be a problem if multiple sites are connected and those not involved in the conversation fail to mute their microphones. Training on how to operate the conferencing equipment, including when to open or mute the microphone, is necessary for all parties involved in the videoconference.

Guidelines for Use

Supervisor and supervisee training in the use of online and conference technologies is a simple solution to many of the aforementioned technical issues. The necessity of such training is addressed in *Technical Competencies for Counselor Education Students: Recommended Guidelines for Program Development* (http://ehe.osu.edu/paes/couned/technical_competencies.htm) published by the Association for Counselor Education and Supervision (ACES). One implication of these guidelines is the need for counselor education programs to provide direct technology training, increase the frequency of technology-based assignments, and ensure that graduates can communicate effectively (Alleman, 2002). A lack of program responsiveness does not absolve counseling students from the responsibility to acquire technical competencies (Mallen et al., 2005).

Supervisors who opt to deliver live, remote supervision over wired or wireless systems must be familiar with the operation of the computer system they are using and with the procedures used to connect and participate in a videoconference. They must know protocols for providing a user ID and password to access the videoconference or the network. They must further be able to establish connections to the camera/microphone in the counseling room and to focus the camera (if this option is available). Supervisors must also know and use videoconferencing etiquette (e.g., communicating in a personable manner, allowing adequate time for others to finish speaking).

Insuring the security of audio/video transmissions is a critical consideration. Authors recommend consulting with information technology specialists and commercial vendors to identify a system that provides the use of firewalls and encryption software to protect sessions from unauthorized access. Using videoconferencing equipment and software from the same vendor may ensure compliance with HIPPA requirements (J. Paolucci, personal communication, September 2007; Williams, Ellis, Middleton, & Kobak, 2007).

Conclusion

Live, remote cybersupervision is a technological marvel whose emergence holds enormous promise for the counseling profession. Advantages of this approach appear to outweigh limitations, which can be addressed through education, policy, and practice. Live, remote cybersupervision has the potential to enhance the quality, quantity, and effectiveness of supervision while making it more accessible and efficient with reduced expenditures of time, money, and resources.

References

Alleman, J. R. (2002). Online counseling: The Internet and mental health treatment. *Psychotherapy: Theory/Research/Practice/ Training, 39,* 199-209.

Evans, W., Miller, K. L., & Miller, S. M., & Lucey, C. (2005, October). *Enhancing live clinical supervision through the use of audio.* Poster session made at the National Association of Counseling Educators and Supervisors: Pittsburgh, PA.

Kanz, J. E. (2001). Clinical-supervision.com: Issues in the provision of online supervision. *Professional Psychology: Research and Practice, 32,* 415-420.

Layne, C., M., & Hohenshil, T. H. (2005). High tech counseling: Revisited. *Journal of Counseling & Development, 83,* 222-226.

Liu, H., & Zarki, M. E. (2006). An adaptive delay and synchronization control scheme for Wi-Fi audio/video conferencing. *Wireless Networks, 12,* 511-522. DOI archived at http://dx.doi.org/ 10.1007/s11276-006-6549-7

Mallen, M. J., Vogel, D. L., & Rochlen, A. B. (2005). The practical aspects of online counseling: Ethics, training, technology, and competency. *The Counseling Psychologist, 35,* 776 -718.

Miller, K. L., & Miller, S. M. (2008). An integrated instructional and clinical model for intranet and internet live supervision. In S. P. Ferris & R. Zheng, (Eds.), *Online instructional modeling: Theories and practice* (pp. 223-241). Hershey, PA: Idea Group, Inc.

Miller, K. L., Miller, S. M., & Evans, W. J. (2002). Computer-assisted live supervision in college counseling centers. *Journal of College Counseling, 5*(2) 187-192.

Mora, F., Cone, S., Rodas, E., & Merrell, R. C. (2006). Telemedicine and electronic health information for clinical continuity in a mobile surgery program. *World Journal of Surgery, 30,* 1128-1134. DOI archived at http://dx.doi.org/10.1007/s00268-005-0204-9

Neukrug, E. S. (1991). Computer-assisted live supervision in counselor skills training. *Counselor Education & Supervision, 31,* 132-138.

Trauner, M. & Yafchak, M.F. (2005). *Video conferencing cookbook. Video development initiative.* Retrieved October 23, 2008, from http://www.vide.net/cookbook/cookbook.en/

Wegge, J. (2006). Communication via videoconference: Emotional and cognitive consequences of affective personality dispositions, seeing one's own picture, and disturbing events. *Human-Computer Interaction, 21*(3), 273-218. DOI Archived at http://dx.doi.org/10.1207/s15327051hci2103_1

Williams, J. B. W., Ellis, A., Middleton A., & Kobak, K. A. (2007). Primary care patients in psychiatric clinical trials: A pilot study using videoconferencing. *Annals of General Psychiatry, 6,* 24. DOI Archived at http://dx.doi.org/10.1186/1744-859x-6-24

Article 29

Wikis, Podcasts and More... Program Policy Considerations With Online Teaching

Paper based on a program presented at the 2008 National Career Development Association Global Conference, July 9-11, 2008, Washington, DC.

Debra S. Osborn

There are many reasons why an instructor might consider teaching a course online. Students often seek online courses for the convenience of being able to complete course assignments at their own speed, from the comfort of their own home. Faculty might teach online because of a desire to enhance students' technological skills, enhancing the quality of their courses through technology, expanding course availability for those students whose geographic location makes commuting difficult, increasing flexibility in their own schedule of teaching, in response to student demand, and interacting with their students more frequently (McKenzie, Mims, Bennett, & Waugh, 1999). In addition, some administrators may encourage or offer incentives for instructors to teach online, as a means of increasing class enrollment and freeing up classroom space.

A faculty member should not dive into teaching online without first testing the waters. There are several considerations to keep in mind, for oneself, one's students, one's program, and from the institution's perspective. From a personal perspective, the faculty member should consider the positives and negatives for teaching a course online. Some potential positives include every student being engaged, continued instructor challenge and growth, convenience, ability to engage all learning styles, more time to think about a response (versus thinking on the spot), discussions on multiple topics at the same "time," increased technological capabilities of students (which they can then share as part of their service delivery), and enhancing one's vita (Osborn, 2008). Potential negatives include: the amount of time required to create/deliver/maintain an online course; lack of understanding/appreciation by colleagues and peers; feeling disconnected from students; students' differing technological capabilities and available resources; academic honesty; technological glitches and frustrations; the challenge of teaching to different learning styles; addressing inappropriate comments; incorporating oneself into an initially stale and impersonal course; and the impact on one's professional career, annual evaluations, and tenure (Osborn, 2008).

King, Nugent, Russell, Eich, and Lacy (1998) identified several key issues within seven policy areas that should be considered with distance education. The seven areas included: Academic, Governance/Administration/Fiscal, Faculty, Legal, Student Support Services, Technical, and Cultural. Some of the key issues were technology fees for students, intellectual property of the online course and activities, faculty compensation, technological support, the acceptance of distance education within a program, college, and university, and maintaining academic standards.

If, after considering these policy issues, a faculty member decides to proceed with delivering either a web-enhanced or an online course, the next step is to determine how to either create an online course from scratch, or in most cases, how to translate an existing course effectively into an online format. The best way that I have found to begin is by taking the current syllabus, and outlining the activities that are traditionally used to ensure that students have learned the related objective or skill. Once I have outlined this, I then begin the brainstorming process of how to translate that activity into an online activity that would hopefully result in the same pedagogical outcome.

Consider the slide below:

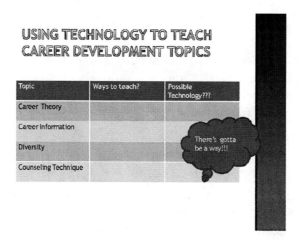

The topics listed above are commonly found in a graduate career development class. You'll notice the caption that says, "there's gotta be a way." Having a philosophy such as this is imperative to developing an effective online course, and for ensuring that you don't use the same online tool for each activity. The next slide shows a completed grid with potential ideas.

USING TECHNOLOGY TO TEACH CD TOPICS

Topic	Ways 2Teach?	Possible Technology???	Tools
Career Theory	Lecture	Video Lecture	Camtasia
	Case Studies	Insert video/audio into PPT	
		Case study responses	Windows movie maker
	Role plays	-via chat (provide info first)	
		-online quiz	Audacity http://audacity.source
	Reflective paper	-threaded discussion or blog	forge.net/
		Roleplay	
		Personal analysis	Elluminate
		Experiential	
			Google pages, blogspot
Career Information	Review main sites	Online Scavenger Hunt	Any homepage site
	Occupational Comparison		
Counseling Technique	Observe Roleplays	Video presentation Online roleplays (pairing)	
Diversity	Reflective paper	Course wiki	PB Wiki

I've created several video lectures that accompany the assigned readings. These lectures range from ½ hour to 1 hour in length (broken up into fifteen minute segments), and cover key issues in the reading as well as additional information I want students to know. Sometimes, it will include a demonstration of a skill. The purpose of the video lecture is to let the students see and hear me in a traditional lecture format. I create PowerPoint slides in a guided note format that accompany the video lecture so that students can follow along. Another option is to create an audio podcast of your lecture, which would allow students to play it on their iPOD or mp3 player.

If you use a pre-made course shell such as Blackboard or WebCT, you should make use of the discussion board format. (If you do not have such a shell, you can create a blog and have students post replies to the blog). For larger courses, you might consider creating smaller workgroups and having students give two suggestions to a question, and then one member post a summary of the group discussion to the main discussion board. This will allow you to quickly check off that a student has made two original contributions, but only respond to the group summaries on the main page.

You can use an online chatting format such as provided through Elluminate, or ILinc, or netmeeting, where students can chat verbally. The benefit of a verbal chat is that you don't lose slow typers. A drawback is when a student has failed to make sure the microphone/speakers work, when they forget to join the chat, or when there is a computer failure (on the instructor's side or student's side). If you have a verbal chat room, you can use it in much the same way as a regular chat room. You can roleplay with a student, send them into breakout rooms to roleplay or discuss a case, talk through a PowerPoint or have them make presentations.

A wiki is a webpage that students can edit. This is useful for covering information that is of interest to the students, and when time does not allow for in depth coverage in class. For example, some students are very interested in the military, or career development and offenders. These are topics that receive only a cursory overview in the class because of other objectives that must be covered in depth. In my career development class, I have assigned different groups a wiki to develop. They have a group page, and then each has their own individual page. Some ideas for wikis include: fan page of their favorite career development theorist/theory, specific career development topic, best strategies for working with a particular population, an FAQ page on a specific topic, or responding to a case study. Students can add text, links, video and audio, diagrams and pictures. For a sample way to grade a group wiki project, see the rubric below:

SAMPLE WIKI GRADING RUBRIC

20	Individual Contribution	Averaged by group rating of individual members' contribution and instructor rating. The group must include a link to a page of acknowledgements on which individuals list their contributions.
GROUP GRADE		
20	Content	Covers the topic in depth with details, demonstrations, examples, images, etc. Content is factually accurate. Demonstrates complexity of the topic. APA citations used appropriately and correctly when paraphrasing, quoting, or summarizing, in text and in references.
10	Organization	Content is well-organized, uses headings or bulleted lists as well as a table of contents.
10	Hyperlinks to sources	Provide working, appropriate hyperlinks to sources that provide additional information about the topic.
15	Original, intelligent wording	Provide a summary of key points, findings, etc., related to the topic. Do not copy! Always cite appropriately.
15	Accuracy (-1 each up to 15 points)	No spelling, grammatical, or APA errors. No HTML errors in wiki (e.g., broken links, missing images). APA citations used appropriately and correctly when paraphrasing, quoting, or summarizing, in text and in references.
10	Visual Appeal	Graphics are used as needed and add to the message. Graphics are not distracting and are used to further explain a topic. It does not look cluttered.
	Extra Credit (Up to 10 points	Uses technology in a creative way, or in a way that is above and beyond what is expected. For example, links to a well designed PowerPoint created by the work group or includes a link to a video of one participant demonstrating a particular skill or technique.

An instructor can make use of the various technological tools out there to create experiential activities for students. For example, a simple PowerPoint can be adjusted with internal hyperlinks to create a *Career Jeopardy* type of game (Osborn, 2005c), or an experiential way to teach career theories (Osborn, 2005a). To see examples of each of these, go to http://careerresource.coedu.usf.edu/linkcareerlab/interactivelab.htm, and click on either "Career Jeopardy" or "Virtual Career Counseling Experiment."

Another creative idea for using technology is to create a virtual career scavenger hunt (Osborn, 2005b) to teach students about various career information sources. This is a great way to teach students about common questions that clients may present with, and to increase students' awareness of the variety of resources available. An example scavenger hunt question is presented on the following slide. You will see that the instructions are very specific about how to go about finding the correct answer. By being this descriptive, you will avoid students spending hours searching for the answer to one question and still achieve the goal of student exploration. As the student goes through each step, they will see other links that they might be interested in exploring. The process of discovering the correct answer – and the multitude of other tools and information sources available, far exceeds the simple benefit of a earning a few points on an assignment.

SCAVENGER HUNT QUESTION

You are working with a student who says she is no good at math, but wants to go to college. Further probing reveals that none of her friends like math, and aren't enrolling in the advanced math class, so she doesn't want to, either. You recall seeing a statistic about **the percentage of college jobs that are closed** for students who do not take advanced math in high school.

From the Career Resources Page , you go to the self -assessment site to the link of the site that will encourage her to think about career opportunities in math. Once on that site, you click on the techquest link and then the Career & Technology Facts where you find your answer:

? 20%

? 40%

? 60%

? 80%

In summary, an instructor can be excited by the plethora of online tools, and challenged by the question of how to transform traditional activities into virtual ones that address and achieve the same pedagogical purpose and outcome. At the same time, it is wise to remember the old cliché that *all that glitters is not gold*, and avoid the temptation to put every bell and whistle into an online course and miss the emphasis on learning. In other words, each online activity should be tied in with one of the course's objectives, and not just be technology for technology's sake. An instructor should regularly evaluate the usefulness of each online activity. Finally, the wise instructor of an online course should consider policy issues outlined earlier in the manuscript.

References

King, J. W., Nugent, G. C., Russell, E. B., Eich, J., & Lacy, D. D. (1998). Policy frameworks for distance education: Implications for decision makers. Retrieved August 11, 2008, from http://www.westga.edu/~distance/king32.html

McKenzie, B. K., Mims, N., Bennett, E., & Waugh, M. (1999). Needs, concerns and practices of online instructors. Retrieved August 11, 2008, from http://www.westga.edu/~distance/ojdla/fall33/mckenzie33.html

Osborn, D. S. (2005a). A virtual career counseling experience. In M. Pope & C. Minor (Eds.), *Experiential activities for teaching career counseling classes & facilitating career groups, Vol II.*, Tulsa, OK: National Career Development Association.

Osborn, D. S. (2005b). A virtual career scavenger hunt. In M. Pope & C. Minor (Eds.), *Experiential activities for teaching career counseling classes & facilitating career groups, Vol II.*, Tulsa, OK: National Career Development Association.

Osborn, D. S. (2005c). Creating a career jeopardy game in PowerPoint. In M. Pope & C. Minor (Eds.), *Experiential activities for teaching career counseling classes & facilitating career groups, Vol II.*, Tulsa, OK: National Career Development Association.

Osborn, D. S. (2008). *Teaching career development: A primer for presenters and instructors.* Tulsa, OK: National Career Development Association.

Article 30

Web-Based Research Tools and Techniques

Paper based on a program presented at the 2007 Association for Counselor Education and Supervision Conference, October 11-14, Columbus, Ohio.

Annette C. Albrecht and Dennis G. Jones

According to Sedwick (2004), "the Internet is gaining in popularity as a research tool through the use of e-mail and the World Wide Web" (p. 35). Most people who use e-mail or "surf the Web" have received a solicitation to complete some type of web-based survey. Many of the early web-based surveys were from companies conducting marketing research. However, as noted by Siah (2005), "the speed, ease and cost of conducting an internet-based study has attracted an increasingly large number of researchers to the medium for data collection" (p. 115).

Advantages of Web-Based Research Techniques

Like Siah (2005), numerous researchers have noted a plethora of advantages of using the Internet to collect research data. The following table briefly summarizes reasons noted by various authors for collecting data through a web-based interface.

Web-Based Research Data Collection: Advantages
- Ability to reach larger population (Betz Hobbs & Farr, 2004; Wright, 2005)
- Capability to reach participants with certain physical disabilities (Wright, 2005)
- Ease of completion by participants (Ahern, 2005)
- Flexibility and control over format (Granello & Wheaton, 2004)
- Improved accuracy and simplicity of data entry (Ahern, 2005; Granello & Wheaton, 2004; Van Selm & Jankowski, 2006)
- Increased participation (Sax, Gilmartin, & Bryant, 2003; Van Selm & Jankowski, 2006)
- Incorporation of rich media such as audio, graphics, and video (Tourangeau, Couper, & Conrad, 2004)
- Interactive nature of Web (Sax et al., 2003)
- Methodological rigor (Ahern, 2005)
- Lower cost (Betz Hobbs & Farr, 2004; Fricker, Galesic, Tourangeau, & Ting, 2005; Granello & Wheaton, 2004; Parks, Pardi, & Bradizza, 2006; Tourangeau et al., 2004; Sax et al., 2003; Van Selm & Jankowski, 2006; Wright, 2005)
- Popularity among certain populations such as college students (Carini, Hayek, Kuh, Kennedy, & Ouimet, 2003; McCabe, 2004; Sax et al., 2003; Van Selm & Jankowski, 2006)
- Rapid access to participants (Betz Hobbs & Farr, 2004; Parks et al., 2006)
- Saves time (Ahern, 2005; Granello & Wheaton, 2004; Sax et al., 2003; Wright, 2005)
- Simplicity of administration (Betz Hobbs & Farr, 2004; Wright, 2005)

Disadvantages of Web-Based Research Techniques

Despite the number of advantages cited for using the Internet to collect research data, several investigators have expressed concerns related to using this approach. The following table briefly summarizes reasons noted by various authors for not collecting data through a web-based interface.

Web-Based Research Data Collection: Disadvantages
- Concerns with data integrity (Sax et al., 2003; Wright, 2005)
- Initial development time or costs (Ahern, 2005; Sax et al., 2003; Van Selm & Jankowski, 2006)
- Issues related to data security (Sax et al., 2003)
- Limited Internet access for some sub-populations such as nursing home residents, people with certain disabilities (Granello & Wheaton, 2004; Sax et al., 2003)
- Technical troubles experienced by users (Ahern, 2005; Granello & Wheaton, 2004; Sax et al., 2003)

Methodological Issues

Whether collecting data using a web-based survey or any other method, researchers need to consider methodological issues related to the data collection technique being employed. However, the use of web-based survey tools for data collection has forced researchers to address methodological concerns that are unique to this electronic medium. The following table briefly summarizes methodological matters noted by various authors that must be addressed when conducting web-based research.

Web-Based Research: Methodological Issues

- Ability to follow-up with participants who did not complete survey (Granello & Wheaton, 2004)
- Capability to provide participants with immediate feedback such as individual response summaries (Sax et al., 2003)
- Eliminate interviewer bias (Parks et al., 2006; Van Selm & Jankowski, 2006)
- Increased generalizability of data (Ahern, 2005)
- Lack of control over test setting (Ahern, 2005)
- Limited generalizability of data (Granello & Wheaton, 2004; McGothlin, 2003; Sax et al., 2003; Stafford & Goiner, 2007; Wright, 2005)
- Measurement errors (Granello & Wheaton, 2004)
- Subject recruitment bias (Ahern, 2005; Wright, 2005)

A methodological issue not explicitly cited in the literature that has been expressed to the authors during conference presentations on this topic is related to the challenges of receiving approval from Institutional Review Boards (IRBs) for research involving web-based data collection. Over the years, the authors have received reports from conference attendees of not receiving approval for web-based research projects due to IRBs' apprehensions related to study participants' inability to complete institutionally required informed consent documents. In general, it appears that some IRBs do not comprehend the unique nature of web-based data collection. This conclusion has some support from a recent study by Kotzer and Milton (2007) which reported that many investigators believed that IRBs do not understand their studies.

A paramount issue for many researchers is the ability to generalize results from a sample to a larger population. As noted above, various authors disagree concerning the generalizability of results from research designs that utilize web-based data collection techniques. When developing the methodology for a web-based research project, it is essential for researchers to address this issue in the study's design.

Ethical Issues

In addition to addressing methodological concerns unique to online data collection, researchers must consider ethical issues that are of special concern when conducting web-based studies. The following table briefly summarizes ethical issues documented by numerous authors that must be considered when conducting web-based research.

Web-Based Research: Ethical Issues

- Ability to address sensitive topics such as alcohol abuse, eating disorders, HIV (Link & Mokdad, 2005; Parks et al., 2006; Van Selm & Jankowski, 2006; Wright, 2005)
- Ensuring anonymity to participants (Ahern, 2005; Sax et al., 2003)
- Lack of ethical guidelines related to conducting web-based research (Hamilton, 1999)
- Participant concerns about confidentiality (Ahern, 2005; Madge, 2007; Sax et al., 2003)
- Personalization of invitations to participate in surveys related to sensitive topics (Heerwegh, Vanhove, Matthijs, & Loosveldt, 2005)
- Promotes increased access to cultural groups (Ahern, 2005; Betz Hobbs & Farr, 2004)
- Underrepresentation of racial or ethnic minority groups (Sax et al., 2003)

All researchers should be concerned about these ethical issues. However, with the special attention given to research in the

American Counseling Association's Code of Ethics (2005), it is important that counselor educators and supervisors adhere to these ethical principles when conducting web-based research.

As noted above, various authors disagree concerning the impact of web-based research on inclusion of participants from racial or ethnic minority groups. As counselors, this issue should be of particular concern and must be considered prior to conducting web-based research.

Web-Based Survey Tools

The increasing availability of web-based survey tools now provides researchers with a variety of options when selecting a tool to best meet the data collection needs for a particular project. However, having a broad understanding of the types of web-based data collection applications available can assist in narrowing the options from many applications to a few tools, then ultimately selecting the best product for the project.

Based on the collective experiences of the authors in designing numerous web-based surveys using a variety of web-based data collection applications, the following matrix provides researchers with a relative comparison of web-based survey tools.

Web-Based Survey Tools: Relative Comparison						
Type of Tool	*Hosting Location*	*User Control*	*Ease to Customize*	*Turnaround Time*	*Analysis Tools*	*Researcher's Cost*
Web Hosted Survey Wizard	External	Medium to High	Low to Medium	Low	Low to Medium	Medium
Web Survey Wizard	Internal	Medium to High	Low to Medium	Low	Low to Medium	Low
Custom Design	Internal	Low	High	Medium to High	Low	Low

Types of Tools

Web-based survey applications can generally be divided into the following three broad categories with great variation of features available for each tool within a category.

1. *Web Hosted Survey Wizard.* These applications are generally housed on a web server that is outside of the researcher's organization. Companies make these tools available for use by businesses for market research as well for individuals who use these products for data collection. Most of these companies charge investigators to use these tools on a per respondent basis (i.e., more responses = more money).

2. *Web Survey Wizard.* These products are generally housed on a web server that is inside the researcher's organization. These tools are similar to "hosted" options except that the institution maintains the hardware and software application. Most of these applications are one-time purchases with the organization paying an annual service fee for software upgrades and support.

3. *Custom Design.* Rather than purchasing a web survey product, some institutions have built their own applications in order to complete an individual web-based survey. Conceptually, building this type of tool is fairly straightforward because the product has two components: (a) a database for collecting the data, and (b) a web-based interface for data entry. However, in reality, designing custom tools can be both expensive and time consuming.

Issues to Consider

The factors involved in selecting a web-based survey tool will vary greatly from research project to research project. However, five general matters need to be considered when differentiating between products.

1. *User Control.* The ability for the researcher to manipulate the "look and feel" of survey items is often an important consideration. For example, the ease of editing the contents of a survey item or manipulating the layout of the survey is imperative. Many survey applications include templates of standard survey items (e.g., select only one, select all that apply, text response boxes) that the researcher uses to build the survey.

2. *Ease to Customize.* In many situations, templates of standard survey items are suitable. However, due to the nature of some research questions, standard survey items may not be appropriate for collecting some types of data. Therefore, it might be important for the researcher to use non-standard data collection items (e.g., rank order a series of items) that cannot be created using templates.

3. *Turnaround Time.* The timeframe between when a researcher receives initial approval to conduct a study (e.g., IRB, funding agency), and the time that the investigator needs to begin data collection is often an important consideration. This is especially true if the researcher needs to conduct any type of pilot test during the early stages of the project.

4. *Analysis Tools.* Many researchers prefer to extract data from the survey tool and conduct the analysis using a stand alone software application (e.g., SPSS). However, some web-based survey tools have built in reports that allow the investigator to review summary results while the survey is still active (i.e., no need to export data from the survey application and import it into another product). Most of these internal reports provide basic demographics (e.g., number of respondents, percentage responding "yes" to a certain item).

5. *Researcher's Cost.* The cost of using varying survey applications will be dependent upon the arrangement the researcher negotiates with external vendors or organizational policies related to cost recoupment for use of institutional resources. For many research projects, cost considerations become a primary factor in selecting a survey tool.

The ultimate selection of an application for a web-based survey might be determined by considerations other than those outlined above. However, identifying the best product to collect data for a research project must always be carefully contemplated. Following are examples of web-based data collection applications.

- http://www.activewebsoftwares.com
- http://www.advancedsurvey.com
- http://www.askget.com
- http://www.classapps.com/SelectSurveyOverview.asp
- http://www.freesurveysonline.com
- http://www.hostedsurvey.com
- http://www.infopoll.com
- http://www.prezzatech.com
- http://www.questionpro.com/web-based-survey-software.html
- http://www.raosoft.com
- http://www.supersurvey.com/?sezbcom_software
- http://www.vovici.com (was http://www.websurveyor.com)
- http://www.zoomerang.com

Note: Inclusion in this set of examples does not represent the authors' endorsement of the product.

Conclusion

As outlined above, web-based data collection is growing in popularity for a number of reasons. However, prior to diving into web-based methodologies, it is important for researchers to weigh the advantages and disadvantages of this approach as well as be prepared to address methodological and ethical issues unique to this medium. Ahern (2005) concluded that the advantages outweigh the disadvantages. Nevertheless, each investigator needs to consider these factors individually and reach his or her own conclusion. Finally, if web-based data collection is selected as the preferred method for a particular study, researchers need to identify the best application available to collect the type of data needed for the particular project.

References

Ahern, N. R. (2005). Using the Internet to conduct research. *Nurse Researcher, 13*(2), 55-70.

American Counseling Association. (2005). *ACA code of ethics.* Available from http://www.counseling.org/Files/FD.ashx?guid =ab7c1272-71c4-46cf-848c-f98489937dda

Betz Hobbs, B., & Farr. L. A. (2004). Accessing Internet survey data collection methods with ethnic nurse shift workers. *Chronobiology International, 21*(6), 1003-1013.

Carini, R. M., Hayek, J. C., Kuh, G. D., Kennedy, J. M., & Ouimet, J. A. (2003). College student responses to web and paper surveys: Does mode matter? *Research in Higher Education, 44*(1), 1-19.

Fricker, S., Galesic, M., Tourangeau, R., & Ting Y. (2005). An experimental comparison of web and telephone surveys. *Public Opinion Quarterly, 69*(3), 370-392.

Granello, D. H., & Wheaton, J. E. (2004). Using web-based surveys to conduct counseling research. In J. W. Bloom & G. R. Walz (Eds.), *Cybercounseling and Cyberlearning: An Encore* (pp. 287-306). Greensboro, NC: CAPS Press.

Hamilton, J. C. (1999, December 3). The ethics of conducting social-science research on the Internet. *Chronicle of Higher Education, 46*(15), p. B6.

Heerwegh, D., Vanhove, T., Matthijs, K. & Loosveldt, G. (2005). The effect of personalization on response rates and data quality in web surveys. *International Journal of Social Research Methodology: Theory and Practice, 18*(2), 85-99.

Kotzer, A. M., & Milton, J. (2007). An education initiative to increase staff knowledge of Institutional Review Board guidelines in the USA. *Nursing and Health Sciences, 9*, 103-106.

Link, M. L., & Mokdad, A. H. (2005). Effects of survey mode on self-reports of adult alcohol consumption: A comparison of mail, web, and telephone approaches. *Journal of Studies on Alcohol, 66*(2), 239-245.

Madge, C. (2007). Developing a geographer's agenda for online research ethics. (2007). *Progress in Human Geography, 31*(5), 654-674.

McCabe, S. E. (2004). Comparison of web and mail surveys in collecting illicit drug use data: A randomized experiment. *Journal of Drug Education, 34*(1), 61-73.

McGothlin, J. M. (2003). The infusion of Internet-based surveys and postal mail surveys. *Journal of Technology in Counseling, 3*(1). Retrieved October 16, 2005, from http://jtc.colstate.edu/vol3_1/McGothlin/McGothlin.htm

Parks, K. A., Pardi, A. M., & Bradizza, C. M. (2006). Collecting data on alcohol use and alcohol-related victimization: A comparison of telephone and web-based survey methods. *Journal of Studies on Alcohol, 67*(2), 318-323.

Sax, L. J., Gilmartin, S. K., & Bryant, A. N. (2003). Assessing response rates and nonresponsive bias in web and paper surveys. *Research on Higher Education, 44*(4), 409-432.

Sedwick, J. L. (2004). A comparison of three data collection survey modes among Southern Baptist youth workers. *The Journal of Youth Ministry, 3*(1), 35-46.

Siah, C. Y. (2005). All that glitters is not gold: Examining the perils and obstacles in collecting data on the Internet. *International Negotiation, 10*, 115-130.

Stafford, T. F., & Goiner, D. (2007). The online research "bubble". *Communications of the ACM, 50*(9), 109-112.

Tourangeau, R., Couper, M. P., & Conrad, F. (2004). Spacing, position, and order. *Public Opinion Quarterly, 68*(3), 368-393.

Van Selm, M., & Jankowski, N. W. (2006). Conducting online surveys. *Quality & Quantity, 40*(3), 435-456.

Wright, K. B. (2005). Researching Internet-based populations: Advantages and disadvantages of online survey research, online questionnaire authoring packages, and web survey services. *Journal of Computer-Mediated Communication, 10*(3), article 11.

Appendix I

Authors and Titles of Additional Articles Accepted for Inclusion in the ACA VISTAS Online Library

Addressing Grief and Loss Issues With Children and Adolescents of Military Families
Jacqueline Melissa Swank and E. H. Mike Robinson

Arena for Success: Metaphor Utilization in Equine-Assisted Psychotherapy
Sandra L. Kakacek

Body Dissatisfaction Among Gay Men: A Cultural Phenomenon
Kristin Meany-Walen and Darcie Davis-Gage

The Boy Code Betrays Me: Addressing Societal and Sex-Based Trauma in the Lives of Gay and Bisexual Men
Stacee Reicherzer, Jason Patton, and Alessio Pisano

Bridging the Professional Gap: Mentoring School Counselors-in-Training
Kelly Duncan, Robin Svendsen, Tobin Bakkedahl, and Lisa Sitzman

The CACREP Standards: How Much Do Students Know?
Livia M. D'Andrea and Leping Liu

Cognitive Appraisal and/or Personality Traits: Enhancing Active Coping in Two Types of Stressful Situations
Ming-hui Li

Compulsive Gambling "Action" Inventory
Valerie C. Lorenz

Compelling Counseling Interventions

Counseling Students Learn Adventure Counseling as an Additional Mode of Therapy to Increase Their Repertoire of Counseling Skills
Louise B. Graham

A Counselor's Guide to Child Sexual Abuse: Prevention, Reporting and Treatment Strategies
Kenneth L. Miller, Marianne K. Dove, and Susan M. Miller

'Crash': Modernism Meets Postmodernism
Jerry A. Mobley

Cyberbullying and Cyberbalance: Cultivating a Respect for Technology
Barbara Trolley, Connie Hanel, and Linda Shields

Developing a Regional Supervision Training Program for School Counselors
Alan Bakes

A Discussion of Coping Methods and Counseling Techniques for Children and Adults Dealing With Grief and Bereavement
Candice N. Slate and David A. Scott

Ecotherapy: Theoretical Foundations Leading to Clinical Work With Images and Dreams for Individual, Community, and Planetary Transformation
Patricia A. Sablatura

Everything Counselors and Supervisors Need to Know About Treating Trauma
Lindsay Bicknell-Hentges and John J. Lynch

Exploring Racial Variations and the Impact of Parental Attachments and Psychological Health Among Diverse College Students
Deneia Thomas, Keisha Love, and Kenneth M. Tyler

A Flexible Pedagogy for Counseling Supervision
Jerry A. Mobley

Grief Work: Its Contributions to Healthy Living
Lori A. Russell-Chapin and Rachel B. Bridgewater

Group Therapy to Build Strong Relationships for Same Sex Couples
Lamerial Jacobson, John Super, and Kara Pappalardo

Horses as Healers: Equine Facilitated Therapy for Grieving Children
Laura Strom and Jennifer Wilson

The Impact of Cyber Bullying: A New Type of Relational Aggression
Jennifer M. Johnson

*The Impact of Relaxation Techniques on Third Grade Students'
Self-Perceived Levels of Test Anxiety*
Colleen M., Johnson, Heidi A. Larson, Steven R. Conn,
Lincoln A. Estes, and Amanda B. Ghibellini

*The Impact of Skills-Based Training on Counselor Locus of
Control and Emotional Intelligence*
Jill Packman, Marlowe Smaby, Cleborne Maddux, Craig Farnum,
Colin Hodgen, Elisabeth Liles, and Becky Rudd

*Is There A Magic Bullet? Pharmacologically Assisted Addiction
Management: What Counselors Should Know*
Benjamin P. Kelch

*The ISLLC Standards: A Unifying Force in School Administrator
and Counselor Preparation*
Gene Wright and Neal D. Gray

Joining Forces for Students: School and Community Counselors Unite!
Rebecca N. Earhart and Sharon Mindock

Leading Mutual Aid Support Groups: Difficult Members and Other Challenges
Lawrence Shulman

Living With Learning Disabilities: Strategies for Family Support
Carol J. Dolan

Multiple Addictive Behavior Questionnaire (MABQ) Validation Project
Victoria L. Bacon and Theresa A. Coogan

Narrative Approaches in Sand Therapy: Transformative Journeys for Counselor and Client
Dee Preston-Dillon

Out of the Ivory Tower and Into the School-Based Practicum
Marielle A. Brandt and A. Jonathan Porteus

Outcome Study of a Community Based Training Clinic: Are We Serving Our Clients?
Darlene Daneker

Pharmacological Treatment of Childhood and Adolescent Depression: What School Counselors and School Psychologists Need to Know...
Carrie Lynn Bailey

Physical Wellness Self-Monitoring Project
Darren A. Wozny and Julia Y. Porter

Possible Selves: Concepts, Applications, and Implications for Career Practice and Policy
Anne Marshall and Fran Guenette

Predictors of Body Dissatisfaction Among Adolescent Females
Melissa Hall

The Professional Counselor and the Diagnostic Process:
Challenges and Opportunities for Education and Training
Mary Beth Mannarino, Mary Jo Loughran, and Deanna Hamilton

Promoting International Counseling Identity: The Role of
Collaboration, Research, and Training
Wendy J. Hoskins and Holly C. Thompson

Promoting Professional Development Among Students and
Professional Counselors
John McCarthy, Amy J. Thompson, and Teresa E. Fernandes

Racial Ethnic Identity and Career Development Concerns of
College Students From Immigrant African and Hmong Families
Aneneosa A.G. Okocha

The Relationship Between Psychological Birth Order and
Romantic Relationships
Nicole A. Healy, Tammy H. Scheidegger, Amy L. Ridley Meyers,
and Karen Friedlen

Situating Supervision in the Context of a Social Justice Paradigm: A
Convergence of Bernard's Discrimination Model and Social Justice
Melissa Odegard, Linwood G. Vereen, and Nicole R. Hill

Social and Emotional Needs of Gifted Students: What School
Counselors Need to Know to Most Effectively Serve this Diverse
Student Population
Carrie L. Bailey

Social Justice, Advocacy, and Counselor Education Pedagogy
Kaye W. Nelson, Marvarene Oliver, and Rochelle Cade

Strategies for Effectively Teaching Career Counseling
Aaron H. Oberman and Jeannine R. Studer

Compelling Counseling Interventions

Support Systems for Parents of Children with Special Needs
Chiharu Hensley

Taking a Multifaceted Approach to Retirement
Vera S. Maass

That's Just Plain Silly! Channeling Outrage to Champion Change
Roberta Neault

A Tool of Facilitating Courage: Hope Is a Choice
Mark Blagen and Julia Yang

Training Counselors to Be Consumers of Supervision
Irene Mass Ametrano, Devika Dibya Choudhuri, and
Diane L. Parfitt

*Traumatic Brain Injuries and Substance Abuse: Implications for
Rehabilitation Professionals*
David A. DeLambo, Kananur V. Chandras, Debra Homa,
and Sunil V. Chandras

Uses of Bibliotherapy for Adoptive Children and Their Families
Claire A. Kavanaugh and Jody J. Fiorini

*Verification- To Check or Not to Check: The Use of Criminal
Background Checks in Counselor Training Programs*
Gloria Dansby-Giles and Frank Giles

Wellness and Academic Performance of Elementary Students
Mary A. Hollingsworth

*Women Counselor Educators: Level of Job Satisfaction While
Raising Children*
Carrie Alexander-Albritton, Nicole R. Hill, and
Brooks Bastian Hanks

Appendix II

Accessing VISTAS Online

VISTAS Online is a database established collaboratively by ACA and Counseling Outfitters in 2004 to capture the resources and information exchanged during the annual ACA conferences. In 2006, NCDA elected to participate through the solicitation of papers from its annual conference. This year marks the first year ACES elected to participate as well.

The *VISTAS* database contains the full text of all 395 articles selected for inclusion in print versions of *VISTAS* as well as articles that met *VISTAS* standards for quality, but could not be included in the print versions due to space limitation. ACA members can access the *VISTAS Online* database in two ways through the ACA website (www.counseling.org). After signing in as a member, click on "Library" under the "Resources" tab at the top of the home page. To conduct a database search, simply type in your criteria in the "Start your search now for:" box and click *go*! The *VISTAS Online* website organizes articles by year and can be accessed directly under "Other Links" found at the bottom of the ACA Library page. The ACA Online Library also contains the full text of 182 *ERIC/CASS Digests* as well as 24 new ACA *Professional Counseling Digests*.

For information on how to submit articles for *VISTAS* or proposals for ACA *Professional Counseling Digests*, go to counselingoutfitters.com or send an email to counselingoutfitters@comcast.net.

The print edition of *Compelling Counseling Interventions: VISTAS 2008* (# 72878, $44.95; $34 Member Price) can be ordered from ACA.

Phone: 800-347-6647 x222
Fax: 800-473-2329
Web: www.counseling.org